A Light on the Path
A Journey Home

William Clark

Parson's Porch Books

www.parsonsporchbooks.com

A Light on the Path: A Journey Home

ISBN: Softcover 978-1-946478-85-6

Copyright © 2018 by William Clark

All rights reserved. No part of this book may be reproduced or transmitted in any form or by any means, electronic or mechanical, including photocopying, recording, or by any information storage and retrieval system, without permission in writing from the publisher.

This book is dedicated to those who are seeking their missionary journey.

"For we wrestle not against flesh and blood, but against principalities, against powers, against rulers of the darkness of this world, against spiritual wickedness in high places."

Ephesians 6: 12

Contents

Foreword 7
Chapter 1 – Late Autumn Ushers in Winter 9
Chapter 2 – When Morning Comes 16
Chapter 3 – Questions 22
Chapter 4 – Looking for Answers 31
Chapter 5 – Maggie Valley 35
Chapter 6 – Sunday in Maggie Valley 55
Chapter 7 – Lydia 73
Chapter 8 – Lydia's Arrival 77
Chapter 9 – Back in Indiana 89
Chapter 10 – Home Sweet Home 106
Chapter 11 – The Arrival 115
Chapter 12 – The Search 122
Chapter 13 – Spring Takes a New Turn 126
Chapter 14 – Family and Friends 129
Chapter 15 – Base Camp 133
Chapter 16 – The First Visit 140
Chapter 17 – Return to Base Camp 146
Chapter 18 – The Second Visit 154
Chapter 19 – One More Valley to Cross 168
Chapter 20   The Third Visit 175
Chapter 21 – New Beginnings 182
Chapter 22 – Spiritual Reunion 191

Foreword

We have news reporters to cover the White House, The United Nations, and correspondents who cover national and international news. We don't have anyone to cover heaven. The Apostle John was given a vision of heaven and wrote about it. The Apostle Paul saw the third heaven, but he wasn't allowed to talk about it; that was 2,000 years ago.

The world is now changing drastically, and my friend, Anderson McCollister, is right in the middle of the changes. Anderson is an unpretentious family man, who wouldn't have the faintest desire to have a story written about him. However, I believe his story should be recorded and shared.

Anderson is the most conscientious person I know. He is compassionate and somewhat idealistic; he wants the best for everyone! I've known him, since he moved from Indiana to retire in Tennessee. He and his wife, Ruth, bought a house and land in Sevier County over twenty years ago.

Some people don't believe the story about Anderson; however, many people reject the stories in the Bible. Anderson's experiences were told to me by his sister, Lydia, and his best friend, Kenny, from Maggie Valley, North Carolina. When I first heard about Anderson, it took a while for my finite brain to process the phenomena.

I finally realized that the incredible report did make sense; largely, because I'm living in a fast-changing world (and it isn't getting better). Just a few months after my community and the rest of the world started drastically changing, I believe Anderson got caught up in the middle of those changes.

I was told that Anderson had some serious concerns about his sister, daughter and his best friend. I know that Anderson is a man of prayer, and I believe God heard his prayers. One day I would like to see Anderson again, and hear him tell about what happened. Fortunately, you can read the story for yourself, and determine the veracity of Anderson's journeys.

His Friend,
John Smith

Chapter 1 – Late Autumn Ushers in Winter

Anderson is sitting by himself, thinking "why did this happen? The delight of my life has been taken away." The hum from his house full of guests fills the air, as Anderson sits in his own silence after his wife's funeral.

"Anderson, do you want anything to eat or drink?' Anderson's sister, Lydia, broke his silent contemplation.

"Oh, a cup of hot, green tea would be nice, Lydia."

"I'll get it right away," she replied.

As Anderson watched Lydia walk to the kitchen, he thought that his sister is a lost breed of a demure person, who is so very thoughtful and compassionate. He fell right back into thinking about his wife, Ruth. As if she were right there by him, he could see her warm and loving face with her winsome smile. Lost in his thoughts, it was almost like he did not sit at the edge of a noise-filled great room.

"Here's your tea, Anderson." It seemed like Lydia had only been gone a few seconds. "Thank you, Lydia. I suppose I have ignored my friends and relatives these last few minutes."

"Don't worry about that, Anderson. They've been busy with their food and conversations."

"I haven't even thought about everyone who was able to come after the funeral and committal service."

Lydia replies, "Your daughter and her family; my son and daughter and her kids, your pastor, your neighbor, a couple from your church and Kenny."

"I didn't even realize there were that many people here."

"Yes, and most of them will be leaving soon. Paul and his family will have to leave by 5:00. Nashville is on Central time, but they won't get back home until 9:00 this evening."

"Oh yes, I can almost guess that my daughter and Stephen will leave about the same time. They always leave early enough to get half way home, and then stay in a motel before they get back to Greenfield, Indiana."

"Yes, I know that routine," replied Lydia. "It seems that they only stay part of a day with you, then go to the Smokies or somewhere and stay the night on the road."

"That's right. I think Angela has always resented me being gone a lot on business while she was growing up."

"Anderson, if you're up to it, why don't you circulate with your guests before they have to leave."

A Light on the Path

"Good idea. Don't go away, Lydia. It's great having you here"

"I'll be here. You know that I have a problem with driving after dark now, and Crossville is over two hours from here."

"You're always welcome here, Lydia. You can use the guest room tonight. I'm glad you can stay."

As Anderson turns to greet his guests, his friend Kenny, an elderly but stocky man with bronze colored skin comes up to him. With a clear and deep voice, Kenny says, "My friend, I must leave soon to have time to go through the gorge and get back to Maggie Valley before the sun sets." Kenny has a small farm there that Anderson has visited many times in the last twenty-five years.

"God bless you, Kenny. Thank you so much for coming. Do you want to take some food with you? There's plenty."

"I might grab a diet soda, and some of those great snickerdoodle cookies for my ride back home," replied Kenny.

"Let me get a container for you," replied Anderson. Kenny gets a soda out of the fridge while Anderson gets a container for the cookies. "There you are my brother. Have a safe trip home." Anderson steps out on the front porch with Kenny.

"It's a cold, but clear evening, Anderson. The moon is already looking down on us."

"It is at that, my friend," answered Anderson.

"Are you doing alright?" asked Kenny. Anderson smiled and nodded his head. "I'm sorry that you are going through this heartache. Do you need anything?"

"No, and thanks for asking. I will call you this week."

"Not if I call you first!" replied Kenny. They both laugh and give each other a quick hug and handshake.

Anderson watches Kenny walk toward his car. Since Anderson lives in the foothills near the Smokies, between Sevierville and Newport, Tennessee, Kenny would get home to his farm between Maggie Valley and Waynesville, North Carolina, in an hour or less. As he walks back to his guests, he thinks about how fortunate he is to have a close friend like Kenny.

As Anderson walks back into the house, Angela meets him just inside the door.

"Dad, I was looking for you. We'll have to go soon. I should have asked if you wanted us to stay tonight."

"I'm fine, Angela. Lydia is staying tonight."

A Light on the Path

"Oh, Dad, I miss Mom not being here," she said as she throws herself into her Dad's arms. Her beautiful, crystal blue eyes well up in tears, as she looks at Anderson and says, "I know that you also miss her a lot."

"Yes, dear, there's no one that I could miss anymore," replied Anderson as his eyes begin to tear also. His lanky frame bends down, and he gently kisses his daughter on her cheek.

As they part their embrace, Stephen, Angela's husband, walks up to them. "I'm sorry, Anderson, that we had to meet under these circumstances; everyone loved Ruth so much."

"Thank you, Stephen. She thought a lot of you," replied Anderson as he looked up at Stephen. Anderson didn't look up at a lot of people, but Stephen stood at 6'5", a couple inches taller than Anderson. Clint, Angela and Stephen's son, stands 6'7" and is four inches taller than Anderson. He played small forward at the University of Tennessee. He just finished his masters at UT, and got a job teaching health and assisting the basketball coach at Indiana State.

Clint also walked up to Anderson and gives him a hug. "You're in my prayers, Grandpa." "I will stay in touch," said Clint.

"Thank you, Clint. I will look forward to hearing from you."

At the front door, Anderson watches as his daughter, and her gangly husband and son walk toward their car. "Be careful," Anderson yells.

Angela replies, "Good night, Dad; I love you." Anderson notices the daylight is fading fast. He realizes the rest of his guests will be leaving soon.

As he goes into the great room, he notices the level of conservations has died down, and that some of his friends are getting their coats.

His pastor comes and gives him a hug; a portly man with a great sense of humor. "God bless you, Anderson. If you need anything, don't hesitate to call."

"Thank you, Pastor Don. If I don't see you Sunday, I will be visiting Kenny in Maggie Valley."

"Well, either way, I will be praying for you every day. I will talk with you soon."

Anderson replies, "Have a good night, Pastor," as he opens the door for a dedicated man, who brings joy to everyone he meets.

Within a few minutes, Anderson says goodnight to the rest of his guests with Lydia's help. His friends from church, John and Wilma, say good night, as well as his neighbor, Conard.

A Light on the Path

His last guests to leave are Lydia's family: her son and daughter, Paul and Rachel, and Rachel's daughter and son, Faith and Eli. Faith is a striking young lady with coal black hair, big brown eyes and a flawless complexion. Eli is as intelligent as his sister is beautiful. Lydia said a school official told Rachel years ago that Eli's IQ is 140. He didn't make top grades in high school and college, but he went on and got a master's in business, and for his age, he has become very successful in international marketing.

As they step outside, Anderson hugs Lydia's family good night, and as always tells Faith and Eli how proud he is of them.

"Good night, Anderson," said Faith and Eli in unison. "Good night. Mom. Good night, Grandma," they said as the sun sets behind the Tennessee foothills. The lavender and pink colors of the sunset radiate into the distance on the Great Smoky Mountains.

As they leave, Anderson and Lydia stay on the front porch, and wave as their white SUV backs out of the driveway. After a few minutes on the porch, Anderson and Lydia start shivering. Anderson's loyal cat, Pockets, starts meowing at their feet. "Want a treat, Pockets?" asks Anderson. "It must be under 35 degrees already, we need a coat out here. Lydia, do you mind making us some coffee, while I get Pockets a treat?"

Lydia answers, "That sounds good to me".

They go back inside to a quiet house. In the country kitchen, painted in a light tan with knotty pine wood trim, Lydia picks out two mild roast coffee cups. Soon the smell of coffee fills the kitchen.

After giving Pockets a treat, Anderson comes back into the kitchen. "Nothing like the rich smell of coffee," said Anderson. "Why don't we sit down in the great room with the coffee and just relax and talk for a while."

"I would enjoy that," replied Lydia.

Lydia's divorce had been nine years ago, and she always enjoyed her talks with Anderson. He helped her get over her loneliness. It reminded her of how Anderson always looked out for his younger sister while they were growing up. As they sit down with their steaming coffee, Lydia says "I don't think I every told you how much I appreciated you helping me while we were growing up. You were always concerned about my safety and well- being."

Anderson replies, "Mom and Dad were so busy that I think I reacted by making sure that their lack of time didn't affect you."

"Maybe I didn't notice their lack of attention so much, because you were always there."

A Light on the Path

"When I left for college, I remember thinking that you would be okay, since you were going into your junior year at Hartford City High," replied Anderson.

"Those were some good years: a lot of relatives in Hartford City and Muncie: family reunions; great Christmas celebrations and a simple and more pleasant society than what we know today."

"That's right, Lydia. It seemed like people had more class, honesty and respect than society today."

"Say, Anderson, when things settle down, I want to talk with you about something."

"What do you want to talk about?"

"It will have to be later, because I need to do an evaluation of my finances."

"Are you having problems?"

"Yes, but I haven't decided on any solutions yet"

"You told me a long time ago that you had to take out an equity line on your home," replied Anderson. "Does that have something to do with it?"

"Yes, but since it's not a good time to talk about it now…and also I'm not quite prepared to talk about it yet."

"I understand," said Anderson as he nodded. "We'll talk about it soon. I was thinking about our families' birthdays and ages. Maybe you can help me catch up on them, while we finish our coffee. Also, update me on your grandkids' jobs, and on any boyfriend or girlfriend. I know that you'll be 78 in January, and I will be 80 in April."

"That's right. Paul will be 51 in August and Rachel will be 48 in October. Faith will be 27 in May and Eli will be 25 in February."

"Time goes so fast," replied Anderson with a puzzled look on his lined face. Clint will be 24 in June. I think Stephen will be 53 in October and Angela will be 50 next month."

Lydia laughs, "My grey hairs tell my age."

Anderson lightened his look and said, "But you have hair and plenty of it!"

"Faith is still a V-P at the small regional bank in Nashville. She met a young doctor at her church. He's her age, and just finished his internship at the Vanderbilt Medical Center. He's going into allergy. Faith told me that he started out in engineering at MIT and switched to pre-med in his junior year. He went to Emory University for medical school. Eli is still dating around.

He recently broke up with a girl he dated for six months, because he suspected that she is an alcoholic."

"Eli sure doesn't need that. How did he find out?"

Lydia replies, "He said he eventually noticed that she had a lot of liquor at her house. At first, he thought she was sipping on ice tea, but realized later it was liquor. Eli said the longer he knew her, the more he noticed erratic behavior."

"Those sure are signs of alcoholism."

"Eli has been working for the international company out of Atlanta, but they have a six-month job for him in Singapore. He thinks they're going to fly him there by early spring."

"Wow, it sounds like a great experience! I was never sent to cities like Singapore, Tokyo, Beijing and Hong Kong. Del Ware sent me to several cities in Europe, as well as to Charlotte, Nashville and Denver," remarked Anderson.

"I remember the post cards you sent from cities like London, Helsinki, Brussels and Frankfurt. You must have had an exciting career," replied Lydia.

"Yes, a lot of different experiences. It was interesting, but also tiring. Speaking of getting tired!"

"I'm ready to hit the sack too, but you didn't update me on Clint".

"Oh, yeah; long, tall Clint…He is doing well. You know about his new job at Indiana State, and I think he is still trying to date the same girl from Knoxville. If he keeps dating her, I will get to see him more often. He has dated her regularly for about a year, and I haven't heard any talk about engagement yet."

"Alright, I'm glad we got updated. I'm sure they will do well," replied Lydia."

"I will get up between 5 and 6 and do my regular routine of making a pot of coffee and then I'll do devotions. If you want to get up around 7, I will make turkey bacon and eggs for breakfast."

Lydia smiled and said, "I will look forward to it."

"Do you need the remote or anything?"

"No, I know where the towels and everything are." They both got up. Lydia walked over to Anderson and gave him a hug. "I will say a prayer for you".

Anderson looked down at her and smiled, "have a good night, sis." Anderson walked into his bedroom; closed the door; and laid down before

A Light on the Path

he got ready for bed. He thought to himself, "I actually feel exhausted". He kept seeing Ruth in his mind.

He feels so alone in the big king bed. He thought that there must be something more than just the loss of his wife. He felt that Ruth passing on could not be the end of things as he knew them. He could not prove it, but he knew that his wife was still out there, at least somewhere, if not only in another dimension. Losing his wife was the hardest thing he had ever been through.

One thought haunted him. He knew he had to find some way to get it out of his mind. He envisions a gruesome scene of his lovely wife buried in the coffin; in the vault under the cold, hard ground of late autumn. He doesn't want to see the vision in his mind, but he can't help it.

He knows that Ruth's soul is not buried, but he struggles giving up his faithful and loving companion of half a century. He tells himself that he must concentrate on faith in God; on prayer and the promise that his wife is in heaven. Anderson thinks, "How do you give up the person that you loved a lifetime and made you laugh? She was always there and always had an assuring word." He thinks that he must come to terms with his wonderful companion being gone.

He feels that he is in a stupor and must shake it off. He tells himself, "I need to get ready for bed and just pray". Anderson gets up; goes into the bathroom and changes. He turns out the lights; goes to bed and is asleep before he realizes it.

Chapter 2 – When Morning Comes

Anderson wakes up on his own. He looks at his cell phone: 5:14. He thinks, "I don't even have to set an alarm anymore." He struggles somewhat to get out of bed, then stumbles into the bathroom. As he throws water on his face and freshens up some, he thinks it would be refreshing again to be much younger. He wouldn't have the sore and stiff muscles all the time. He doesn't have the severity of fibromyalgia and arthritis that his sister has, but he felt that he has plenty of it.

He grabs a robe and heads to the kitchen to make a pot of coffee. He also puts a cup of water in the microwave to make an early cup of green tea. He gets an almond granola bar out of the pantry and takes it and the cup of green tea to the recliner in the great room. He gets his Bible and devotional; turns on the vibrator pad and gets comfortable on the recliner. He reads then he turns out the reading light and prays. He usually dozes off for a while, but never for more than an hour. He wakes up before 6:30 and decides that he'll get an early start on preparing breakfast.

He turns the light back on; grabs the remote and turns to his favorite news channel. As he gets the eggs, butter and turkey bacon out of the fridge, a breaking news item catches his attention. He goes back to the remote and turns up the volume, so he can hear what's going on while he fixes breakfast.

He slows down his normal pace of preparing breakfast, so he can hear the news report more clearly. The reporter is saying something about the world monetary system changing. Anderson is very intrigued, but he can't hear the details while he fixes breakfast. He thinks, "Be patient. I can hear more in a few minutes after I finish with breakfast and get Lydia up".

He finishes cooking the bacon and eggs; turns the heat down and goes down the hall to wake up Lydia. He knocks on the guest bedroom door, "Lydia, are you awake?" He hears a muffled and sleepy reply. "Breakfast will be ready in one minute. There is a very interesting report on the news that you will want to hear."

As Lydia gets up, Anderson puts the bread in the toaster to complete breakfast. He pours two cups of coffee. Lydia comes into the kitchen with tousled hair and wearing a white robe. "Can I put the bacon and eggs on the plates?"

Anderson says, "Sure thing. The toast is ready, and I'll take our coffee into the great room, so we can find out what's going on in the world."

As Lydia picks up the plates, she says, "What's the big news story?"

A Light on the Path

"It's something about the international monetary or trading system being changed."

Lydia replies, "That doesn't sound good".

Anderson says a short prayer, and they sit down to their breakfast. Anderson turns up the volume on the television. "It looks like they're coming back from a commercial. I'm sure we'll know in a few minutes the gist of the report."

The news commentator comes back on, "we have been reporting a major story that we received by 6 AM this morning. We have learned that China, Russia and sixty-eight other countries, central bank governors and finance ministers met Friday through Sunday in Frankfurt, Germany, and have voted to change the world monetary trade system. Reginald Zeigler, World Bank President, said, "This was not an overnight decision. We have met numerous times during the past nine years discussing this move. The growing changes in the international economy find an increasing need to change the trading currency from the dollar, especially for oil trading."

The news reporter continues, "There has been worldwide reaction to this change. American and Great Britain leaders are outraged, because their global trading has been based on the American dollar. We have reports from a number of American banking leaders saying this decision will cause great dollar devaluation and inflation to world economy".

The commentator, Chet Sumley, says "We are now going to Charles Steinberg, owner of a leading Wall Street investment firm. Charles, we thank you for being with us this morning. Would you please sum up for us how this world monetary decision impacts most Americans"?

"Good morning, Chet. Thank you for having me on your program again. I wish it was under better circumstances. Many American banking and political leaders have been in denial about this approaching financial storm in the last nine years, since this world council of banking leaders have been meeting. They have met about a dozen times in the past nine years, and they never invited or informed the United States, Great Britain and Israel about their meetings. Also, most of our leading politicians and bankers have not wanted to talk about the implications of our national debt approaching 22 trillion dollars. Our stock market opens in about one hour. We expect there to be widespread selling of most stocks, and buying of gold, silver and other precious metals. We are expecting to see today a large dip in the devaluation of the dollar and to see wholesalers and retailers significantly raising their commodity prices."

"I have two questions for you, Charles. Why were our country, Great Britain and Israel not invited? My second question is your opinion about the amount of increase in prices of necessary products like gas and food?"

"First of all, Chet. The three countries not invited would have been vehemently opposed to such a change. If they had been in the mix, they would have used every leverage possible to have stopped a majority vote for the change. The U.S., Great Britain and Israel suffer economically by not having the dollar as the world trading currency. Secondly, it is hard to predict the increase in retail prices until the market opens. Commodities like gas and food could go up immediately. Before the end of the day or by tomorrow morning, we could see even higher increases."

"Thank you, Charles. I know you must get ready for the opening of the market. Thanks for taking time out of your busy schedule to be with us."

The reporter announces, "We will be right back with more on this breaking news after these messages".

Anderson mutes the remote and says to Lydia, "I've tried to tell people for several years that this was coming".

"Wow," replied Lydia. "This is unbelievable … earthshaking!"

"We don't know the whole story yet about price increases. By tomorrow, gas and food prices could be much higher or even double." replied Anderson.

"I'm glad I bought extra last week!" exclaimed Lydia.

"Me too. I usually get gas and groceries early in the week, but I buy extra too. I've also told people for years to put most of their money in annuities or similar investments that have a guarantee. Most investments like 401Ks are tied directly to the stock market without any guarantees. I hope people don't lose half or more of their retirement investments with this blow."

Lydia said, "We can talk more about it on the phone today or tomorrow. I should leave for Crossville in about an hour, and I need to shower."

"There is strawberry shampoo and conditioner in the shower; I hope you like it," replied Anderson.

"I love that fragrance! Well, I better get to it."

"I'll try to get more information from the news, while I finish up in the kitchen."

Lydia replied, "Let me know, if you need any help."

A Light on the Path

While Lydia tosses aside the white robe on the garden tub, and gets in a warm shower, Anderson turns the TV volume back on, and cleans up the kitchen. Anderson hums one of his favorite gospel songs and listens to the continued news report off and on.

Anderson looks out the kitchen window to where his bird garden is. He loves watching the birds feed and fly in and out of the bird bath. His cell phone rings.

He sees Kenny's name come up on the phone window. "Hi, Kenny, I bet you've been watching the news this morning."

Kenny answers, "I sure have. Our suspicions were right about the eventual change in the world trading currency, and our economy."

"Lydia and I were watching the news around 7 to 7:30, then she had to get ready to go back to Crossville. I've been cleaning up the kitchen while trying to get more information from the report. Recently I heard something about the countries that attended, and the new world currency. Did you get to hear that in the last 10 minutes or so?"

Seventy countries attended; sixty-two voted for the change and eight abstained. I think they said Japan abstained and a couple of the European countries. Did you hear that the U.S., Great Britain and Israel were not invited?"

"Yes, I did. What about the new world currency?"

Kenny continues, "They said it would be a mix of the euro, the ruble, the yuan and the yen. They decided that the main standard for the new currency would be gold. As you know, the Chinese have been stockpiling gold for years. Even though Japan abstained from voting on the currency change, it appears that they are permitting the yen to be part of the new currency mix."

"The decision does not surprise me. I know that Iran had already been dealing with another currency for oil trading. I've also heard for several years that Saudi Arabia, Russia, China, India, Brazil and a number of other countries wanted to change from the dollar."

Kenny replied, "That's right. A friend of mine from Maggie Valley called a few minutes ago and said that gas there is already $4.19."

"What a big jump! I was there about two months ago, and the gas was around $2.29. Kenny, it sounds like Lydia is about to go. I want to call you by tomorrow about visiting you before Christmas. I would have to come there within a week, so I could stay two or three days."

"That would be fine," replied Kenny. "We can set the dates tomorrow."

A Light on the Path

"Okay, my friend. I will call you then."

"Until we meet again," said Kenny as he signed off.

Lydia's thick grey hair was still partially wet from the shower. "Was that Kenny on the phone?"

"Yes, I'm planning to visit him within a week."

Lydia walked over to one of the kitchen windows, and said, "Look at that bird party!"

Anderson looks at the bird garden with her. "Yes, the tufted titmouse is well represented with his friend the black-capped chickadee. Let's see: there is also the morning dove, the cardinal, the winter junco and the cedar waxwing."

"Lydia, there is plenty of food left from the gathering yesterday. Why don't you take whatever you want"?

"I might just do that. I'll pull some bowls from the fridge and see what is left."

As Lydia puts some of the leftovers on a plate, Anderson says, "Kenny says that gas in Maggie Valley has already climbed to $4.19."

"Jeepers, Creepers! I wonder what it is in Crossville," replied Lydia.

"On your way back, will you check the gas signs and let me know the prices?"

"Sure thing," said Lydia as she covered her leftovers with foil. "I'm pretty well ready to hit the road."

"Have you checked your tires and oil lately?" asked Anderson.

"They're in good shape, brother. How are you feeling this morning?"

"Not bad. I'm just trying to keep busy," replied Anderson.

"Well, give me a hug," said Lydia as she went to get her purse in the great room. As they hugged, and kissed each other on the check, Lydia said, "I want you to call me anytime, day or night; okay?"

"Okay, sis." Anderson followed Lydia outside. Anderson thought with all her sore muscles and achy bones, she still has something of a spring to her step. Just before she got in her car, Anderson yelled, "watch out for the other guy!"

Lydia yelled, "I will. Love you." She closed the door of her denim blue Honda Accord. As Anderson looked at the car, he was surprised that she took it on the two-hour trip. She bought it new almost thirty years ago. It still has the original engine. He always noticed that it had the headlights that flip up, when they're turned on. It was also one of the last models to not have cup holders.

A Light on the Path

As Lydia drove off, she peeped twice and waved.

It was beginning to be a nice day. Anderson thought that it felt a little warmer than yesterday and the sky was clearer. He couldn't believe that it was almost 10:00 already. With Crossville being on central time, Lydia would probably be back home around 11:00 her time. Anderson walked back into the house.

As he walks into the house, he thinks of something that he wants to tell Ruth. He wonders what room she is in. A second later, he realizes Ruth is not there, and she will never be there again. Anderson can't believe that she is gone. His home feels unbearably empty. The only company he has is the creaking of the hardwood as he walks over the knotty pine floors. His eyes begin to tear, and he says out loud, "oh, God, help me!" His mind goes blank, then he thinks if he turns the news back on, it will help remove the loneliness.

He sits down in the cabin style great room, as the news comes back on. He thinks about his daughter; wondering if she is back in Greenfield. As he thinks about his daughter and her family, a news reporter is talking about the increase in prices.

The reporter says, "We have talked with retailers in New York, Charlotte, Atlanta and Chicago, and they are telling us that by 9 A.M. Eastern standard time, prices on food and gas have nearly doubled. New York City is reporting gas at $4.34 a gallon and Chicago is reporting $4.29. In Charlotte and Atlanta, we have been told that staple items like milk, eggs and coffee have virtually doubled. At two major food chains, a $4.00 can of coffee is selling for over $7.50 a can; a $2.99 gallon of milk is selling for $4.99. A $1.39 dozen of eggs is selling for $2.79."

Anderson pushes the mute button on the remote, and thinks, "I can't handle this news right now". He decides to select a music channel. It puts it on light jazz. He can't help but wonder what will happen to utility prices and interest charges. He feels sorry for anyone who is not on a fixed interest loan. He leans back in his recliner and dozes off.

Chapter 3 – Questions

Lydia pulls up in her driveway. She feels a little depressed, when she sees that long, wide crack in her concrete drive. She also notices the rusting pole on the old basketball goal, that hasn't been used for many years. As she walks to her front door and gets her door key out, she remembers that the storm door lock doesn't work anymore. As she unlocks the wood door, she notices how the sun has dried out the lacquered finish on the door. She steps inside and can't believe that her eyes go immediately to the corner of her living room. Near the corner of the wall, a crack goes from the ceiling to the floor. She thinks, "Oh well, what can you expect from a house that was built fifty-five years ago?"

As she puts down her purse and takes off her coat, she starts thinking that spring will be here sooner than she thinks. She wonders how she will take care of the yard. It's getting harder for her to mow. She has a hard time keeping the bushes trimmed around the house and keeping the weeds out of the bed. Her quick answer is to make a cup of coffee.

She puts a french vanilla coffee cup in the coffee maker. Once she fills the side tank with water, she starts thinking about Anderson. After she makes the coffee, she says to herself, "I need to call Anderson about the gas prices that I saw."

She puts creamer and sweetener in her coffee and gets her cell phone out of her purse. She dials Anderson and it rings several times. Anderson wakes up from a sound sleep on the recliner and grabs his cell phone. He sees that Lydia is calling.

"Hello".

Lydia replies, "That's the sleepiest "hello" that I've ever heard!"

"I fell asleep on the recliner after I turned on some music. What time is it?"

"It's almost 12:15 your time."

"You've got to be kidding!" Anderson says, "I've been asleep two hours."

"Don't worry about that, brother. You've been through a lot. I remember three gas prices that I got for you on the way home. In your area, the gas was $4.15. In Knoxville it was $4.17, and here in Crossville it's $4.22".

A Light on the Path

"It's hard to take in, isn't it? I shouldn't be surprised. I've told people that one day things will change overnight".

"They'll be calling you, 'the prophet'."

Anderson replied, "I wouldn't call myself a prophet, but I do believe God's Word."

"Yes, you do, and I need more of that belief myself."

"You can start practicing it at any moment, sis. I will be praying that you do."

"Thank you. Do you have any plans today?"

"I think I will call Kenny after I figure out when I can stay in Maggie Valley this next week."

"When you settle on the dates, let me know. I'm going to work on my finances. Maybe we can talk about them after you get back from Maggie Valley."

"Sounds like a good plan."

"Anderson, let me know if you need anything. I'm ready for a nap myself."

"Okay, sis; sweet dreams."

"Goodbye."

Anderson thinks that he needs to get up and get the blood circulating. It has been three days since he has walked in his woods. On the back side of his house, from the southeast to the southwest, Anderson has 120 acres of mostly wooded hills. From his house and from some of his hills, he can see Douglas Lake. About 1/8 mile, southeast from his house, a wooded area on his property touches Douglas Lake for about 200 feet. Since his property is virtually land-locked, Anderson has thought many times that no one is likely to build on it beyond his lifetime.

Anderson grabs his favorite cap while he verbally checks off his list for the hour hike on his trails. He puts a hunting knife and sheath on the left side of his belt and a small .38 handgun and holster on the right side of his belt. He grabs a small leather shoulder bag for a bottle of water, small first aid kit, emergency fire starter, and leather work gloves. His last and most important hiking tool is his sturdy walking stick. He makes sure he has his house keys and cell phone.

He puts on his coat and heads out the back door. He steps out on his porch-like deck. His back and front porch/decks extend the length of the house. He enjoys the decks as much as any room in his house. Here comes

Pockets; she has heard him come out of the house. Anderson says to Pockets, "Are you ready for a walk?" He bends over and runs his hand down her back. He calls her the tuxedo cat; white for the shirt and black for the coat. She walks with him almost every time.

Anderson's Trailhead

They step off the deck and Pockets follows Anderson down the hill to the fire pit. They walk by the fire pit clearing to the trail head that goes up a steep hill. Even though the trail winds in and out, Anderson considers this part of the walk to be high impact.

He always notices the trees. His favorite are the pines. In past years he planted Leyland Cypress near the road and on the sides of his yard, but in the woods, the loblolly pine dominates the pine trees. The loblolly pines are also taller than the other trees. A lot of them are 50 to 70 feet tall. A few are over 70 feet tall. There are also many younger pines that are under 25 feet. Their bark reminds him of alligator skin. Several years ago, while reading about the pine, he was amazed to learn that pine cones are male and female. He kidded with Kenny that the male cones have a band below their center and the females have the lower band and a band around their top. He read some about how the cones pollinate, but then he started reading more about the trees and birds that he sees.

He loves the sweet birch tree as well. Most of the trees in his woods besides the sweet birch and the loblolly pine, are the southern red oak, the white oak and the southern hickory. The red maple, sassafras, black walnut,

A Light on the Path

and horse chestnut are also common. As Anderson walks along the trail, the sunlight dances between the trees. Anderson likes to keep walking, but the main two reasons for stopping are to pet Pockets and to observe the trees and birds. He also notices a lot of the newer saplings are now three to four feet tall.

Being near the Smokies, he gets different warblers flying through, but they are hard to identify in the woods. He usually can't get close enough to see them well, since they are usually on the move. In the Smoky Mountains, near Clingmans Dome, he got a good view of the black-throated blue warbler and the black and white warbler. The easily identified birds in his woods are the red tail hawk, the crow, the blue jay, the big pileated woodpecker, several types of other woodpeckers, the eastern bluebird and sometimes the tufted titmouse. He sees more birds as he gets closer to clearings.

Anderson never gets tired of seeing an occasional woody the woodpecker (the pileated woodpecker). He usually identifies more types of birds in his bird bath and bird garden, like the male and female scarlet tanager, the indigo bunting, the spotted towhee, the Carolina wren, the wood thrush, the hermit thrush and different types of finches. In and near the bird garden he also sees the downy woodpecker, the hairy woodpecker and the red bellied woodpecker.

"Come on, Pockets," yells Anderson, as they get farther into the woods. Anderson just turned on a trail heading south that is not too far from a coyote den that is just east of him; in a ravine covered with fallen branches. In this area he keeps his eyes on Pockets more often. He usually doesn't see a coyote, but some days he hears them howling and yipping off and on. Even though tradition says that coyotes are more afraid of you than you are of them, Anderson continually keeps a watchful eye in all directions as he hikes in the woods. He knows he has his handgun, walking stick and hunting knife as back-up.

There isn't much wind in the woods today, and the early afternoon feels like it is warming up to the high thirties. Anderson thinks, "What a beautiful day!" He thanks God for such a picturesque day. He continues down the south trail, which is getting ready to make a slight swing to the west, as he passes a big, old white oak tree that he calls the civil war tree.

He continues to keep his eye on Pockets as he turns more to the south on the trail. Now and then he hears a squirrel running over the leaves, but at times when he hears the leaves, he sees the white tail of a mountain deer running through the woods. There is a long ravine that now runs south to

A Light on the Path

southwest between two hills; goes into a clearing and gradually turns to the southwest. Anderson is on a trail above the ravine, but off and on for years, he has also made a path through the ravine.

He looks around again for Pockets. She follows the trail most of the time, but she gets off it to run on fallen branches. Now and then she'll climb six to twelve feet up a tree. She lays back, but she's not far away. Anderson yells, "Come on!" She starts catching up. He waits for her, since she likes to be petted, when she is in the mood. As he pets her, he says, "Good girl. You're a good walker." Anderson continues down the path. He made the trails, so they would circle around on his property.

His trail and the ravine below start to turn more to the southwest. So Anderson can make a broad circle on his hike, he will be coming down to a clearing soon, which is near the southern edge of his property. Water flows down the hills and over boulders protruding from the hills into a creek that meanders on his property and runs under a barb wire fence into a horse pasture. Most of his neighbor's hills have been cleared for grazing. Anderson sees the familiar pinto, and he also see a black horse, a brown one and a brown mule. His neighbor said that the mule helps protect the horses from coyotes and other intruders. Even though the mule is more aggressive than a horse, the horses can also be aggressive toward coyotes and unwelcomed dogs.

The ravine that Anderson has been following opens into the clearing by the horse pasture. The ravine continues again as it goes between hills that circle to the south and southwest. Rather than hike through the ravine, Anderson and Pockets, go up another trail that also turns to the southwest and later to the west. Most of the time, the trail that Anderson is following will also run above the ravine. At times it goes deeper into the woods, but eventually it comes closer to the ravine again.

He hears a loud rushing sound speeding between some smaller brush and through the dry, fallen leaves; it's a couple of wild turkey. They're fast, and hard to see when they're running. Anderson would like to see them roosting in the pine trees. They start roosting at dusk, and Anderson likes to get out of the woods before dusk. He sees them the best when they come into his yard or near the road. He has been walking steady for almost 30 minutes. He decides to take a minute break. He pulls off the leather carrying pouch and gets out the water. He finishes about half a bottle before he takes off. Pockets is still enjoying her walk on the fallen branches near the trail.

A Light on the Path

The path starts to get closer to the ravine again. It leads Anderson to the southwest. In a few minutes the ravine will go between two other hills, as his path starts to turn to the west. He is about half-way back. Anderson guesses that the hike will take a little over an hour.

He will be glad to get back and eat a late lunch. He can tell that he will need to rest his muscles after lunch. Fibromyalgia is a peculiar ailment. When he lays down to rest, he can feel his muscles quivering inside his body. Anderson stays focused on the trail, as he thinks about calling Kenny this evening.

Pockets is catching up to be petted again. Anderson obliges her. The trail is winding to the west, while they continue at a steady pace. Anderson knows that as he heads west, he only has about 25 minutes left. He is amazed at how long the ravine is, if the clearing by the horse pasture is counted as part of the ravine. One of the reasons he likes late autumn to early spring is the visibility in the woods. On a normal day he can see his surroundings 100% better without the leaves on the trees and the underbrush.

Soon he will be headed northwest. Anderson thinks, "What a wonderful sky-blue day, with a scattering of puffy white clouds. He notices an occasional plane leaving its cloudy streak in the sky. Most of the planes are heading to or coming from the Knoxville Airport. He feels a little tired as he walks northwest.

Once the trail curves to the north, he will have circled back, and will soon be walking down to the fire pit. The long ravine finally gives in to a big hill, as Anderson's path curves to the north. He can see the part of the trail now that leads down to the fire pit. As usual, Pockets has kept up with him. She knows that she will get a treat as soon as they get home. She usually lays down on the front porch, while Anderson goes inside to get her treats.

Anderson is now on the part of the path that will go downhill to the clearing below his back yard. As he gets closer to the clearing, he notices more birds chirping. He sees a white breasted nuthatch on the side of a hickory tree. As he starts to go down the trail head he can see the log seats around the fire pit and in a clearing to the side. He carefully places the walking stick on the ground ahead of him, as he goes down the steep hill. Pockets sprints down the rest of the hill and past the fire pit. She crouches down behind a log seat and waits.

As Anderson passes the fire pit, Pockets springs out and follows him up a short trail beside the house, and across the front of the yard to the porch. Anderson unlocks the door and goes in to get Pocket's treats.

A Light on the Path

Anderson thinks, "Where does time go? It's almost 2:00." He thinks about what he can fix for lunch. He's ready to lay down for a while. After he gives Pockets her treats, he grills a cheese sandwich and puts a bowl of chicken and noodle soup in the microwave. After lunch, Anderson decides he needs to stretch out on his bed and take a short nap.

As Anderson wakes up, he hears a truck go by the house. He looks at the clock on the dresser. He thinks, "3:20, I have plenty of time to get the business news on before the close of the market. I need to call Kenny after I catch up on the news."

Anderson is wondering again about the change of the economy and what the ramifications might be. He turns on the business news. He finds out real soon that it didn't take until the end of the day for some prices to more than double. The business reporter said that the price of gas in California is $5.65. He found out that New York City's price is already $4.99. The unpredictable, rising prices remind him of the old carnival show saying: "and where it stops nobody knows".

As Anderson listens to the business report, he wonders what kind of civil unrest will be caused by steep inflation. He thinks, "There is no doubt that the unemployment numbers will go up." He expects protests, even though the protestors can do nothing to change the economy. He also assumes that there will be no big government bail outs, like the feds did about ten years ago. The federal government has their back to the wall with the twenty-two trillion-dollar debt in addition to the demise of the dollar, as the international trade currency.

He decides to also listen to some of the national and world news before he calls Kenny. Before he turns to the regular news, he sees that the Dow Jones Average has already dropped 4,800 points, almost 20%. The reporter says that is only 2% less than the initial drop of the 1929 Great Depression. Anderson says to himself, "it sure sounds scary." He goes ahead and turns channels, since it's almost 4:00.

"I can't believe it!" exclaims Anderson. The news reporter is already talking about unrest in a lot of the major cities across the country. Some protestors are not only shouting about the increase in prices, but they're showing protestors in downtown Baltimore and in the streets of Los Angeles looting and burning cars. Anderson wonders if Kenny has been watching the news a lot after his morning chores were done.

A Light on the Path

He thinks that he will go ahead and call Kenny. He knows that Saturday through Monday will work for him in Maggie Valley. He also thinks that Kenny may have heard a lot more news than what he has.

Kenny answers Anderson's call, "Hello, my friend. Can you believe what is happening in the country right now?"

"It is hard to believe, Kenny. The inflation is bad enough. What do the protestors expect to accomplish with protesting, looting and vandalizing?"

"They may not be expecting it, but they're asking for martial law," replies Kenny.

"I haven't seen a lot of news, since we talked this morning. Can you fill me in on what you've heard?"

Kenny says, "I came in about 11:30; fixed a quick lunch and turned on the TV. There are so many astonishing reports that I left the TV on after 11:30."

"I didn't have it on between 11 and 3:30," replied Anderson. "I heard a few minutes ago that there were protests, looting and fires started in Baltimore and Los Angeles."

"Unfortunately, brother, what you heard just scratches the surface. Those things are happening in most major cities across the country. The only states where I haven't heard those kinds of reports are Hawaii, Alaska, Montana, North and South Dakota and a few other states with sparse population."

"Have you heard about violent protests in Tennessee, North Carolina and Indiana?"

Kenny replies, "I've heard Indianapolis and Gary mentioned. I also heard Memphis, Nashville and Charlotte mentioned. Evidently you haven't heard that most states are calling up their National Guard units. It sounds like the states who activate the National Guard will call for a curfew and possibly martial law. I don't know if the curfews will be for the whole state or just for the cities where there are violent protests."

"We need to do a lot of praying."

"And possibly preparing for civil unrest in our own areas," replied Kenny.

"I understand what you're saying: if things get bad enough there may be a lot of breaking and entering."

"That's right, my friend. If you are still coming to Maggie Valley soon, I'm guessing the roads will be clear. I doubt that there would be problems now driving through Newport or into Maggie Valley."

A Light on the Path

"We don't know what will happen in another week, but I wanted to ask about your schedule for Friday through Monday. I wouldn't get there until about noon on Friday and would come back about 1:00 or so on Monday. As always, I'll stay at the Maggie Valley Inn".

"That sounds good," replied Kenny. "If you don't feel safe there, I can put you up in my cluttered, spare bedroom!"

"I'll check things out Friday night, and then we can decide. I was thinking we could go to the Maggie Valley Chapel for Sunday morning worship service," said Anderson.

"Sure thing," replied Kenny. "I'm sure we'll go to the Blue Ridge Parkway and also walk around Lake Junaluska."

"By all means, and I always look forward to our meals at Salty Sea Restaurant."

"Yes, and also the Butter and Roll Restaurant!' replied Kenny.

"How are things on the farm?" asked Anderson.

"Pretty normal. You know, "no news is good news".

"How true that is! Brother, I almost hate to listen to the 5:00 news."

"I know what you mean," replied Kenny. "We live in good areas, but still be safe and double check your locks."

"I will, and I will also call Lydia and Angela, and make sure that they are taking safety precautions. Especially Angela; she teaches at a college in Indianapolis."

"Tell her to take a hard look wherever she goes."

"I will, Kenny. Have a good night."

"You too. Until we meet again," says Kenny as he hangs up.

Anderson reluctantly picks up the TV remote and turns the mute off. He's not looking forward to hearing the alarming and morbid news. He thinks of how devastating violence and arson are. Before Anderson sits down, he goes into the kitchen to get Pocket's food. He goes outside, "Here's your supper, Pockets!" She comes running across the lawn and starts gobbling up the food. "I'll get you some fresh water, Pockets." Anderson finishes taking care of Pockets and goes to his recliner thinking, "I sure hate to hear these news reports."

As he sits down to watch the news, he thinks, "I should be checking on Angela and Lydia now, but I'll call them in a couple hours." He starts watching all the reports on protesting, looting and arson. Anderson watches the news for about fifteen minutes, then prays, "God, please help the country". As he prays, he falls asleep.

Chapter 4 – Looking for Answers

Anderson wakes up and dials Angela on her cell phone. She answers right away, "How are you doing, Dad?'

"I'm coping alright. How are you and the family?"

Angela answers with tension in her voice, "Oh, dad, it's a mess in Indianapolis. I taught classes today, but with Central Indiana College being near downtown, I saw some of the protesting.'

"Do the college officials and campus police think that it is safe to conduct classes?"

Angela replies, "For now they do. Dad, I'm sorry that I haven't called before now. We got home at 11 this morning, and I left right away for a 12:00. I had a 2:00 also, and I left the campus by 3:30. I didn't want to be any longer than I had to be."

"I'm glad you left early. Don't feel bad about not calling yet: I've been talking with Lydia and Kenny. Angela be careful wherever you go and at home as well. The police have had a training film for people to take a hard look around whenever they get out of their car and in their car."

"I will, Dad; that's a good reminder. I'm so upset that I don't even know who to blame for this mess."

Anderson replies, "I know that you usually like to blame the conservatives, but this problem overreaches media propaganda."

"You're right, Dad. I know that you don't like the slant from most of the media. I really do believe that the conservatives or the liberals can't be blamed for this one. I think it started years ago, when our foreign trading practices with countries like China took a lot of jobs from our country."

"China has been preparing and building for years. With their quest for the number one economy and Russia's greed for other countries, I'm not surprised. Also, there is no love lost on the part of most mid-eastern countries. I've told people for years that things could change overnight."

"I know you have, Dad, and I probably should have listened more."

"While the looming debt took our country downhill, China kept stockpiling gold."

Angela asks, "Not to change the subject, Dad, but is it safe where you are?"

"As you know, this is a good neighborhood and semi-remote. The closest small town is about four miles from here. There's one way into this neighborhood, and one way out. I think for now that it is safe. Kenny said there were protests and some violence in Memphis, Nashville, and Charlotte. Charlotte, the closest of the three cities, is about four hours from here."

"That's good to know about your neighborhood. Can I do anything for you?"

Anderson says, "There is one thing. If you don't have other plans, I would like to fly to Indianapolis and spend Christmas with you."

"We would love to have you. Is there enough time to get your flight booked?"

"There is; I will use my Knoxville connections! I'm thinking about flying in on the 23rd or early on the 24th and leaving on the 26th. Would that work for you?"

Angela replied, "Sure it will."

"Do you think that you or Stephen could pick me up at the airport?"

"We're both off during that time, so both of us will probably be there. We will definitely pick you up."

Anderson replies, "Thank you, honey. Keep me posted about your work location, and about your area of Greenfield."

"I will. I will be waiting to hear about your flight arrival."

"Thank you. I'm praying for you, and I wish you would pray."

Angela replies, "I know how you believe, and I probably should pray."

"Be safe, Angela. I love you.'

"I love you too, dad. Take care."

Anderson hangs up and thinks, "I'm glad I can be with Angela during Christmas, but the state of the country is just too much for me to think about now after losing Ruth. I better call Lydia now and see how she is doing." Anderson dials her cell phone.

"Hi, Anderson."

"I just talked with Angela. She said things have been rowdy with protestors not far from the campus."

"How are they doing?"

Anderson replies, "She and her family seem to be doing alright. She said that they're safe for now. How are things in Crossville and in your neighborhood?"

"Things seem normal in the neighborhood, but I heard there were a few thugs in the downtown area causing problems. The local news hasn't reported any arson problems, but the thugs were bothering people and some people were robbed."

A Light on the Path

Anderson comments, "It makes you wonder if things will get worse before they get better."

Lydia replies, "That's so true. There was some news today forecasting even higher prices. I think that is the opinion of some bankers and economists."

"It's nerve-racking. I was just thinking that there are times that I just can't handle thinking about it. I think it's because I miss Ruth so much."

Lydia replies, "I understand. I don't like thinking about it either."

"Lydia, do you feel safe? Are you checking locks on the house and taking precautions?"

"I am. I also have a small handgun, and today I made sure that it was loaded and handy."

"That's good. How is your family?"

"So far, they haven't had problems. Faith said that her doctor friend saw some fires in Nashville, but no one in my family has experienced any altercations."

"I'm glad to hear that. I know that you want to talk about your finances sometime. I'm going to visit with Kenny this Saturday through Monday in Maggie Valley. Do you want to get together after Monday?"

Lydia says, "Yes, I will work on them this week. Would you want to get together at your place next week?"

"Sure. What days are good for you?"

Lydia replies, "I could use a change. Could I stay there Thursday through Saturday? I will want to come back home by Saturday afternoon."

"That's a date. I will write it in my calendar book. What time do you want to arrive next Thursday?"

"I think 1:00 would be good."

"Great! If you feel like walking in the woods, maybe we can walk awhile on Thursday and Friday."

"I will do what I can to be ready for a nice walk!"

Anderson says, "I'm flying to Indianapolis on the 23rd or 24th, and I'm coming back on the 26th."

"That will be nice. Are you staying at Angela's house for Christmas?"

"Yes."

Lydia says, "My family is coming here for Christmas Eve and early Christmas day."

Anderson replies, "I'm glad to hear that. I'm praying that you will keep looking up."

A Light on the Path

"I should probably talk with you about that, Anderson, when we get together next week. I feel like I'm missing out on something, and maybe it's my lack of faith."

"Are you praying?"

Lydia replies, "I think I do need to try that. It's hard for me to pray. When we were growing up in our home church, I felt closer to God. Maybe I was disillusioned with how my marriage turned out. I was disappointed with my ex-husband. Maybe I blame God. I just don't know."

"Why don't you just try praying by faith? The Bible says, "Whatever is not of faith is sin.""

"Really? Do you know where you found that verse?"

Anderson replies, "Romans 14:23".

"I remember where Romans is. I think I will read that chapter."

Anderson says, "I will be praying for you. You remember the old hymn "Trust and Obey". Try to keep looking up. Have a good night. I can't believe its 9:00 already."

Lydia replies, "I know. I'm starting to wind down. Have a good night. Love you."

"Love you," Anderson hangs up and says a short prayer for Lydia.

Anderson thinks, "I will listen to the eerie news just a few minutes before I go to bed." After he turns on the TV, he almost wishes he hadn't; things are still getting worse. He hears reports about violence in Philadelphia and Detroit. The reporter shows fires that have been set by arsonists in Houston and Dallas.

Anderson wonders about the rising prices while he watches the news. He hasn't even heard the world news. He wonders what kind of impact the changes have had on third world countries. In his life he has supported missions in Hong Kong, Kenya, Nigeria, Zambia, the Philippines, Nicaragua and in several other countries. As weariness sets in, Anderson says a prayer especially for third world countries.

He turns off the TV. As he walks to his bedroom, he thinks, "What is the world coming to?"

Chapter 5 – Maggie Valley

Anderson finishes with breakfast in the kitchen and gets ready to feed Pockets. He looks at the large national parks calendar on his kitchen wall. He thinks, "Friday, my last day to get things done before I leave for Maggie Valley." He opens the front door; Pockets is stretching on the screen door as she waits for him. "Good morning, Pockets, are you ready for breakfast?" He pours the "no preservatives" cat food in her bowl. "I'll get you some fresh, warm water." Anderson sees that they got a dusting of snow last night.

After he takes care of Pockets, he freshens up and dresses, so he can run several errands in town. He puts on his red and black checked coat and locks the front door. Going down the sidewalk, he notices Pockets paw prints in the light snow. He thinks, "I can brush this light snow off my truck in less than a minute".

He gets in his 1999 Ford F150. He still likes the army green color with the tan trim. He has a 4x4, so he can drive the hills in his area during any type of weather. It's hard for him to imagine that Christmas is just two weeks away. He thinks, "Now I have to get ready for my Maggie Valley trip and take flowers to Ruth."

As he starts out on the four mile trip to Mount Holly, he sees his neighbor in front of his house. Anderson yells, "What are you up to, Conard?" Conard's toboggan hat accentuates his ruddy complexion.

"Hey there, Anderson. The morning paper is always late. I should probably cancel my subscription."

Anderson pulls over. "I haven't seen you for a few days".

Conard replies, "I've been gearing up for the deer season, and I've been in Knoxville part of the time visiting my son and daughter-in-law. How are you doing?"

"I'm doing alright. I'm getting ready to leave for Maggie Valley in the morning. Could you keep your eye on the place until Monday?"

Conard says, "Sure I will. I wanted to ask you about when I can hunt on your land. Since you're leaving tomorrow, would it be alright if I hunt there Saturday and Sunday?"

Anderson replies, "That will be fine. Let me know how you do. Will you make sure Pockets is okay?"

A Light on the Path

"I will. She always comes over. Be safe on your trip, and I'll keep a watch on things."

Anderson replies, "Keep lookin' up, brother!"

"I will. Take it easy." Conard waves as Anderson pulls out on the snow-covered road. Anderson thinks, "Conard is the most unassuming and sincere person I know. I sure am fortunate to have him for a neighbor."

Mount Holly is the closest town to Anderson, but he is glad they have a large grocery store, a general discount store, a pharmacy, a public school, a bank, a nursing home, a veterinarian, two restaurants and two gas stations. The last he heard, the population in Mount Holly is about 2,400. Anderson brags that they have two red lights and one flashing yellow light.

Anderson first winds through his neighborhood area. Next is a long curve that winds around to the back of his property. There he passes the horse ranch, and a hedge row that he calls the blue jay stretch. Every time he gets to the hedge row, he sees blue jays flying in and out of the area.

Now and then he sees deer and their fawn on the side of the road. As he passes the hedge row, it looks like a doe and two juveniles are crossing the road ahead of him. Only a couple of months ago, he was coming home on that stretch of road, when he had to stop for the wildest turkey sighting he had seen. They were crossing rank and file, and their line was almost done crossing, when he came to a complete stop. Anderson counted the twenty he could see, and others had already gone into the woods.

It only takes him about ten minutes to get to the Eat Rite grocery store in Mount Holly. Right before he gets to the edge of town, Anderson passes an old factory that use to make transistor radios! After Anderson passes the factory, he starts thinking about Willie. About three years ago, Willie started working in produce at Eat Rite. Anderson talks and kids with most of the staff there. After he got to know Willie, he found out that he is a retired pastor; works at Eat Rite part-time and drives a school bus.

Just a couple months after he met Willie, Anderson told him about a dream he had years ago. After the dream, he looked up a scripture that was not familiar to him. Through the years he shared it with people now and them, but they too were not familiar with it. When he shared it with Willie, he quoted the book, chapter and verse it was from. Anderson was amazed! He remembers saying, "Willie, I shared that scripture with a good number of people through the years, and you have been the only one who knew it."

Before Anderson went back to Eat Rite after that experience, he prepared a difficult question from the Bible for Willie. When he asked Willie

A Light on the Path

the question, not only did Willie know the book, chapter and verses, he quoted a long part of the passage! Anderson was flabbergasted!

Willie said, "I noticed how surprised you were the first time I knew about the scripture you shared. At that time, I didn't tell you something."

Anderson had replied, "What's that?"

Willie said, "I have the New Testament memorized."

Once again, Anderson was completely astonished.

Willie said, "I don't mind if you ask me now about any scriptures in the New Testament."

So, Anderson asked him about two different passages that he was familiar with. In each case, Willie quoted a good part of each chapter.

In the past three years, Anderson knew that some people he told had trouble believing it. He was glad that his neighbor, Conard, could confirm it. Anderson also met an author at Eat Rite years ago, and the author could confirm Willie's ability as well.

Anderson pulled up in front of Eat Rite and got out of his truck. As he walked in the store and got a cart, he thought, "Willie might be working this morning." As Anderson turned the cart down the first aisle, which was produce, there stood Willie.

"Hey there, brother!" exclaimed Anderson.

"Hi Anderson. How are you doing?"

"I'm still looking up."

Willie replied, "I heard about your wife. I'm so sorry, Anderson. Is there anything I can do?"

"Just keep on being my friend, Willie."

"You can count on that."

"Thank you, brother," replied Anderson. "Hopefully, I will see you soon."

Willie said, "Take care, Anderson."

Through the years, Anderson found out quickly that Willie was not only knowledgeable and pleasant, but also learned he was very resourceful.

The next item was flowers for Ruth. They have a small section of flowers right after produce. The rest of the items were for home and the trip. He always took bottled water, granola bars and nuts on his trips. For home, he was sure to get potatoes, onions and thin cut pork chops for stir fry that he made. It was every one's favorite meal that he cooked.

The other items he got were coffee, eggs and bread. This is the first time he has been to the store, since the world trade currency was changed. He is shocked to see that most of the items are more than double what they were a week ago. The eggs are $3.79. The bread that he buys is only 55

A Light on the Path

calories a slice, and it's made without high-fructose corn syrup. Normally the bread is $2.49 a loaf, but it's now priced at $4.99.

As Anderson checks out, he kids with the cashier about all the extra money that she and the store are making. As Anderson walks the grocery cart outside. He notices an officer in a police car near the front of the store. He wonders if the officer is stationed there, because of the trouble throughout the country. Before he goes to the Gardens of the Valley cemetery, he pulls into the gas station to fill up. He also sees another officer in a police car at the gas station.

As he gets out of his truck, he laughs to himself, because he calls his truck an old man's truck. He thinks, "Even though it's a 1999 model. I wouldn't trade it for anything." As he is paying for the gas at the pump, he sees the officer nearby getting out of his car. Anderson projects his voice, "Excuse me, officer."

The officer looks at him, and as he walks toward Anderson, he says, "Can I help you, sir?"

Anderson replies, "I was wondering if you and the officer at the grocery store are stationed here, because of all of the trouble in the country."

The police officer answered, "Yes, sir. Our chief wants customers, business owners and their employees safe."

Anderson replies, "Thank you, officer; that's good to know."

As the officer walks away, Anderson thinks, "Man, the officer is as tall as my grandson, Clint, and about twice as wide. I bet nobody messes with him!"

The gas pump handle clicks off, and Anderson returns the handle to the pump and tears off his receipt. Anderson gets in his truck and heads toward the Gardens of the Valley. The cemetery is literally in a valley on the other side of Mount Holly. As Anderson pulls into the peaceful cemetery, the light snow gives it an even more ethereal appearance.

There are Dwarf Evergreens and Dwarf Alberta Spruce planted near the grave sites. The markers are even to the ground. Anderson is glad that there are no markers sticking up and looking ostentatious. Anderson climbs out of the truck and gathers up the flowers. He walks over to Ruth and pulls up the bronze vase that is inserted into the marker. He secures the flowers in the vase and looks at the marker. His name is already on the marker: Anderson L. McCollister, April 11, 1938 - _____. Beside his name is Ruth M. McCollister, January 30, 1939 – December 7, 2018.

Anderson continues to stand by the grave on the cold, hard ground. He envisions Ruth looking at him with her warm and loving smile. He can imagine hugging her. He starts to pray for her and for the time that he can

A Light on the Path

see her again. After Anderson pauses for several minutes, he looks at the marker and flowers once more and turns to walk to his truck.

All the way back home, Anderson only thinks of Ruth. Going through town and over the winding, hilly roads are only a blur to him. As he turns onto his snow-covered drive, he notices good, ole' faithful Pockets sitting in front of the porch, looking at him. It's already 11:00, and he wonders if he is going to walk in the woods today. He thinks, "The sun is beginning to come out. Maybe I can take a shortcut in the woods today and make it a 45-minute walk."

He pets Pockets and looks at the thermometer on the edge of the porch; 34 degrees. With the sun coming out, Anderson decides that he will rest, then walk in the woods. On purpose, he walks pass the TV and the remote. He lays down on his bed to enjoy the silence and to take forty winks.

Anderson wakes up from a dream. He hears the high-pitched song of a tufted titmouse near his window. He sees the sun is shining, and it's time for walking. Anderson gathers his walking aids. After the walk, he plans to spend the rest of the day preparing for the Maggie Valley trip.

The last thing that Anderson grabs before he walks out the door is his walking stick. The snow is still melting. From his back deck, he sees that the winding trailhead is painted from the snowfall. The trail winds up the hill into the woods. The trees are sparkling as the sun shines on their snow-covered branches. The branches look like long arms that are lifted to heaven with praise to God.

Here comes Pockets; ready for a hike. Anderson takes a few seconds of playtime with her, and they swat at each other. As Anderson approaches the trailhead by the fire pit, he thinks of how he misses the fires he builds during autumn. He loves sitting by the fire while he watches the flames and glowing coals.

At the top of the hill, Anderson notices how the fallen leaves glisten in the sun as the snow has left for another day. The thawing ground crunches under his feet as he walks deeper into the woods. Anderson has forged another trail, so he can observe his property in the deeper part of the woods. He won't be seeing his creek today or the neighbor's horse pasture.

He looks around and sees Pockets hanging back about 20 yards. "Come on, Pockets," he yells at times. Anderson thinks, "It looks like she is digging again in the middle part of the trail. It might be her way of helping to keep the trail clear."

As he passes a little shelter he built for a campsite, he is headed due south, instead of the perimeter route that takes him to the east then to the southeast. Near the campsite, he notices the stoic beauty of the sweet birch trees. They stay dressed in their small, light brown leaves during the winter. In early spring, they change into their more fashionable green leaves.

He notices an occasional squirrel that keeps a tree trunk between Pockets and him. Even though Pockets likes to crouch and stalk them, the squirrels are confident that they are faster than cats and climb higher. As Anderson keeps a good pace, he prays, "Thank you, Lord, for another wonderful day!"

It's a beautiful, but uneventful walk for Anderson. He is thinking about his imminent Maggie Valley trip. He keeps an eye on Pockets, as she jumps from one fallen branch to another.

Before he knows it, the trail is gradually curving to the southwest. Soon he will be headed west, which will join the northwest trail closer to the perimeter of the woods. Anderson has been walking for about thirty minutes. He looks at a tree just ahead of him by the trail. He rests his walking stick against the tree and relieves himself. He's thankful for the convenient rest areas.

He's ready for a short rest and knows that he will be coming soon to the two small, benches that overlook most of his backyard and the back of his house. Most of the journey has been quiet and peaceful. He sees the two russet benches under the large red oak tree. He leans his walking sticking against the red oak and sits on the bench next to the tree. Pockets is right behind him. She goes under the bench next to him and lays on the ground.

Anderson enjoys the rest, as he looks at his surroundings. The wind is almost absent; at the most at 1 m.p.h. Suddenly, a gust of wind blows in at over 7 m.p.h. It is constant and brings with it a euphony of sounds and rhythms. There were just one or two maverick leaves dancing on their twigs, but now all the leaves have become part of the symphony. The wind seems to create its own polyphony of sounds, not to mention the cool breeze that refreshes Anderson.

As the gust blows for about three minutes, the rush of the wind sounds more like a section of violins than a horn section blowing into their brass instruments. The wind rests as quickly as it began. Anderson thinks, "Wow, that was like one long crescendo. If I could have recorded those sounds, it would have been a very pleasant new age song and video."

Anderson gets off the bench; grabs his walking stick and heads for the trail to the fire pit. Once again, Pockets rushes through the leaves and passes Anderson before he gets to the trailhead. As he nears his house, he notices that only patches of snow are left on the ground.

He puts up his walking gear; fixes a quick lunch and sits down to rest. He thinks, "It's almost 2:00, and I haven't listened to the news for about 24

A Light on the Path

hours. I really need to get updated." He turns on the remote, even though he doesn't want to hear about the new problems in the country.

Anderson hears about more curfews being set in some large cities. Some states are still talking about using more national guard in some of their larger cities. The newscaster is also warning people to keep their doors locked. Some of the locals they interview are talking about having their guns loaded and ready. Anderson discerns that most food and gas prices nationwide have more than doubled.

After the commercial, they start talking about world bankers discussing a new global currency besides gold. Anderson is ready to turn the TV off and to start packing. He assumes Kenny is getting the latest news and can probably inform him of what he has missed. He plans to call Kenny by 7 or 8:00 to confirm his arrival time. Anderson will be getting to Maggie Valley before he can check into the Maggie Valley Inn. He's sure that he will visit with Kenny at his farm before he goes to the motel.

Anderson packs and works on everyday things around the house. He washes the dishes; brings the mail in; gives Pockets extra food and water and cleans up some throughout the house. He makes some stir fry. He cuts up the thin cut pork and starts cooking it in olive oil. Next, he cuts up a potato and puts that in with the pork. His last ingredient is half of a sweet, yellow onion. He cuts it up and adds it. He adds lite salt and a little pepper off and on as he stirs it.

After supper it's almost time to call Kenny. Anderson goes to a spare bedroom (his office and study) and finds his cell phone on the desk by the computer. He calls Kenny.

"Hello, my friend."

"Hi, Kenny. How are things down on the farm?"

"Doing well. What time are you arriving tomorrow?"

"It looks like I will get to Maggie Valley by 11, but I can't check in until 2:00."

Kenny replies, "Why don't you come here at 11. I will be finishing my chores, then we'll have a light lunch here."

"That's perfect. I haven't listened to the news much. Do you have any special reports for me?"

Kenny says, "There are two significant things that have been reported today. Reports are coming in that panhandling and robbery are rampant nationwide. The other development is world banker meetings about making a new global currency besides gold."

"I heard a little about the world banker meetings. I'm not surprised about the panhandling and robbery. I went to Mount Holly today. One officer was stationed outside the grocery store in his squad car and another officer was stationed at the gas station. The police officer at the gas station said they're stationed there for the safety of the customers, owners and employees."

Kenny says, "You will probably see the same thing in Maggie Valley tomorrow. If we go to Cherokee, we're likely to find the same thing there."

"Okay, brother. Let me know more about the national news and any world news tomorrow. I'm starting to wear down right now. It's been a busy day, so I'll probably go to bed early."

"That sounds like a good plan. Have a safe trip tomorrow; until we meet again."

"Thank you. Have a good night," replies Anderson. He puts the phone down by his recliner. He thinks, "Where has the day gone? Its 7:45 and almost bedtime." Anderson gets up and checks on Pockets. He comes back in; walks down the long hall way and goes into the master bathroom. He brushes his teeth; changes his clothes and tunes into relaxing music on the Sirius Spa channel. It's only 8:30 by the time Anderson turns out the lights in the house and gets under the covers. He turns the remote off; prays and falls to sleep.

His cell phone alarm goes off at 6 AM. He thinks, "I did pretty good last night. I only got up one time; that's pretty good for an old man." He goes into the kitchen and makes his daily cup of hot green tea. He takes it to the recliner with a high protein granola bar; reads from a daily devotional and reads some chapters in Ezekiel and the gospel of John. After he reads, he does some deep breathing exercises and then prays for a long list of people and needs.

Anderson goes in his office and turns on his computer to check the extended forecast for Maggie Valley. It's usually a few degrees colder there. It looks like the average low will be in the mid-twenties and that the average high will be in the low to mid-forties. It says they might get some light snow tonight. He is already packed for the trip. He'll load two small luggage bags in the truck after he checks the house. He always turns on a few lights outside and inside for security lights. He double checks locks and outlets, and he heads out the door.

He makes sure that Pockets has plenty of water and food. He pets her and grabs his bags. He starts up the truck. While it warms up a little, he gets out his snacks. He pulls out an aspartame-free diet soda and some mixed nuts with almonds. As he pulls out of the drive, he notices the patches of snow are gone, and the road is nice and dry. It's a few minutes after 10:00, and he has plenty of time to get to Kenny's around 11.

He stops at the highway that goes to I-40 Mount Holly and Sevierville are to the right, and Newport and I-40 are to the left. Anderson is in Newport before he realizes it. He's been thinking about Ruth and his upcoming trip to

A Light on the Path

Indianapolis. He turns at the Asheville-I-40 East sign and merges onto the interstate. For a Saturday morning, the traffic is not bad. Soon the Tennessee Mountains are ahead of him. He sees there is still snow coverage in the higher elevations.

As he starts through the gorge in Tennessee, he knows he will soon be crossing into North Carolina. Most of the mountains along the gorge are in North Carolina. Anderson thinks, "The snow-covered mountains are majestic! How could anyone not appreciate God's splendor?" He crosses into North Carolina and soon he passes the state's rest area. The Maggie Valley exit is just ten miles away.

He turns on exit 20 and merges right on the road to Maggie Valley. It's a quiet and scenic four lane highway. When he comes to the stop light, Maggie Valley is to the right and Kenny's farm is to the left; off Soco Rd. He has always enjoyed looking at the hills that surround Maggie Valley.

Anderson turns left and has a little over five minutes before he gets to Kenny's farm. Right away he passes Lake Junaluska, and another two miles to the left is the road to the farm. He turns onto Walnut Rd., which is a lot narrower than the highway lanes. He passes a gravel road and a paved county road, and in two miles on the right is Kenny's place.

Anderson always thinks of it as the farm from the past. The land has some level areas and the rest is small rolling hills. One of his favorite sites on the farm is just ahead of him.

To the right is an old barn, where someone has excavated the ground and made an earthen ramp into the barn, which is on a slight grade. The ramp to the barn is just a few yards to the right of the drive way. The ramp and barn as well as Kenny's small orchard, which is straight ahead, remind Anderson of a family friend and his farm in central Indiana. As a young kid in the 1940s, Anderson would go to that farm with his family. It also had an earthen ramp, which was between a dirt country road and the barn. It also had a small orchard near their house.

Kenny's orchard is just about twenty-five yards to the right side of his house. As Anderson pulls up to the front of the house, it's 11:03. There is Kenny on the front porch with his lap dog, Scooter, a frisky and loveable, amber Pomeranian. It looks like Kenny just finished his chores. He has on his grey coveralls and a green John Deere cap.

Kenny waves as Anderson gets out of the truck.

"Did you just finish your chores?" asks Anderson as he leans down to pet the wagging Scooter.

"I did, my friend. How was your trip?"

A Light on the Path

Anderson replied, "Very pleasant; I always enjoy the scenery. Kenny, I've meant to ask you something before now about your orchard, barn and ramp."

"What's that?"

Anderson said, "Do you know when the barn was built, and how long the fruit trees have been bearing?"

"Well, the house and barn were built in 1912, and I assume the original owner excavated that ramp, when the barn was built. Guessing the age of the fruit trees, I would say that either the original owner planted them much later or the next owner may have planted them. The abstract says that another owner bought it in 1938, and his son ran the farm until 1998, when I bought it. I'm guessing that the trees are roughly seventy to eighty years old."

Anderson replied, "That's very interesting. The earthen ramp I saw as a kid always intrigued me. Do you think they used something like an excavating blade on a tractor to make the earthen ramp?"

"I don't know if they had that kind of accessory back then. It's clear that it was done by hand or by machine," said Kenny. "I know farms by 1912 were using gas powered Ford tractors, and John Deere tractors became popular a few years later."

Anderson said, "I always meant to ask you, if you have only the apple and pear trees in the orchard."

Kenny replied, "That's most of them. On the perimeter I have a few black walnut and pecan trees. After lunch we'll have time to walk in the orchard, and I'll show them to you."

Anderson said, "That will be nice."

Anderson followed Kenny and Scooter into the hundred-year-old house. Anderson noticed that the white front door not only had Victorian scroll work, but also a black, metal door knob. Anderson had noticed many times the old, porcelain white door knobs on the inside doors. He loved the fragrant pipe odor inside the house. Anderson's eyes always went to the old upright piano in the living room. It was a pristine, burr walnut Wm. Knabe & Co. piano. Anderson's favorite piano was a restored Knabe concert grand that he played at a friend's house in Knoxville. He always remembered how clear and full-bodied the bass was on the Knabe.

Kenny said, "Have a seat at the table. I'll make some coffee and get out some food that we can have for lunch or a snack. Kenny had cut up some celery and apples that he put on the table. He also put out baby carrots, deli black forest ham, mustard and gluten free crackers. As he set a couple cans of diet soda on the table, he said, "Here's something we can drink, if we want something before the coffee is ready."

A Light on the Path

Anderson laughed, "Kenny, I have this kind of food at home and like it. I also get the same kind of crackers and deli ham.

Did you know that eating this processed ham with gluten free crackers is like eating a candy bar with a diet soda?"

Kenny laughed too, "You know, my friend, that's true! I never thought of it that way."

Anderson said the blessing, and they both attacked the food. Anderson remarked, "Wow, this hits the spot. Thanks for the lunch. It makes me think of where we want to have supper tonight."

Kenny replies, "I would guess the Roll and Butter Restaurant or the Salty Sea. Seafood sounds good for this evening. What do you think?"

Anderson says, "The Salty Sea it is! So, what's the latest that you've heard on the news?"

"It's really bad in Los Angeles. Last night a news reporter said that property damage from fires has surpassed the property damage done by hurricane Katrina. Los Angeles officials are reporting over $90 billion in property has been destroyed throughout Los Angeles and surrounding counties. It sounds like the governor of California has no choice, but to declare martial law in Los Angeles."

"That's appalling!" replied Anderson.

Kenny said, "I would bet governors of other states will call for more curfews and probably for more martial law in some cities. It looks foreboding in Chicago, Miami, St. Louis, Detroit, Baltimore and a few other cities."

"Do you know how many cities are under curfew?' asked Anderson.

"Besides Los Angeles, Chicago, Baltimore, Miami, Detroit, and St. Louis, I think there are also curfews in Indianapolis, Milwaukee, Philadelphia, D.C., New Orleans, Memphis and Nashville."

Anderson replied, "Wow! There may be more curfews than that in place by now."

Kenny continued, "An investigative reporter in D.C. said insurance companies are lobbying congress for more curfews and for more martial law. There have been serious problems in many other cities, including Phoenix, Houston, Birmingham, Atlanta, Cleveland and Buffalo."

Anderson remarked, "I bet the insurance companies are behind an eight ball. When did you hear about all of these things?"

Kenny answered, "I got all of these updates between 5:00 and 9:00 last evening."

"Well, brother, you know what we have talked about off and on the past several years; these kinds of problems, the civil unrest and more."

"Yes," replied Kenny. "I know you believe even more is connected to it spiritually."

A Light on the Path

"I believe it is. I know that you also believe in the Great Spirit, but I don't know how that connects with your belief in Christ and His Word."

Kenny replies, "I think I know what you're saying. I've had a similar thought. I know that part of my belief in the Great Spirit is from my ethnic background. I descend from the Cherokees who hid out in the neighboring mountains from the time of the Trail of Tears until the end of the Civil War. We became known as the Eastern Band of the Cherokees. The federal government eventually approved the Qualla Boundary Reservation, commonly called the Cherokee Reservation, after the Civil War.

My Great Spirit belief developed as I followed Cherokee practices like the sweat lodges all my life. Our culture is different than the white man's. We still have medicine men, and we have certain beliefs about animal and plant life. I do believe in Christ and I believe in the triune God. It's true that I don't know a lot about the intricate beliefs of Protestants and Catholics, but I do believe the story of Christ and of heaven and hell."

Anderson replies, "I know what you're saying. You have traditional Cherokee beliefs, yet you believe the basic tenets of the Christian faith."

Kenny says, "That's correct."

"I respect that Kenny, and you know that I respect you and the Cherokee people. You also know that following Christ is my life. I believe in nature too, but my great admiration for nature is not part of my faith in Christ. As your friend, I ask that you study the gospels and the epistles of the New Testament. Hopefully, we can talk more later about what Christ taught."

Kenny replies, "That's fair. I will try to read and meditate more on the books of the New Testament."

Anderson says, "I will be praying for you, and you know that I always wish you the very best."

"I know you do, Anderson, and the same here. It's after 12:30 already. Do you want to look at the orchard and maybe walk around the farm some?"

"I would love to," replied Anderson.

Kenny walks by the fireplace and a small pile of neatly stacked wood. He opens the front door. Scooter rushes out first and lets out a couple barks.

"She knows she is going to walk and run around," said Kenny.

As they walk toward the small orchard, Anderson says, "The orchard is laid out well."

Kenny replies, "Whoever did the planning, or the planting knew what they were doing." When they got next to the orchard, Kenny stopped and said, "There are four rows of five trees in a row. The first three rows are apple trees. When they were planted, I think they were a lot more limited on variety. All of the trees are either Jonathan or Golden Delicious." As they

A Light on the Path

walked into the orchard, Kenny said, "the last three trees of the fourth row are Bartlett pear trees. The first two trees of the fourth row are pecan."

Anderson replied, "Very nice. The orchard is picturesque, almost alluring. I could walk in the orchard every day. Whoever did the planting knew about cross pollination."

"They did know about cross pollination. You're so right about the orchard being alluring. I do walk through the orchard every day."

"Wow! Twenty fruit trees; it's absolutely beautiful," exclaimed Anderson.

"As you know, the farm is sixty acres. I think it's laid out well. I could show you the scheme of things."

"Sure!' replied Anderson enthusiastically.

Right now, we're on the southeast corner of the farm, which is the house, the garden area, the orchard and the barn. If we walk near the road you can see the lay out better. As you look to the north and to the west, you can see that the land is hillier. The farm was laid out to take advantage of the most level ground for the house and garden area and for the crop land. Of course, you're familiar with the chicken coup, which is to the northwest of the house. About an acre was laid out behind the house for the yard and garden."

Anderson asked, "How many chickens do you have now?"

"Right now, I have twenty hens and one rooster. The hens are producing about 90 eggs a week or about 7 ½ dozen. I use about eight to ten eggs a week, and I sell the rest of them to a little country, convenience store. There's about thirty acres of crop land. I lease it out by cash rental. Like most farms, I rotate corn with soy beans annually. Thirty acres doesn't bring in a lot of money, but it sure helps. You can see all of the crop land from here."

Kenny points to the north and swings his arm around to the west and says, "that whole area is all of the crop land."

"Very nice," exclaims Anderson. "From what you tell me, it sounds like you have more woods than I thought."

"The southeast corner, where the house and barn are, sets on roughly four acres. I'm including the orchard, garden, chicken area and yard areas. The rest of it is about twenty-six acres."

Anderson asks, "How much of that is woods?

Kenny replies, "Over ninety percent of it. The woods are mostly on the small hills that run behind the crop land from the north to the west. When we get back to the house, you can see part of the woods behind the garden area. There are clearings here and there, but there is plenty of woods for hunting."

"Oh yeah. You probably have a lot of deer and wild turkey."

A Light on the Path

"Yes, and once in a while I see a coyote, but I try to eliminate them."

Anderson says, "We should go hunting or hiking through the woods sometime."

Kenny replies, "Turkey season is in April. We could hunt for turkey then or just take a walk through the woods. We'll have some nice sixty to seventy-degree weather in April."

"I would like that. You know that you are welcome to hike in my woods anytime."

"I appreciate that," replied Kenny.

"It's almost check-in time. It will be after 2:00, when I get to the Maggie Valley Inn. Do you want to meet at the Salty Sea around 4:30 or 5:00?"

"Sure. Let's meet at 4:45."

Kenny looks at Scooter and says, "Let's go back inside, Scooter," as Scooter starts barking and jumping up and down."

As they walk back through the field to the house and car, Anderson says, "Scooter and Pockets are great companions." Anderson gets in his truck and says, "Salty Sea at 4:45!"

"Until then, brother." Kenny waves as Anderson drives down the fifty-yard driveway.

It only takes him ten minutes to get to the Maggie Valley Inn. It's almost 2:30 when he parks at their check-in area. He walks through the door and says, "Patty, I'm surprised to see you working this early."

Patty, a mainstay of Maggie Valley, says in her raspy voice, "Bonnie called me at noontime and said that she had to pick up her daughter in Waynesville by 2:30, so I came in an hour early. How are you doing, Anderson?"

"I'm still recovering. I lost my wife just over a week ago."

"I'm so sorry. I know that I hadn't seen you for a while. In fact, I remember you saying around August or September that she wasn't doing well."

"Unfortunately, she succumbed to heart failure on December 7th."

"Are you in town visiting Kenny?" asked Patty.

"Yes, I just left him. We're going to meet for supper in about two hours."

Patty says, "That's good to hear. Your card is on file, and we have the same creek side room for you. Just sign here for tonight and tomorrow night."

As Anderson signs, he says, "What do you think of all the steep price increases?"

Patty replies, "It's really sad, Anderson. Most people can't afford it. Police are stationed at grocery stores and gas stations; at shopping areas like

A Light on the Path

Market Square, at banks and at ATMs. This week has been a lot slower. Our regular prices have gone up from $69.99 to $129 through the week, and from $89 on Friday and Saturday to $149. Holiday weeks and weekends will be outrageous!"

"It's a hardship and very troubling. It's always good to see you, Patty."

"You too, Anderson."

"I will unload my bags and move my truck."

"Take your time," replied Patty.

As Anderson gets the luggage out of his truck, he thinks, "Everyone likes Patty. I wonder how many come back to this motel, so they can visit with Patty." Anderson decides to call Lydia as soon as he moves the truck. As Anderson goes back outside, he can tell things are cooling down. He thinks, "It sure smells like snow is in the air. I won't be surprised if it starts snowing before we're done with supper."

He goes back to his room and opens the curtains wide to watch the rushing water in the creek. He sets down on the bed, and calls Lydia on his cell phone.

"Hi, Anderson. Are you in Maggie Valley?"

"Yes, I just checked in. I had lunch with Kenny at his farm."

Lydia replies, "Right now I'm being a little lazy, but I have most of my financial statement and evaluation done."

"That's good. Are you still coming over Thursday?"

"Yes. If it's alright with you, I'll arrive around 11:30 Thursday morning and leave about 1:00 or 1:30 on Saturday."

"It will be good to see you. What do you think about the state of the union?"

"It seems surreal; like it should be a dream. The high prices and the violence are just incredible. Anderson, I hate to say it, but it looks like an unabated crisis."

Anderson replies, "Kenny and I have been talking about some of the problems. I've been busy with other things today. Have you heard any new reports?"

"Yes, about noon today I heard that the governor of California declared martial law in Los Angeles. It's just mind shattering. In our lifetime, we have never seen anything like this in our country," replied Lydia.

"That's sad to hear. Kenny said they were considering martial law. The other drastic measure was what happened when we just had forty-eight states. When you and I were young children, the Japanese in this country were locked up in internment camps during World War II."

Lydia replies, "I was a preschooler then, but I remember hearing about it, when I was seven or eight years old. It was another sad time in our country."

Anderson asks, "How is your family doing?"

"Everyone is fine. Eli is preparing for the Singapore trip. Faith is still dating the young doctor at Vanderbilt. Evidently, she likes him a lot."

"Anderson replies, "and he won't find anyone as beautiful. As Faith got older, I thought only Elizabeth Taylor and Esther of the Old Testament might be as beautiful."

"I agree. We have some attractive people in our family, but not like that. She must get some of it from Paul's side of the family."

"How are you doing, Lydia?"

"The arthritis is about the same and the fibromyalgia is still as bad as always."

Anderson asks, "Do you still have to sit in a tub of hot water to go to sleep?"

"Yes. A good night is just two or three hours in the tub. As you know, when the water gets cool it wakes me up, and I must run more hot water. A bad night is when I have to be in the tub much later than midnight."

"When you take Lyrica or Cymbalta, do you still have to have hot water to fall asleep?"

"Yes, and I also need one of those prescriptions. Are you still able to take ibuprofen for fibromyalgia?"

"Yes, I try to take less than the maximum dose. On some rainy and cold days, I must take the maximum dose," replied Anderson. "It's hard for me to imagine what you go through, because my muscles get so exhausted."

"You know the saying, "getting old ain't for sissies," remarked Lydia. "I know that you have some of the same symptoms: your muscles get so tired that you can hardly walk, and you can feel your muscles quivering inside your body, when you lay down to rest."

Anderson replies, "So true. Speaking of getting old; I need to take a nap! About 4:30, I'll be leaving to meet Kenny. We're having supper at the Salty Sea. You'll have to come with me sometime."

Lydia says, "I would like that. Tell Kenny that I said "hi" and have a good night."

"Good night, Sis. Take care." Anderson puts down the phone and stretches out on the bed.

It's a little after 4:00, when he wakes up. He freshens up; grabs his coat and heads out the door by 4:30. He walks by Patty and tells her that he'll be back around 6:00. As he walks to his F-150, he notices it's even cooler than

A Light on the Path

a couple of hours ago. As he gets in his truck, he shivers a little and thinks, "It must be close to 32 degrees already."

He'll be early, but he likes it that way. He passes the library and town hall, where he walks on their track, and in a minute, he sees the colorful Salty Sea sign ahead. He always gets a kick out of the sign. The neon lights show a sea captain and his mate on a large boat pulling a tuna out of the sea. He pulls in their lot and knows that Kenny will be pulling in soon.

There he is in his navy Jeep Cherokee. They're both ten minutes early. They get out of their trucks. Anderson said, "I knew we would be early."

Kenny lets out his robust laugh, "I thought the same thing. How do you like this refreshing night air?"

"It woke me up in a hurry!"

They walk in and one of the waitresses in her pirate uniform with a black bandana and wide black belt says, "Ahoy, mate. Take a seat of your choosing."

In perfect obedience, Kenny and Anderson find their favorite table. It looks like they've beat the Saturday evening crowd. The same cute, Caribbean waitress hands them menus and says, "What be the drinks, mateys?"

Kenny smiled and said, "I would like the ice tea of the day, mate."

Anderson said, "I would like the water of the day without lemon."

The waitress replies, "Blimey, buccaneers, there's just the same ice tea and water every day!"

Everyone laughs. Anderson says, "Are ya tryin' to gat a good tip out of these old sea dogs?"

The waitress laughs again, "We could banter back and forth like this all night! Do ya old sea dogs want an appetizer?"

In unison they say, "No thanks."

As she walks away from the table, Kenny says, "I think she has earned a good tip already!"

Anderson replies, "What's ya gonna order, you old sea dog?"

Kenny says, "I bet we order what we always order: the catfish with shrimp, hush puppies and coleslaw."

Anderson chimes in, "with cocktail sauce and tartar sauce on the side!"

The waitress bounces back and serves the drinks, "What it be, mateys?"

They order, and the waitress says, "Aye, aye, mateys!"

Anderson asks Kenny, "When you had your state trooper meetings in Charlotte, did you ever go to a fish camp?"

Kenny hesitates and says, "That term sounds familiar, but I can't place it."

Anderson says, "As you know, I traveled to Charlotte a lot for many years; Del Ware had one of their biggest offices there. One of the first times

I went there, around 1964, one of their local employees asked me if I had been to one of their fish camps. I assumed that fishing and camping grounds must be popular there. When I replied that I like to camp, but I don't fish much, they laughed. I was told that a fish camp is what they call a seafood restaurant. In fact, one of their local celebrities, Captain Hook, was a host at one of them.

Kenny replies, "I remember now. I don't think the troopers and I ever met at one."

"It must be a regional term. They were popular in Charlotte and Gastonia, and the counties of Mecklenburg and Gaston. Outside of that area, I haven't heard of seafood restaurants being called fish camps. If Salty Sea were there, it would be one of their best fish camps!"

They both look at the waitress bringing the food. Kenny says to Anderson, "Wow, that was fast." Kenny says to the waitress, "Blow me down; that was some fast cookin', matey."

She says, "I hope you rascals enjoy the grub. Ring that bloomin' bell, if you need anything."

Anderson says, "So be it, mate." Anderson says to Kenny, "This is the only restaurant, where I've seen a bell with a rope above the table."

Kenny says, "You've gotta love it! Will you say the blessing?"

After the blessing they both dig into the catfish and shrimp. After a couple minutes of concentrated eating, Anderson says to Kenny, "I would like to get your confidential input about something."

Kenny replies, "Fire the cannon, buccaneer!"

Anderson can't help but smile, then he gets a serious look again. "You've met my sister, Lydia, and you know a little about her, but I want to share what she is going through. I also want your response to how I'm thinking about helping her."

Kenny replies, "Sure. Take your time. We should slow down from inhaling this food."

"She told me that she is having some financial difficulties. She's coming over Thursday and staying a couple days. I'm going to look at her financial situation. Her husband left her for a younger woman nine years ago. He was 69 then and he left her for a younger woman, who was working at a fast food restaurant, where he met with other older men in the morning. The woman must have known he was retired. She was in her late forties and still had a 29-year-old millennial living at home."

Anderson continues, "During the past nine years, I think Lydia's financial situation has gradually gotten worse. They still owed some on the house, and several years ago she took out a significant equity line. I know that she had to spend $10,000 at that time on a new roof. Lydia is the most kind

A Light on the Path

and considerate person I know. She was a beautiful girl, and she has the most sanguine attitude. Letting her go would be like trading a Mercedes for a wrecked pinto."

I think you know that she suffers with fibromyalgia and arthritis. I haven't told you how severe the fibromyalgia is. Even though she has a prescription for it, she must rest about half of the day, and she has a problem at night relaxing her muscles, so she can sleep. She has to get in a tub of hot water, so she can go to sleep."

Kenny exclaims. "Bless her heart."

Anderson says, "I want to help, so I'm going to decide what to do after I look at her finances."

Kenny surmises, "I bet you will want her to stay with you."

Anderson answers, "The solution might be selling her house, and having her move in with me. It helps me to think things over by sharing and getting your input."

Kenny answers, "If my sister had a need like that, I would do the same thing."

They talk about it for a couple more minutes while they finish their favorite Salty Sea meal.

The waitress comes over to check on them, "How ya doin', gents?"

Anderson says, "We thank ya, lass, for the jolly voyage and good grub."

The waitress returns, "Well blow me down, mate; you are quite welcome. I will rustle up the tab."

They get up, put on their coats, and give the waitress the money for the tab and tip.

She greets them goodnight, "Ye ole' sea dogs be careful out there. Don't ye go fallin' into Davey Jones' Locker!"

They say goodnight. "A lass the last laugh," says Anderson. They open the door to a cold night with snowflakes swirling in the air. Anderson says, "Well I guess I will see you a little before eleven at the Maggie Valley Chapel."

Kenny replies, "Yes, and you won't have far to go." After they're in their truck and Jeep, they honk at each other as they pull out on the road to the farm and to the Maggie Valley Inn.

Anderson pulls up by Patty's special edition Mazda. As he walks to the door, he watches his breath in the cold air. As he opens the door, he lets out a "Brrrrrrr". "It's so cold, Patty, that milk cows are giving ice cream!"

Patty says, "Are you ready to come in out of the cold?"

"I sure am," replies Anderson.

"How was Salty Sea?"

A Light on the Path

"Real good, like always; but like everything else, their prices have almost doubled," replied Anderson.

Patty replies, "I hope the business here stays solvent, and I hope I keep my job."

"I think a lot of people are hoping the same right now. I hope that for you too. I guess I'll turn in early. Have a good night, and I'll see you later tomorrow."

"Have a good night, Anderson."

Anderson walks into his creek side room; closes the curtains and lays down on the bed. He thinks, "I need a respite from all the crazy things happening in the world. I should listen to the news, but I'm going to lie here in perfect repose."

He plans for the earlier part of the morning; before he meets Kenny. He decides to listen to the news after he goes to their breakfast bar early. He plans enough time to catch up on the news; walk and shower before he meets Kenny at church.

As Anderson thinks about tomorrow's activities, he drifts in and out of sleep. He finally sets his alarm for 5:45 and gets ready for bed. He turns out the lights after 9:00, and thinks, "Good, I'll get about eight hours of sleep."

Chapter 6 – Sunday in Maggie Valley

Anderson wakes up right before the alarm goes off. He sits up on the edge of the bed and stays there a moment to get his bearings. He throws cold water in his face and brushes his hair. He puts on his clothes from yesterday, so he can go in the breakfast room, when it opens.

Before he goes to the breakfast room, he finds the news channel. There's no one else in the breakfast room. He goes straight for the coffee and adds one cream and one sweetener. He looks over the breakfast bar and decides on a banana, two boiled eggs and a small blueberry muffin. He sits down and eats the eggs with the blueberry muffin. He gets a second cup of coffee and takes it and the banana to his room.

As he walks in, he thinks, "Oh boy, I've got the news channel tuned in, but I hate to hear about conflict." He sees that its 6:45. He still has plenty of time for a walk before church. He relaxes with the coffee and starts to listen for new information. He hears that more cities have curfews, and that a few more of the larger cities are still considering martial law. It looks like things haven't gotten any better. He wonders if there have been any more price increases.

Before he gets up to do his stretching exercises, he starts listening to a report about meetings for a new world currency. It sounds vague to him right now, but he's not fully awake yet. He goes ahead with the exercises and goes outside to walk. He thinks, "There's not enough snow to keep me from walking." At 8:00 it's still getting light outside, and Anderson thanks God for the beauty of the snow in the valley and on the mountains.

Anderson pulls into the lot for the library and town hall. He parks toward the front of the library. Being a Sunday, the lot is not cleared yet, but there is only about ½" of snow. He feels invigorated in the clean, crisp air. He is familiar with the course around the building and by the small park behind the buildings. He knows if he walks for thirty minutes on level ground, he will cover at least 1 ½ miles. He loves looking at the snow reflecting the lights, which have a glory of their own during early morning.

At 8:45 he's back to Maggie Valley Inn early enough to get a third small cup of coffee. He cheats on himself and grabs one more blueberry muffin. Now there's a few people that he greets in the breakfast room. He goes to his own room; drinks the coffee and gets ready to shower.

He is ready for church an hour early. He decides he'll leave about 10:30, so he can talk to some of the early birds at the church. The Maggie Valley Chapel is only two blocks from the motel. He likes that part of Maggie Valley. It's close to the mountain that goes up to the Blue Ridge Parkway, and back down to Cherokee.

A Light on the Path

He parks his truck and goes inside about 10:35. There are only a few people in the sanctuary. He guesses that Sunday School hasn't dismissed yet. He admires the compassionate subjects and vibrant colors of the stain glass windows. An elderly lady comes up to Anderson and greets him. She says, "Welcome, haven't you been here before?"

Anderson replies, "Yes, my wife and I have been here a couple times. Kenny, who is meeting me here today, came with me another time." She said, "There is coffee in the fellowship hall."

Anderson replies, "Thank you, but my friend may arrive early, and he's meeting me inside the front doors." Anderson walks back to the entrance to the sanctuary. He looks for Kenny to walk in any minute. Sure enough, Kenny is fifteen minutes early.

Anderson says, "Good morning, brother. You're on Lombardi time!"

"Yes, I know we both like it that way."

Anderson replies, "I was ready so early that I came ahead. It looks like Sunday School has dismissed. Go on in, and we'll find a seat.

They sit about five pews from the back. The pastor greets everyone, and the congregation starts singing joyously their opening hymn:

"Have Thine own way, Lord! Have Thine own way!

Thou art the Potter, I am the clay.

Mold me and make me after Thy will,

While I am waiting, yielded and still."

It's an upbeat service. The pastor preaches about Paul's message to the Athenians. Paul points out that they have a statute to the unknown god, and shares that there is one true God. After the service they shake hands with several people. When they step outside, the sun is shining, and the little bit of snow is melting.

Anderson asks Kenny, "Do you want to have lunch at the Mountain View Restaurant?"

"Good choice, brother. It's a good restaurant, and it's on the way to the Parkway. Why don't we take my Jeep, and I'll bring you back here, when we come back from the Parkway."

"Sounds like a plan," replied Anderson. They get in Kenny's Jeep and head to another frequented restaurant.

Anderson asks, "Do you remember when we first met?"

Kenny replies, "I sure do. You were getting ready to retire, and I was thinking about retirement in a couple years. I had a patrol that afternoon near Maggie Valley, and it was near suppertime, when I had to go back to Cherokee to finish my shift. We ended up at tables next to each other at the Mountain View."

A Light on the Path

"Do you remember the owner's little daughter, who would refill the coffee cups?"

"Kenny replies, "She was the cutest little brunette. Her head wasn't much higher than the table top!"

As they head up the mountain, Anderson says, "It looks like we're almost here." They pull into the lot, and once again they enjoy the mountain view. "It looks like some of the snow is hanging onto the mountain."

Kenny replies, "I never get tired of this view."

They walk inside the comfy, rustic restaurant. A fire in the fire place is warming the reception area. Ginny, the owner, greets them, "Good to see you, boys! Seat yourself and we'll get your drink order." They take a seat at one of the shiny, wooden tables.

Kenny says, "It feels like a second home here."

"Yes, you and I, as well as Ruth and I, have a history here."

The owner's oldest daughter, a friendly lady with a bright smile, comes over and asks for their drink order. They both order coffee and water.

Anderson says, "Yes, I remember very well the day we met. I have no doubt that we connected soon after we met each other."

Kenny replies, "Yes, I could tell that we connected with our love for nature. I think we both discerned that we like people."

The comely waitress brings their drinks and takes their orders. Anderson says, "The coffee smells really good! Thank you, miss."

She replies, "I'll keep it filled up. Let me know if you need anything else."

Kenny asks, "When I met you, and you were getting ready to retire, were you still going to Europe a lot at that time?"

Anderson replies, "My trips to Europe were becoming less frequent. Del Ware had already begun the transition between the new European Marketing Director and me. He had been working with me for about eight years. My trips to Charlotte had become more frequent, because they were gradually moving the home office from Nashville to Charlotte."

Kenny asks, "Were you still living in Indiana during the time you were the European Marketing Director?"

"Yes, my residence was still there, but for years they had me traveling a lot. The last ten years, I spent more time in Nashville, Charlotte, Frankfurt, Brussels and Helsinki than I did in Indiana. Del Ware moved their plant operations from Delaware County, near Muncie, Indiana, to the Nashville area in 1965, just five years after I started with them."

Kenny replies, "Tell me again about what they did and how they grew. It's been so long since you shared that with me.

A Light on the Path

"When I joined them in 1960, they were just in kitchen wares. They had already grown a lot. They were worth about $200 million at that time. They had some of the state-of-the-art cooking devices that were popular. The CEO and board wanted to expand, and they were already thinking about getting into food and beverage packing before 1965. I was on the ground floor of those plans, and we expanded that operation from Nashville to Charlotte and to Denver through the years. By 1968 we were the fifth largest food and beverage packer in this country, and when I left the company in 1995, we were the second largest food and beverage packer in the country."

Kenny asks, "Who was the largest?"

"It was Unibelle. They started in the beauty aid business before the turn of the century and expanded before we did into food and beverage packing. When I retired in 1995, our company was worth $14 billion, and they were worth about $35 billion. They were a very large industry. We did become the largest food and beverage packer in Europe about five years before I retired."

"Here you are, gentlemen. Does everything look good?"

Kenny replied, "It couldn't be better."

The waitress said, "I will be right back with more coffee."

As Kenny and Anderson said a prayer and dug in, the waitress filled their cups to the brim.

Kenny said, "Thank you, hon."

As they enjoyed the pork chops and mixed vegetables, Anderson asked Kenny, "Your question made me think about you at the time we met. I know you were two or three years from retirement, but what made you decide on being a state trooper?"

Kenny answered, "As you know, I was a MP in the army. After basic training in 1958, I trained to be in the military police. During the twenty years, I was stationed at Fort Benjamin Harrison in Indianapolis; Seoul, South Korea then at Fort Bragg in Fayetteville, N.C. A lot of MPs go into law enforcement after they're discharged."

Kenny continues, "After I came back home to Cherokee, I heard that the North Carolina State Trooper office was looking for someone with a law enforcement background, who could communicate well with the reservation law officers. They picked yours truly."

Anderson exclaimed, "Good choice! Did you start with them in 1978?"

"It was the latter part of 1977. It was uncanny that the position became available right after I returned home. Not long before I left the army, I was thinking about building a house outside Bryson City. When I interviewed for the job, they said they wanted someone to patrol the highways in the Bryson City, Cherokee and Maggie Valley areas."

Anderson replies, "That is uncanny! It must have felt like it was fate."

A Light on the Path

"Yes, I felt that it was in the cards."

"So, you retired before 1998?"

Kenny replies, "Yes, I retired in January of 1997 to get my twenty years."

Anderson says, "You had a great career!"

Kenny says, "And so did you, and a very interesting one!"

"That's true. I was very fortunate and blessed," replies Anderson. "I know you went ahead with building a nice house in Bryson City. When did you move to your farm?"

"I sold the house and two acres in March of 1998 and bought the farm the same month."

"Brother, how time flies! I've known you almost twenty-five years, and you've already had the farm for over twenty years."

Kenny replies, "Time does go by too fast. Did you and Ruth move to Mount Holly in 1995?"

"We started looking in that area of Sevier County and Jefferson and Hamblen counties in 1995. I think it was March or April of '96, when we bought our home. Originally, the house was on sixty acres, but about fifteen years ago my rancher neighbor needed the money, and I bought the other sixty acres from him. Since the woods are land locked, it was a good deal."

Kenny exclaims, "I'm stuffed!"

Anderson replies whimsically, "Someone may try to mount you on their wall."

Kenny replies, "I'll check my back."

The waitress returns and asks, "Desert, gentlemen?"

Kenny says, "I'll take desert, if you carry me out on a stretcher."

As the waitress laughs, she says, "Okay, I will get the checks."

Kenny says to Anderson, "How about we take a spin on the Parkway in my Jeep?"

Anderson replies, "Let's do it!"

They pay for their lunch and head to the Parkway. The Blue Ridge Parkway entrance is only a mile from the restaurant. As they ride in the Jeep, they continue to exchange wits and reminisce.

As they turn onto the Parkway entrance, they take a left, which goes east to Asheville. As Kenny enjoys the drive, Anderson says, "Did I tell you about my long stint with red-tailed hawks?"

Kenny replies, "No, tell me about it."

"About twenty years ago, I started noticing red-tailed hawks more."

Anderson continues, "Not long after that these experiences started, they seemed to develop into a phenomenon. One day I stop at a convenience store in the country. They were busy, so I had to park way pass their building and sidewalk; parallel to their curb. When I came out of their building, I noticed that something large was on top of my car. When I got close enough to see what it was, this red-tailed hawk flies away!"

Kenny exclaims, "Great ghosts, brother! I know a little bit about hawks and that's spooky!"

Anderson continues, "When I got close enough to make it out, it was perched on the roof above the driver's seat before it flew away. For several years after that, when I would go outside to walk, there would be a red-tailed hawk flying in front of me. One day I stepped outside the front door, and I heard this loud sound of flapping wings, and this red-tailed hawk takes off right above me."

Kenny replies, "The hawk symbolizes different things to different tribes. The consensus is "messenger". If you were Cherokee, we could call you, "red hawk".

Anderson answers, "If I were Cherokee, they would call me "sore foot", because I've always had foot problems!"

They both laugh, and they continue bantering back and forth and telling stimulating stories. After they drive east for over thirty minutes, Anderson looks at his watch and says, I can't believe it's after 2:30 already."

Kenny says, "Let's head back, and go to Lake Junaluska. There we can get out of the car and take the two mile walk around the lake." "Sounds good," replies Anderson. "The overviews here are still captivating in the winter, but these overviews during autumn are absolutely mesmerizing. I wish I were a painter just to capture their beauty and autumn colors."

"You've got that right," replies Kenny. "I know that we both have a whole picture catalogue of the overviews in autumn."

Anderson says, "This stretch of the Parkway is one of the closest roads to my heart. Even in the winter, the snow-covered pines on the mountainside have a grandeur of their own. Kenny, like a kid, I'm fascinated with the many smooth curves in the road. When you come upon a curve, do you wonder what's around the next bend?"

Kenny replies, "All the time. I thought that was in my Cherokee blood, but maybe it's from that true love of nature. After a rain or when the sun is melting the snow and ice, you never know what kind of trickle or waterfall is going to run over the rocky mountainside. There are just so many intriguing, natural wonders around the next bend."

Anderson says, "No truer words have been spoken. Even though we finished eating an hour ago, my mind is wandering to food. How could I be thinking of food at a time like this?"

Kenny replies, "Man's stomach has a bee line to his brain."

A Light on the Path

They both laugh. Anderson says, "After our walk, what do you think about having supper at the Roll and Butter around 4:30?"

Kenny replies, "Probably our best choice since it's near the lake. We'll stop at the church and get your truck. After supper, I know we'll want to retire."

Anderson says, "Yes, we'll have to catch up on the news. In the morning you have chores, and I'll be walking at the library and town hall. Before I go back home, do you want to meet at the Roll and Butter around 11:30 for lunch?

"That would be good," said Kenny. They turn off the Parkway and go down the mountain road to Maggie Valley Chapel.

Right before they get to the church, Anderson says, "Not to sound down on a beautiful day like this, but I sure miss Ruth."

"I know you do, Anderson," replied Kenny. "Even though God gives us a wonderful day, I know you miss Ruth a lot."

As they pull into the church lot, they notice most of the snow in the valley has melted away. When Anderson looks at his truck, it reminds him of home. Anderson said, "Well, thank you for the Parkway ride. Now we get to walk around the serene lake. I'll follow you there."

Kenny replies, "We can stretch our legs in a few minutes."

As Anderson gets under the wheel of his truck, he thinks, "home sweet home; tomorrow afternoon it will be nice to be on the road to home." As He follows Kenny's Jeep, he thinks, "Lake Junaluska is not only very pleasant but it's a great location between Maggie Valley and Kenny's farm."

In very little time, they're at the lake. Anderson pulls up near the front of the book store next to Kenny. As they get out, Anderson says to Kenny, "Ruth and I usually parked here too, because it's near the beginning of the rose walk." The roses are by the sidewalk for many blocks.

Kenny replies, "Me too. Even though they're not in bloom this time of year, I got into the habit of parking here. I only park in one of the two big lots, if this is filled up from a meeting or another event."

Even though the sun is out, it's cold and they bundle up for the two-mile walk. Kenny remarks, "What a tranquil place!"

Anderson replies, "I love it here." They start walking along the rose walk.

Kenny says, "It's sad that we don't see the colorful life of the roses in the winter."

Anderson replies, "Spring will be here soon. We'll enjoy their new life then."

A Light on the Path

"In a bizarre way, when you said life, it reminded me of a news report that I heard before I left for church this morning. It was the first time I've heard of a death toll from all the rioting, arson and robberies."

"Oh, Lord, I haven't heard about deaths from the unrest," replies Anderson.

Kenny says, "Nationwide they reported 326 deaths from the violence. The reporter commented that some of the deaths were related to robbery with either the homeowner or business owner killing the thief, or the thief killing the resident or residents. They reported that three men broke into a big residence in Beverly Hills and killed four people in the opulent house."

Anderson replies, "I had hoped that it wouldn't come to this, but you and I have talked several times about how the decline of the dollar can lead to civil unrest."

Kenny remarks, "What bothers me at this moment is the irony of thinking about the turmoil in the country, while we're in such a peaceful setting."

"Yes, it's interesting we didn't talk about the latest news earlier in the day. I can understand that being by such a pleasant lake could remind anyone of how unpleasant the national crisis is. This place of peace can remind us that much of the world is not at peace."

Kenny replies, "I agree. It's also a reminder that all of us need a place of peace in our lives."

Anderson replies, "That's right. All of us also need not only good news but "the good news"."

"I know what you're saying, brother," replied Kenny. "Wow. We've already walked by the roses, and soon we're be at the turn by the swimming pool." Kenny continues, "The report I heard this morning about fatalities was not very detailed. The reporter did say some police officers and national guardsmen had to shoot looters who had guns."

Anderson replies, "The city and county authorities probably have not released much information yet on fatalities."

As they turn at the pool and take the walkway to the bridge, Anderson asks, "How are things in your area?"

"Things have been calm around the farm and in my rural area. I talked with two officers I know in Maggie Valley. They said some people have tried panhandling at gas stations. When they see someone pull up at a pump and get out of their car, they approach them for money. You know the old story: "I have another 80 miles to go before I get home and I ran out of gas". The officers said there hasn't been any violence so far. They just tell the panhandlers to get off the premises. They tell them not to panhandle in Maggie Valley.

A Light on the Path

As they cross the Lake Junaluska wooden bridge and admire the swans and beauty of the lake, Anderson says, "I've wondered about my trip coming up. I'm driving to the Knoxville airport, and Lydia and Stephen are picking me up at the Indianapolis airport."

Kenny replies, "I would fill up in Maggie Valley or in Mount Holly. I would only stop at the airport in Knoxville. Airport security should be tight. Not only will Homeland Security be stepping up and local authorities, but the National Guard is helping at some bigger airports. I feel confident that our country will not jeopardize national security."

They still enjoy the walk over the bridge, even as they discuss the serious problems in the country. Anderson says, "It's a little cold, but the air is exhilarating!"

"Man, I love a refreshing walk!" exclaims Kenny.

The bridge walkway ends at a sidewalk that goes up a hill and continues between the lake and a residential neighborhood. After several minutes, they walk across a big parking lot, and then the path goes around a chapel and big meeting hall. As they walk up a hill to the sidewalk they started on, they can see the book store and their truck and Jeep.

Kenny says, "Not bad for a little over two miles; we walked for an hour."

Anderson replies, "Really? The time went fast." He looks at his watch. "I can't believe it's almost 4:30!"

"Yes sir, brother, it went by fast. They're probably waiting on us at the Roll and Butter."

Anderson says, "Let's roll on over there and see if they have some good, warm food for us."

They take off, and Anderson follows Kenny to the restaurant. They park in front of the quaint and well decorated Roll and Butter Restaurant. As they head toward the door and see their breath in the air, Anderson says, "You can tell that we're close to the first day of winter by the short days."

As Kenny opens the door for them, he says, "By the time we finish supper, it will be dark."

A very jovial and copious young lady greets them. She sets them near the back of the restaurant. They can see autographed pictures of Hank Williams, Patsy Cline and North Carolina's Randy Travis. A good-natured waitress brings their menus and takes their drink order. Kenny and Anderson both look over the country menu. Kenny says, "I'm seeing barbecued pork, black eyed peas, black beans and rice and sweet potato pie."

Anderson replies, "How can you have room for all of that? I'm going to order the same!"

A Light on the Path

The waitress returns for the meal order. Kenny says, "It looks like were both going to have the same." They place their orders with the smiling brunette in a red and white flannel shirt.

After they order, Anderson says, "I've always liked the country atmosphere here, like their red and white checkered tablecloths. They look good next to the red brick walls. I'm sure you've noticed that the waitresses' red and white plaid shirts go with the décor. It looks good how they wear the plaid shirts like a jacket."

Kenny replies, "I certainly have noticed. I like the red and white plaid shirts better than the tablecloths and brick walls!"

As they smile at each other and nod, Anderson says, "I don't disagree." Anderson hesitates a few seconds as he looks down at his glass of water. "Kenny, I hate to turn the conversation to a serious note, but I've been wanting to get your take on the possible outcomes of this change in the economy and the national crisis we're in."

Kenny replies, "It doesn't bother me to talk about it." Anderson notices Kenny's change of disposition as he begins to reflect. "I was in law enforcement for over forty years; the army then the state police. I can't help but think like a law man, because that's what I am. In the face of a crisis, local or national, facts are not released right away. In this case, facts like the dollar amount of property damage and destruction, and facts like deaths and injuries."

Anderson asks, "What about the property destruction total that was announced from Los Angeles?"

Kenny replies, "As far as we know right now, Los Angeles has been the worst case. The property damage was so devastating that they we're forced to request martial law. We may only know about half or less of all the destruction and loss of life in the nation."

Anderson says, "Yes, it's logical that the public doesn't receive the details right away. You would know from your experience in law enforcement."

Kenny starts to make a reply, when the waitress returns with their order. "Okay, guys, here's your country orders."

Anderson exclaims, "It sure looks like a country boy's delight!"

They all laugh. The waitress says, "Dig in, boys, and let me know if you need anything."

Anderson asks Kenny to say grace, then they start to devour the southern cooked food! After they dig in and come up for air, Anderson asks, "Where were we in the conversation?"

Kenny says in jest, "I think we were somewhere between the barbecue and the sweet potato pie!"

A Light on the Path

Anderson continues with the jest by saying, "I got lost somewhere after my first bite of those delicious black beans and rice."

Kenny replies, "I think you were saying that it's logical for the authorities to not divulge the facts right away during a crisis."

Anderson says, "Yes, you have experienced that during your life. Do your experiences give you an insight as to where this crisis is headed?"

Kenny replies, "The first thing that comes to my mind are the third world countries I visited while I was stationed in South Korea. I usually didn't have time to go home, when I was on leave. Since I was overseas for over four years, I usually visited countries in that part of the world during my furloughs. Like some countries in South America and Latin America, most people in Thailand and the Philippines had very little. The Philippines has received a lot of help from our country, but who helps a philanthropic country like the United States, when they need help? As I see it, the country that helped many other countries for over a hundred years will being doing good to help herself."

Anderson replies, "I have similar thoughts. At some point during this crisis, I think America's hand will be forced to virtually become an isolationist nation."

They continue to finish their country cooked food. Kenny says, "It sounds like we could continue this conversation over lunch tomorrow."

"I think we'll have the right amount of time over lunch to share our thoughts," replied Anderson.

They thank their amiable waitress and hostess for their hospitality and good food, and head out unto the night air. As they say good night and shake hands, Anderson confirms their luncheon meeting, "It has been a great day, Kenny. Have a good night, and we'll meet here at 11:30."

"Until we meet again, my brother," replied Kenny.

As Anderson heads back to the Maggie Valley Inn, he looks at his watch and thinks, "It's getting close to 6:00. Since its Sunday evening, Patty probably won't have many guests at the motel, so I might chat with her for a few minutes." When he pulls into their lot, he parks beside Patty's Special Edition Mazda.

He opens their door and immediately sees Patty behind the front counter. "Good evening, young lady!"

Patty replies, "Hi, Anderson. How are you doing?"

"Just a little cold but feeling pretty good for a man who will be eighty in a few months."

Patty replies, "I wouldn't have guessed it. I thought you were at least five to six years younger than that."

Anderson says, "Thanks for the compliment; I needed that."

A Light on the Path

"My birthday will be sooner than I think. I'll be 68 on May 21st."

Anderson asks, "Does it seem like time is going too fast now?"

"It sure does," replied Patty. "I still have a hard time dealing with being over 60! Are you headed back home tomorrow?"

"Yes, I've had a good time, but I'm ready to get on my Tennessee road to home. Kenny and I are meeting for lunch tomorrow at the Roll and Butter Restaurant, before I leave."

Patty says, "Don't you love how they've decorated the restaurant?"

"Yes. We ate there this evening, and Kenny and I mentioned that. Over supper, Hank Williams, Patsy Cline and Randy Travis were looking down at us."

Patty laughs, "I enjoy that too. I always wonder whose pictures will be at my table. Have you noticed that they have a few southern gospel group pictures too, like the Cathedral Quartet, when George Younce was with them?"

"I haven't noticed that, but George Younce was my favorite gospel singer. I went to see him and the Cathedrals in Muncie, Indiana, and Charlotte."

Patty replies, "He was a great singer and wonderful man. I also loved his sense of humor."

"Me too. Thinking about gospel music, I was at a big church in Marion, Indiana, many years ago and heard Lulu Roman from Hee Haw speak and sing. She sang the most beautiful rendition of "Blessed Assurance" that I have heard."

Patty says, "Yes, I remember Lulu Roman well from Hee Haw. I always watched their show, when I wasn't working. I like a lot of Southern Gospel and Country singers as well as some from the early rock and roll days. Johnny Cash, Conway Twitty and Brenda Lee also had some early rock hits."

Anderson replies, "About thirty-five years ago, I met Brenda Lee at the Charlotte Motor Speedway."

Patty says, "I like the young picture of Brenda Lee that they have at the Bread and Butter. They also have some pictures of the next generation, like The Judds, Alan Jackson and Brad Paisley."

Anderson replies, "It would be nice if they added some of the early rock stars like Elvis, Chuck Berry and Buddy Holly."

One of the guests walks in and heads back to their room.

Anderson asks, "Do you have many guests tonight?"

Patty replies, "No, we just have a few rooms booked, but we'll have the usual breakfast bar in the breakfast room in the morning."

"That's good. I'm usually ready for breakfast by 6 or 6:30. How have you been doing, Patty?"

A Light on the Path

"I've been fine. I've worked too many doubles the last two weeks. I'm just a little tired and need to catch up on my sleep. This week I only have to work forty hours."

"Good," replied Anderson. "It's always great seeing you. Lord willing, I'll see you the next time."

"You take care, Anderson."

You too," replied Anderson. "Keep lookin' up!"

Anderson walks in his room and turns on the television to the news. It's almost 7:00, and it looks like a Sunday night, investigative news program is coming on. Anderson starts getting ready for bed, so he can relax and watch the special report.

The news commentator opens with a report from the White House. He says, "The President is telling the Democrats and the Republicans to stop fighting each other. We will now play that sound bite from the President." The President says, "While our nation is embattled with high prices and civil unrest, politicians from both parties on a national and local level are quarreling across party lines and have exacerbated the national crisis. It's high time for the two parties to stop quarreling like children in a school yard. Any Democrat or Republican, who has a constituency, I am calling on you currently to take off your political agenda gloves and roll up your sleeves and start working to help your country. Our country needs us to be mature and responsible representatives during the current challenges. I expect all party leaders to make sure that your members are doing everything that they can to help, while our local police forces and National Guard are putting their lives on the line."

The news reporter comes back on and says, "This is a current Presidential address that came from the White House today. I hope all Democrats and Republicans will take heed of what our President just addressed to both parties. Now let's look at an update on martial law in Los Angeles and National Guard deployment in other cities, including Chicago, Milwaukee, Philadelphia, Cleveland, Baltimore, New York City, District of Colombia, Charlotte, Atlanta, Miami, Memphis, Nashville, Houston, Dallas, San Francisco, Seattle, Denver, Detroit and Indianapolis. We have just gotten word from the local police and other authorities in Chicago that 260 people have been killed in the past week in South Chicago. We have an unofficial death toll of 566 people, since the civil unrest began in our nation."

"At 8:00 we will be bringing you the latest report about world bank meetings and the debate about a global currency. Stay tuned for more about Los Angeles and other cities after this message." As the commercials come on, Anderson mutes the remote. He thinks, "I don't know if it's my age or what, but this crisis is happening so fast that I have a hard time coming to grips with it." Anderson debates whether he will listen to more or wait to see what Kenny will share tomorrow. Since he is tired from a long day, he decides to turn off the television and read the Bible before he goes to bed early.

After he reads in the Bible, he's not quite sleepy enough to go to sleep, so he flips back and forth between a wilderness show and a wildlife show. He sets his cell phone alarm and turns out the lights before 8:30.

Anderson sleeps through most of the night and doesn't wake up until 4:00. He knows he has been dreaming but can't quite put the dream together. It seemed like he was at a campground with other people, but it's not clear to him. He uses the bathroom and goes back to bed until the alarm goes off at 6:00. He goes through his routine before he goes in the breakfast room. It's the same breakfast bar, and once again, no one else is there at 6:20. He goes back to his room after breakfast; showers; stretches and dresses early for his walk at the library. He looks outside at daybreak. He is thankful that he sees no sign of rain or snow. He sets down and spends time with his devotional and Bible, then he prays; especially for Kenny, Lydia, Angela and the nation. When he gets up, it's only 8:00, so he decides to walk before he checks out.

He goes outside and gets in his truck. At the library and town hall the pathways are dry. He thanks God again for a clear day. He enjoys the invigorating walk. He guesses that it's in the high thirties already. He walks 45 minutes and then drives a few blocks pass Maggie Valley Inn and fills the tank with gas. For his trip back, he gets a bottle of water and a granola bar. He has a habit of keeping wintergreen mints on him.

When he gets back to his room, it's about 9:15. He has time to check in with Lydia and Angela before he checks out. He talks with Lydia briefly and leaves a message for Angela. He checks out about 10:00 so he can browse at the Market Square shops on his way to meet Kenny. He loads his luggage and drives pass the library a few blocks to Market Square. He parks and walks up a few wooden steps to the long wooden walkway in front of the shops. Most of the time he walks in front of the stores, since most of the stores are closed through the week during the winter season. A few of the stores open at 10:00. He walks into those stores and mostly browses. One store owner, Daniel, has become a friend of his, and he goes in and talks with him.

After they visit, it's almost time to meet Kenny. He heads for the Roll and Butter, and after he pulls into their lot, it's 11:17. Sure enough, he sees Kenny waiting in his Jeep. As Anderson gets out of his truck, Kenny gets out. Anderson asks, "What time did you get here?"

Kenny replies, "About two minutes ago."

A Light on the Path

Anderson exclaims, "I could set my watch by you! How are things on the farm?"

"Very peaceful. Scooter and the chickens are doing well."

They walk in and see the same hostess. Anderson asks, "Are you working a double shift?"

The amiable young lady replies, "Not really. I get off at 3:00 today, and I don't return until 6:00 a.m. on Wednesday. Where would you like to sit today?"

Anderson says, "Last evening I was talking with a friend about all of the singer pictures that you have. What table do you recommend?"

She replies, "About mid-way down on the right, we have Dolly Parton, Merle Haggard and Eddy Arnold, the Tennessee Plow Boy."

Kenny exclaims, "That's the table! Who could pass up Dolly Parton? You know, she is still young. She's ten years younger than I am!"

Anderson says, "What a talented songwriter Dolly is! Her hometown, Sevierville, is close to where I live. Her "Coat of Many Colors" is one of the best stories I've heard in a song."

"Okay, gentlemen. I know you'll be right at home here by Dolly."

They thank the hostess. As they sit down, they look at the three pictures. Kenny says, "Man, look at Merle there. What a country icon he is."

Anderson replies, "There was no country singer better than Merle Haggard." They give their drink order to the waitress and look over the country menus. As they talk about what they might order, Anderson says, "We actually ran out of time last night with our discussion. I wanted to get your take on the possible outcome of this national crisis we're in."

Kenny says, "Yes, we did run out of time, but we'll have time to discuss that over lunch."

The energetic waitress comes back for their order. Anderson says, "I think I will have something light today. Give me the grilled chicken salad with ranch dressing, and I just want water."

She says, "You've got it!" She looks at Kenny and says, "What about you, hon?"

Kenny replies, "I've got to have something heavier; I worked on the farm today. Give me the pork chops, mashed potatoes and gravy and green beans."

She replies, "You've got it; anything else?"

Kenny says, "Not now. I just want water, but after lunch I might order some of your sweet potato pie."

"Alright, guys, it should be ready in a few minutes."

She bounces away, full of energy. Kenny says, "that's a good ole' country girl!"

A Light on the Path

Anderson replies, "She is certainly a good, young country girl, who would run circles around you!"

They both laugh. Kenny gets serious and says, "Did you watch any news last night?"

"Yes, a report came on at 7:00, and they showed an address by the President. After the President spoke, the news reporter said 260 people had been killed in South Chicago, since the crisis started. He said the unofficial death toll in the nation is 566."

Kenny says, "I heard those reports also, and the presidential message about the Democrats and Republicans helping the nation, instead of fighting each other."

Anderson replies, "We both know that there has been a lot of hate speech in this country toward Christians and toward others who have traditional American values. We may be coming into an era, when the name callers and judgmental people will have no choice other than rechanneling their focus to survival mode."

"You've got that right," replied Kenny.

Anderson continues, "The other day the old saying, "a chicken in every pot", popped into my mind. I was curious about the details, so I looked it up on line. Herbert Hoover was president just a few years before you and I were born. In 1928, when times were good, he ran for President on the slogan promising, "a chicken in every pot and a car in every garage". Herbert Hoover or anyone else did not know that less than eight months after he took office, the stock market would crash in October of 1929, Ironically, he became known as the "Great Depression President", serving from 1929 t0 1933."

"That is very interesting," replied Kenny.

The waitress returns with their meals and says, "Here it is, guys. Enjoy and let me know, if you need anything."

Soon after they start enjoying their lunch, Anderson says, "Brother, the floor is yours. I've been wanting to hear what you think might be the outcome of the crisis."

With a mouth full of food, Kenny says, "Sure." He thinks for a couple of seconds and says, "First of all, the death toll, injuries and destruction are ongoing. You might find this surprising, but I'm guessing the real death toll is well over 1,000. We know that in the Los Angeles area alone, $90 billion in property has been severely damaged and destroyed. Imagine what the property destruction is nationwide. I believe the insurance companies will be devastated or seriously crippled. How will that affect our country? Soon, our citizens might be hoping there would be a chicken in every pot."

Anderson replies, "These are some of the scenarios that I've been wondering about."

A Light on the Path

Kenny says, "Before the 20th century, our country was basically an isolationist nation. I think there is a good possibility that soon we will be an isolationist nation again. We won't have the deep pockets that we had for years. I believe America will be striving to take care of itself with its own food and own oil. The one deterrent that we must keep for our defense is our large stock pile of nuclear weapons. I think militarily, other nations will leave us alone in fear of us firing the nuclear warheads."

"I agree," replied Anderson. "I think other leading countries were tired of a debtor nation holding a monopoly on the trading currency. I really believe that they did not want America to become an enemy, but they didn't want America to control their trading practices with the dollar."

Kenny adds, "It looks like we agree on the analysis of this crisis. It's good to verbalize that one of three main things will happen: it will improve; it will stabilize, or it will get worse."

Anderson says, "Some people who believe that it will get worse may believe that it's a prelude to an apocalyptic time."

Kenny replies, "Yes, I'm aware of that scenario. If it's God's plan, it will happen that way."

"No denying that," replied Anderson. "If it does get worse, what are some things that you expect to happen?"

Kenny replies, "A new world trading currency or currencies is one thing, but a new global currency is a whole other animal. A new global currency would be like the world is Europe with the euro. It's obvious the euro didn't help Greece or Great Britain, and it's debatable if it's helping the rest of Europe. A new global currency would be more detrimental than the euro in Europe."

Anderson replies, "Are you aware that the Bible indicates there will be a global currency that requires the mark of the Beast?"

"Yes, I'm somewhat familiar with the description in the Bible. If it happens, the economists and scientists have already perfected a chip or "the mark" for the hand, arm or forehead," replied Kenny.

Anderson says, "If that happens after this crisis, the whole situation will seem surreal in a deviant way."

Kenny adds, "If the third scenario happens, things getting worse, we can expect even higher prices and more civil unrest like vandalism, arson, robbery, assault and murder."

"It's a chilling thought," replies Anderson. "At this point, we just have to pray for the best. Since we're about done with the lunch, did you want to order the sweet potato pie?"

"No, I'm full."

A Light on the Path

Anderson continues, "I've been thinking about a suggestion that I made at your home. It's a good suggestion, but a general one. I mentioned reading the gospels and the Pauline epistles in the New Testament. Before you do that, I think I have a good idea. The gospel of John is a powerful book. Think about studying chapters 14, 15 and 16 in John. I also have two scriptures for you." Kenny gets a pen out of his pocket and grabs a napkin to take a note. Anderson continues, "The first is John 14: 6, where Jesus says, "I am the way, the truth and the life. No one comes to the Father, except through me." The other is one of my very favorite scriptures, Revelation 3: 20. I think it will be helpful to study those three chapters and two verses, before reading the four gospels and the Pauline epistles."

Kenny says, "Sounds like a good plan."

Anderson says, "Later on, let me know how that goes."

They put their dishes to the side for the waitress. Kenny says, "I enjoyed our adventures these past couple days."

As they get up from the table, Anderson replies, "I sure did. Come to the old homestead sometime, and we'll walk the trails."

They step outside, and Kenny says, "I will."

As they get close to the truck and Kenny's Jeep, Anderson says, "Take care and keep lookin' up!"

Kenny replies, "Until we meet again. Have a safe trip home." As they pull onto Soco Rd., Anderson waves and honks his horn. He turns off Soco to head to I-40 West. It takes him to the gorge, through the imposing North Carolina Mountains. When he crosses the Tennessee line, the mountains begin to gradually descend. In roughly twenty miles, he takes a left at the Newport exit. In a few minutes, he takes his Tennessee road to home.

Chapter 7 – Lydia

Pockets greets Anderson in the front yard. As Anderson leans down to pet Pockets, he tells his lazy but loyal cat, "home sweet home, Pockets." As Anderson goes inside, his mind automatically goes to Ruth and telling her about his trip. Tears come to his eyes and he thinks, "God bless, Ruth".

He checks the house and goes outside to give Pockets water and food. He looks around the front and back yards, and brings his luggage in. He thinks, "What a good day for a walk. The sun is beginning to peek out and the ground is drying. I'll call Lydia after my walk and begin to straighten up the house." He looks at his wall calendar in the kitchen. He sees that Christmas is just a week away, and he will be leaving for Indianapolis just a day after Lydia leaves.

After Anderson unpacks he thinks, "Man, I was a little too eager to get things done. It's only 2:35, and I have some time left before I walk. I'll take a nap and start walking by 3:30. Anderson sticks with his plan, and he's outside with his walking gear and walking stick by 3:30. He has just enough time to check out the ravine on the backside of his property, since it's a nice day. He thinks that he might have to cut through the woods on the way back to finish by 4:30. This time of year it starts to get dark in the woods about 4:30. He double checks his pack and makes sure he has water, matches and a flashlight.

He starts out by going to the fire pit at the trail head. He looks behind him; sure enough, Pockets is following. He walks up the trail head into the woods. At the top of the hill, he turns left to go east. He checks on Pockets before he starts down the pathway. After Anderson walks for a few minutes, he feels like he is meandering along, even though he is on the trail. He thinks, "Maybe I'm tired from the Maggie Valley trip."

Anderson looks around infrequently, since he wants to finish the hike by 4:30. He concentrates on his pace and the trail ahead. When he does look around, he always looks back for Pockets. If she's not digging or following him on the trail, she's gingerly walking the fallen branches and hopping from one branch to another.

As Anderson walks, he thinks, "most of the trails around the perimeter are well trod, but the path in the ravine is probably rough by now." He mainly anticipates piles of leaves and some twigs. Now and then he knows that he will have to move a branch. He guesses that the path in the main part of the ravine runs close to a mile. Anderson starts turning to the southeast, which means that the beginning of the ravine path is only a few minutes ahead.

Pockets is dragging behind about thirty yards. He can now see ahead where the main part of the ravine begins. He takes a pathway that winds down to the ravine path. As he starts out on the ravine path, the leaves are not too bad. He knows that he can't throw aside every twig, because his time is limited. Before the ravine opens into the clearing, he throws aside three small branches.

Anderson is always glad to see the clearing by the horse pasture. He enjoys the spacious clearing and a needed rest. He takes off his pack and drinks some water. Pockets catches up with him and he pets her and says, "you're a good walker, Pockets; good girl". While he rests for one more minute, he watches Pockets pounce on a leaf or bug just about twenty feet ahead of him.

He throws his pack over his shoulder and starts to walk about sixty yards to the other side of the clearing, when he sees a row of wild turkey marching stoically from the horse pasture up the side of the wooded hill, where the ravine starts again. He counts twenty-one wild turkey and guesses that some are already up the hill and hidden by the trees.

Right before he leaves the clearing, he looks at one of his favorite black walnut trees. It produces every other year, and when it sheds its walnuts, they scatter all over the ground where the ravine begins again between two hills. As he enters the ravine again, it begins to gradually run along the south property line to the southwest. Ahead he can see a larger branch lodged between the two hillsides.

He must take off his pack off to pull the large branch to the side, so he can pass. He puts his pack back on and grabs his walking stick. He takes a second and looks around for Pockets, then he sees her coming around a curve behind him. Anderson continues on the ravine path. He reminds himself that when he comes to the end of the main ravine, he must take the small path up the hill to make it back in time.

After he walks about seven minutes, he is only one or two minutes from the end of the main ravine, when nature calls. He leans his walking stick against a tree, and finds a comfortable rest area, so he can be on his way. Just as he starts out again, Pockets catches up with him. This time she runs ahead of him down the ravine path. When Anderson gets to the end of the wider ravine, he sees that Pockets has found the small path he forged. Pockets is almost to the top of hill, as Anderson walks up the path.

He looks at his watch: it's already 4:07. The branches he cleared, and the short rest stops took a few minutes longer than he expected. Fortunately, he's familiar with his trails, and he knows where he can get on the trail that zigzags to the north. The trail he just took goes west. Where it slightly curves to the northwest, he can pick up the trail that heads north through the woods.

A Light on the Path

Since he left the ravine, he has only been walking for ten minutes, but ahead is the trail that heads north. Even though his watch says 4:20, he knows that he will be on the trail that heads down to the fire pit in about ten minutes.

As he gets on the trail that leads to the fire pit, he notices that the shadows in the woods are getting darker. As he nears the bottom of the trail, he comes out of the woods into the fire pit area. He looks at his watch: 4:37. He thinks, "How lucky is that!" Pockets follows Anderson up the hill to the house. As Anderson approaches his house, he thinks about how dark the woods get after sunset. He thanks God that he isn't in the darkening woods now as the temperature is approaching 36 degrees.

He has no plans for supper. His mind is on calling Lydia. He unloads his packing gear and puts up his walking stick. He gets another bottle of water out of the fridge and quenches his thirst. He decides to have a snack instead of fixing supper. For his main course, he has deli ham and crackers. For dessert he has honey and crackers. After he talks to Lydia, Anderson thinks he might have peanut butter and celery and an apple.

He gets out his cell phone and calls Lydia.

"Hi, Anderson. How are you doing?"

"I wore myself out walking. I hadn't cleared the main ravine path since summer. I thought it would take an hour, if I came back home on the short cut through the woods. It didn't take much longer, but the last few minutes got a little spooky with the dark shadows falling in the woods."

"You're braver than I am. I wouldn't be that far in the woods by myself, and I wouldn't wait an hour before sunset before I started."

Anderson says flippantly, "Wait a minute, who is the big brother or the big sister here?"

Lydia laughs, "I guess the parent is coming out of me."

Anderson asks, "Are you getting ready to come here by 11 or so on Thursday?"

"Yes, I plan to arrive between 11 and 11:30. I went to my regular station today to fill up early, and would you believe a panhandler approached me there?"

Anderson replies, "Oh, no. Did he cause trouble?"

Lydia says, "He didn't have much of a chance to. He had an unkempt appearance, and the station manager must have seen him walking toward me. Just a second after he started to ask for money, the manager was right by him, and told him to get off the property. A cop wasn't there at the time. I have a feeling that more and more people with gun permits are packing heat."

"I'm glad the manager was watching out for you. Police officers were usually stationed at the bigger stations in Maggie Valley. I filled up before I left, and I paid $5.19 a gallon."

A Light on the Path

Lydia replies, "I paid the same. It has more than doubled in the last two weeks. It was $2.39 during the first part of December."

"Before you go back to Crossville, I'm going to follow you to Mount Holly and fill up your car at my station. Sunday evening, I heard on the news that the crisis death toll is up to 566."

Lydia replies, "I know you've been busy today, but now they're saying unofficially it's at 600. I heard two reports today that they are planning to declare martial law in South Chicago and Baltimore. I heard an economist trying to explain why inflation is so high, but he was hard to follow. He believes that commodity prices, housing and interest will go even higher."

Anderson exclaims, "Good grief! The civil unrest will get even worse with more price hikes!"

"I know," replied Lydia.

"Angela booked my flight, and I'm going to reimburse her with a check when I get to Greenfield. I leave Sunday from the Knoxville Airport at 10:35 a.m. The flight arrives in Indianapolis at 2:14. I must go to Charlotte first and wait an hour. I'll get back to Knoxville on Wednesday, December 26th around 1:30."

Lydia says, "We're still fine tuning our plans, but I know the kids and grandkids will be here on Christmas Eve and for most of Christmas."

"If you don't have plans for New Years, why don't you come here on December 29th, and you can go to church with me on the 30th. I could use the company and I was hoping you could stay through January 1st."

Lydia replies, "I would like that."

"I might hang up soon. I need to rest and finish my supper with celery and peanut butter!"

Lydia says, "That sounds good. I know you've had a long day, and I'm going to start supper. It is always good talking with you."

Anderson replies, "Love you, and don't forget your finance papers."

"I will bring them. Love you too. Have a good night."

Anderson hangs up and says, "I'm bushed!" He gets up and decides he'll still fix the celery and peanut butter. Later he watches the news for a short while and gets ready for bed.

Chapter 8 – Lydia's Arrival

Anderson's alarm goes off at 6 a.m. He slowly wakes up and thinks, "The last two days have gone by quickly." I'm glad that Lydia will be here today. As he lies in bed, he enjoys how quiet everything is, and now and then he can hear an owl hooting in the distance. He thinks, "What did that dream I had before I woke up? I remember a lot of people in a very, large building, like a Grand Central Station." He meditates another moment about the dream, but that's all he can remember. He thinks, "I better get up now or the alarm will go off again."

He looks forward to having devotions and enjoying a cup of hot green tea with a granola bar. After he prays, he thinks about the recent news reports on television and about Kenny and Lydia. He looks at his great room clock and sees that it is already 7:15. He thinks, "I must have dozed off for a few minutes." It is just now getting light outside. He looks the house over and makes sure that he has it presentable for Lydia.

He decides to shower before he fries some turkey bacon and an egg. After he dresses, he thinks, "I must be getting slow. It's already 8:00, and Lydia will be here in about three hours." He goes outside and greets Pockets. He gives her food and water. The cold, morning air feels good. Most everything is frosted over. For a few minutes, he stands on the porch and walks around in the front yard. He likes breathing in the refreshing air. As he walks toward the front porch, he notices two mourning doves cooing above the side of his house. He knows when he gets inside, they will be feeding on the bird seed in his bird garden.

After he finishes breakfast, another hour has gone by. He thinks, "I must be anxious to see Lydia." Since it is a little after 9:00, he decides to see if she has left yet.

"Hi Anderson, I just pulled out of my drive. It's a little after 8:00 here, and I should be at your house around 11 your time."

Anderson replies, "Okay. I know you don't speed, which is good. Be careful. See you soon." He thinks, "what else do I need to do?" He decides to cut up some apples and serve them with caramel. He also makes a pot of coffee that they could use for several hours. He cuts some cheese and thinks, "If Lydia wants an early lunch, I'll serve the cheese with some deli ham and crackers."

He goes in the great room and turns on the remote. He selects one of his favorite Sirius jazz channels. He sits down for a while and thinks about today's activities with Lydia. He knows that they plan to go over her finances, and he thinks he told her that they could take a walk in the woods. He also thinks about having a fire in the fire pit, if it is dry while she's here. Anderson looks at his watch, he thinks, "I still have at least an hour before she gets here." He decides to go to his office and look up the extended weather forecast on his table top computer.

He looks up the extended forecast for Newport and Sevierville. Both report little precipitation for the next four days. Today will be mostly cloudy with a high of 39 degrees and a low of 30. Friday there is no chance of precipitation with a high of 45. Saturday is partly cloudy with a high of 44 and a low of 32. He is glad to see that Sunday has a 10% chance of precipitation and wind at 5 mph during the time of his flights. He decides to check weather for Charlotte and Indianapolis later.

While he waits on Lydia, he thinks about building a fire tomorrow, and roasting some hot dogs. He goes outside and checks on Pockets. She follows him down the trail to the fire pit. He walks around the clearing he has made next to the fire pit and two short trails by the clearing. He checks the fire wood he has covered. Pockets is resting on one of the tree stump seats. He checks the time and is surprised to see that Lydia could pull in any minute. As Anderson starts up the trail, he sees Lydia's navy Impala pull in the drive.

As she gets out of the car, Anderson is almost to the top of the trail and yells, "That was good timing!" She turns and looks at him.

She glows with her warm-hearted smile and says, "What do you expect from a perfect sister!"

Anderson laughs, "I wouldn't expect anything less." He walks up to her, and they hug each other. Anderson gives her a kiss on the check. He says, "I'm sure glad to see you."

Lydia replies, "I've missed you too."

Anderson says, "I'll get your bags." He grabs her two bags out of the trunk. They go inside, and Anderson asks, "Do you want me to put the bags in your room?"

Lydia replies, "Yes, thank you."

He comes back in the great room and says, "Okay, young lady, do you want to rest a while and have some coffee and something to eat?"

Lydia replies, "Just some coffee for now." Anderson brings it to her in the great room. Lydia says, "It smells good; thank you."

Anderson says, "Sit on the recliner and relax. How was your trip?"

Lydia replies, "No problems. I didn't stop on the way. I got a little tired when I got to Mount Holly, but I feel better now."

Anderson says, "Well, rest all that you want to. We have the rest of the day. I know we're going over your finances today, and did I mention on the phone that we could take a walk?"

She said, "You did mention the walk. I know you enjoy that, and I need the exercise and fresh air." In Anderson's recliner she takes another sip of

A Light on the Path

coffee. She starts to say something about outside, but her voice trails off and she falls asleep.

Anderson decides to take an early nap, so he takes his shoes off and stretches out on the couch. He dozes off too.

Anderson isn't that tired, and he wakes up about twenty minutes later. When he sits up and reaches for a magazine near the couch, Lydia wakes up. She says, "I guess I conked out."

Anderson replies, "You only slept for twenty to twenty-five minutes. Are you hungry?"

"I'm a little hungry."

Anderson says, "I have caramel with apples, and cheese and deli ham with crackers."

Lydia replies, "You're too good."

Anderson gets up and says, "I'll warm up your coffee." It only takes him a couple minutes to put everything on a plate for Lydia and one for himself.

He puts Lydia's coffee by her, and hands her the plate. He says, "I'll be right back with mine."

Anderson sits back down on the couch and asks, "What do you want to do after lunch?"

Lydia replies, "Right now the rest feels good. I must have gotten more tired from the driving than I realized. If you feel up to it, I could get my finance papers out after lunch. The important things I typed on the computer and printed out copies for you and me."

Anderson says, "Good idea; that will be handy." He and Lydia finish their lunch and Anderson says, "I have plenty of coffee we can sip on while we look over your financial papers."

Lydia gets up; goes to the guest room and pulls a folder out of her bag. She comes back in the great room and gives Anderson the copies he needs. She sits back down in the recliner and says, "I have the finances organized by category and under each category the corresponding lists are in chronological order."

Anderson replies, "This should be easy to follow."

Lydia goes through each paper and highlights mostly monthly expenses and monthly income. She also shows the date she took out an equity line, and how long it would take to pay it off at the current payment schedule.

Anderson says, "I was able to follow you well, because of the copies you made. Let me look at them for a few minutes first. I know I will have questions."

Lydia asks, "Do you want a warm up on the coffee?"

Anderson nods as he begins to look over her finance papers.

A Light on the Path

When Lydia brings back the coffee mugs, she sees Anderson making some notes. It only takes him another four to five minutes. Anderson says, "I have a few questions for you. Do you know what the appraised value of your house is?"

Lydia says, "The last tax appraisal was done about five or six years ago. They valued it at $134,000. When my ex left, most of the house was paid for. Several years later, finances were getting tight, and the house needed a new roof. Because my budget was so tight, I took out an equity line of $35,000, and $10,000 of that went toward the roof."

Anderson says, "It looks like your mortgage balance with the equity line, previous mortgage balance and interest is $53,000."

"Yes, I got the bank to lower the monthly payment on the previous mortgage, when I took out the home equity line."

Anderson says, "You show a total of $1,550 in monthly expenses. Your income is social security and part of his retirement, which comes to $1,400 per month. You have a balance of $3,200 in your checking and savings. Do you have any other savings or investments?"

Lydia replies, "No. The major credit card that has a balance of $3,900 is virtually maxed out. I make the minimum payment per month.'

Anderson takes a couple more minutes to look at two of the papers and makes another note. He says, "First of all, I'm glad we're talking about this now; sooner is better than later. If you downsized in your general area, including Knoxville, the moving cost would be roughly $1,300. The balance left in savings and checking would be $1,900. You're running in the red $150 per month. You would only have enough left for one year to pay all your bills. Of course, if you downsized you would have a profit from your house. If you don't downsize, you have enough left to pay all of your bills for less than two years."

Lydia replies, "It sounds pretty grim. I don't think I want to downsize. I probably couldn't get what I like, and I don't want to rent."

Anderson is listening and smiling. Lydia asks, "Why are you smiling?"

Anderson says, "Do you like it here?"

"Of course, I do. Why do you ask?"

Anderson replies, "The perfect solution is to sell your house and move here!"

Lydia is stunned; she doesn't know what to say.

Anderson is still smiling, "What's wrong, sis?"

Lydia mutters, "I don't know what to say."

Anderson starts laughing, "Say, yes!"

She looks at him bewildered. She hesitates a couple seconds; then smiles and says, "Yes!"

A Light on the Path

Anderson hits the palm of his hands against his legs and exclaims, "Alright, then!" He gets up and says, "Let's celebrate with another cup of coffee!"

Lydia is now overjoyed. She says, "I still don't know what to say, but let's drink coffee!"

When Anderson brings the filled mugs back into the great room, he says, "We can take a few minutes and look at your new financial status, if you want to." Lydia nods and says, "Yes."

He sits back down and looks at his notes again. "For conversation sake, let's say your house sells for $134,000. Your balance after you pay off the mortgage with the equity line would be $81,000. After you pay the realtor, the balance is roughly $72,000. If you pay some of the closing costs, you would have about $70,000 left. A moving company would charge you about $1,500 to move you here. Depending on closing costs, you would still have about $68,000 or more left."

Lydia says, "I'm still stunned. This means that my monthly budget would move from the red to the black!"

"Exactly!"

Lydia asks, "Virtually, you're saving me financially. What can I do for you?"

Anderson replies, "Just be you!"

Lydia gets serious and says, "I could never repay you, but I insist on helping here in some way financially."

Anderson thinks a minute and says, "You could do the grocery shopping and pay for the food."

Lydia smiles again and says, "That's the least I could do. Brother, I love you. A sister couldn't have a better brother." She gets up and gives Anderson a hug. She says, "You have given me new life!"

Anderson smiles and says, "I may have helped, but only One gives new life."

Lydia hugs him again and says, "You're precious."

Anderson looks at the time. "Well, sis, can you believe it's almost 2:00 already? How long of a walk do you want to take?"

Lydia says, "Even though I'm still a little tired, I know the fresh air will help revive me. Why don't we walk for 30 to 40 minutes?"

Anderson replies, "You've got it. I know just the walk for us. We'll be back before 3:00 with plenty of daylight left."

Anderson gets his gear together and hands Lydia her own walking stick. Pockets follows them and as the get to the top of the trail head, they hear a red-tailed hawk call. They look up and see it flying just over the tree tops.

A Light on the Path

Anderson says, "Do you remember when we played in the pine woods as kids?"

Lydia says, "I sure do. The pine needles were so thick on the ground, they were softer to lie on than the thickest carpet made in Dalton."

"Those were part of the good ole' days," replied Anderson." I felt like a Davy Crockett as a kid more than ten years before Disney came out with the movie and music about Davy Crockett. I walked around with my canteen in the neighborhood and in the pine woods like I was an explorer."

"I remember that! You were doing that around age 8 to 9, and I was only 6 to 7. While you were into your Davy Crockett adventures, I was into paper dolls."

As they walk down the trail that turns southeast, they see a box turtle partially covered by leaves. Anderson goes over to it and picks it up. He looks at Lydia and says, "Did you know that the shell on the underside is hard like the top. Tap on it."

Lydia taps on it and says, "It sure is! Is it here because we just passed the Lake?"

Anderson puts it down and covers it with leaves and says, "You'll also find it deep in the woods. It likes a lot of leaf foliage. It gets deep under leaves and hibernates through the winter." They continue southeast. Anderson says, "When we get to the wide ravine, this trail runs above the ravine. When you first see the clearing and horse pasture below, another trail gradually circles back to the north. By taking that trail, our walk will be roughly thirty-five to forty minutes. Anderson looks back and checks on Pockets.

Lydia asks, "Do you see Pockets?"

"Yes, she is just off the trail and lagging behind. She likes to sneak up on us."

"Did I tell you that I cleaned some branches out of the wide ravine?"

"Yes. Isn't that the day you got out of the woods just before dark?"

"That's for sure. The ravine runs a long distance. I think moving the branches took longer than I had planned."

Lydia and Anderson can look down and see the clearing ahead. As they get close to the trail that curves to the right, Lydia says, "I think I see the return home path now."

Anderson says, "That's it."

As they take the trail that curves north, they look at the steel grey clouds in the dark blue sky. Lydia asks, "It looks like snow weather. Is it in the forecast?

Anderson replies, "No, the forecast said it would get to thirty-nine today. If it's only thirty- five or thirty-six, we might end up seeing a few scattered flakes." They pass some sweet birch trees where deer have made

A Light on the Path

their bed out of the leaves. Next is an area that is thick with tall pines. Lydia says, "I love this area. The pine trees are beautiful."

Anderson replies, "We don't get the soft bed of needles here like we had in Indiana, but it is a beautiful area."

Lydia says, "It feels like the walk is giving me energy."

Anderson says, "It will do that. It helps my fibromyalgia, even though I still get a little tired after most walks."

Lydia asks, "Have we put in thirty minutes yet?"

"We're getting close to it," replied Anderson. "In a few minutes this trail will run into the fire pit trail. By the time we get to the front door, I'm guessing we'll turn in a time of 40 minutes."

Lydia laughs and says, "That should qualify us for the Olympics!"

They hear leaves rustling behind them. Pockets rushes by them and darts ahead. Anderson yells, "Go Pockets, go!"

Lydia says, "She is definitely sneaky."

Before they get to the fire pit trail, scattered flakes of snow begin to fall. Lydia says, "The snow falling gives me an ethereal feeling."

Anderson replies, "It does. It's like a little bit of heaven descending to touch us. It feels a little colder than what was predicted for today."

Lydia says, "It feels warmer than freezing. It could be in the mid-thirties."

They head down the fire pit trail. Anderson says, "I haven't planned supper. We could go into town and pick up two big salads."

"I'm not worried about it. I'm not hungry now. Do what you want, but if we get hungry later, we could have soup with crackers."

Anderson replies, "Not a bad idea. We could also have ham and cheese with the crackers. I know we both like chicken noodle soup; I'm well stocked."

They're already near the house. In just another minute, Anderson heads to the master bathroom and Lydia heads to the hall bath. After they're done, they both come to the great room. Lydia looks at the wall clock. "You're right, Anderson. We got back before 3:00."

Anderson replies, "Just in time to take a nap! I'll feed Pockets after we rest awhile. Do you want any music on?"

Lydia says, "Yes, I like one of your Sirius channels. I think they call it 'Spa'".

"That's a good one. It's relaxing music. Some of the music played has the Native American flute in it." Anderson turns on the music. He says, "You take the recliner, and I'll stretch out on the couch." They both doze off.

When Anderson wakes up, he feeds Pockets. He comes back in and heats up chicken and noodle soup. From the kitchen he investigates the great room and sees that Lydia is awake. Anderson says, "Are you ready for soup and crackers?"

Lydia replies, "Yes, that's all I would like right now." Anderson brings their soup and puts it on the tall end tables by the recliner and the couch.

After he sits down and says grace with Lydia, He says, "There's a news program that comes on at 6:00. I thought it would be a good idea to watch the latest news."

Lydia says, "I was wanting to catch up on what's going on."

Kenny and I think the death toll from all the arson, vandalism and robberies is probably a lot higher than we've heard."

Lydia replies, "I agree, and the property destruction nationwide is probably devastating." They enjoy the soup and Lydia says, "This hits the spot!"

"Do you want anything else?"

Lydia replies, "Not now. Later I think the ham, cheese and crackers would be good."

As they finish the bowl of soup, Anderson says, "I don't know why, but after we talked about some things from our childhood, I thought about the poor family that lived in the run-down house that was on our way to elementary school. They had several young children, and the oldest might have been close to your age."

Lydia says, "Yes, I remember the house and seeing the children. I remember us moving to another school district before I went into third grade."

Anderson replies, "That's right. I entered fifth grade in the new school. Off and on all my life, I remember the old refrigerator sitting in their back yard with the door still on it. The sidewalk to school ran parallel with their back yard. I remember being stunned when I heard the news about one of the children suffocating after being trapped in the refrigerator."

Lydia says, "Even though I was two years younger, I remember seeing that old fridge in the yard. Didn't you walk at times from high school with a boy that ended up shooting and killing his sister?"

"Yes. The boy was a year younger than I was. His sister was a year younger than he was. She was a cute girl. One day he even showed me his gun collection. I heard the shooting was accidental. I never heard about the details of the shooting or about his demise."

Lydia says, "We usually don't know what people go through. In junior high school I was in band with a girl, who seemed like a nice, common person. After thirty some years, I saw her on social network, and we got

A Light on the Path

talking awhile about school days. She ended up telling me that most of the time growing up, her dad physically and sexually abused her."

Anderson replies, "How traumatic is that? Some people never totally recover, but there is one that makes all the difference."

Lydia says, "I need to learn from you. I should have been a witness to her, but I didn't even ask her if she knew Christ." Lydia just stares at Anderson for a few seconds.

Anderson says, "What is it?"

Lydia replies, "I really do need to learn more from you about the ways of Christ."

Anderson says, "You've had the same home church background, but we each walk that long, lonesome highway until we find the Lord in our lives. Do you think you need to rededicate your life to the Lord?"

Lydia says, "I probably do."

Anderson replies, "In the time we live in, be prepared. Make things right with the Lord. Thank the Father for the Son and tell the Father that you want to rededicate your life to Christ. We have all sinned and fallen short of God's glory. God forgives, and His grace will keep you."

Lydia says, "I will think about it, and I will regularly pray about it."

Anderson says, "Sis, I love you. Don't wait too long. We're a heartbeat away from eternity. I will continue to pray for you. Remember the childhood prayer that mom prayed with us, when we were real young?"

Lydia recites, "I lay me down to sleep. If I die before I wake, I pray thee Lord my soul to take."

Anderson says, "That's a good prayer." Anderson gets up and takes the bowls to the kitchen. He asks, "Do you want me to leave any food out for you?"

"No thanks," replied Lydia. "I can get it out later, if I'm hungry. Lydia looks at the time and says, "It will be 6:00 before we know it."

"Yes, I'm not looking forward to it, but I need to listen to the whole broadcast and get better informed," replied Anderson. "Have you thought yet, when you might want to put your house on the market?"

"It has crossed my mind. If it's possible, I would like to have it listed not long after New Year's."

Anderson asks, "Do you have any necessary repairs or cracked paint inside or outside?"

"There's a fine crack that runs down the living room wall near a corner. I think spackling and paint would repair it satisfactorily. There's a big crack in the concrete driveway. The old basketball post is rusty, and the outside of the front door needs a coating of polyurethane or something. Also, near the front door is an overhang support that needs paint, and the trim around my back door needs paint."

"Those are mostly minor things. Possibly Paul or Eli could do those repairs. It is required that cracked paint be covered for the sale of a house. I would go ahead and meet with the agent after New Year's, and by the time the repairs are done, the house could be listed. You don't have to provide a seller's warranty, and you can also sell a house "as is"."

Lydia says, "Even though spring is a busy time for the house market, you never know when the early bird will catch an early buyer."

Anderson replies, "That's exactly right. Our winters are usually mild, and someone might be looking for just your kind of house and location. You probably know that most buyers and sellers agree to thirty days before the seller moves. When you get close to the time, let me know, and I'll help you pack."

"That's very nice of you, Anderson. Thank you."

They both look at the time. Anderson says, "We only have two minutes before the news program start." He grabs the remote and gets ready to hear the report with apprehension."

As Lydia and Anderson listen, they squirm in their seats. The beginning of the report is worse than they expected. They start out by giving the latest national death toll at 1,086. The latest they have on nationwide property destruction and damage is $260 billion. Now Los Angeles, Houston, South Chicago, Baltimore, St. Louis and Detroit are reported to be under martial law. The National Guard is in sixty-eight cities and fifty-five of them are the largest cities in the country. The news anchor says the average price increase in gas prices nationwide is 120%, and the average food product increase is 132%. They break for commercials.

Lydia says, "I don't know that this is a good time to sell, but it might be for those downsizing or for first time buyers, who decide to buy less square footage than they originally planned."

Anderson replies, "They also might decide to buy now before the interest rates get worse. The feds are keeping the rates lower than I thought they would. Mortgage interest rates have not gone through the roof yet. Also, the increased price for the house will help pay for food and gas. You might get a lot more than you expect."

Lydia says, "I know you didn't look forward to hearing the bad news. It's sad for everyone." The news anchor comes back on.

He says, "We have a special report tonight. This week we have had several contributing, investigative reporters in the field. We have covered several small towns as well as large cities nationwide. At this time, we will get their reports on "Neighborhood Watch Groups"."

A Light on the Path

The first reporter has covered parts of Los Angeles and San Diego. He talks about gangs and other large groups of people that go in and raid neighborhoods. They're compared to locusts that bring destruction to one block at a time. Other reports in both large cities and small towns are better in areas where gun control is not as strict.

Three other reporters talk about several large cities and small towns, where neighborhood residents have repelled gangs with military rifles, hunting rifles and shotguns. One reporter says, "Even though the gang may bring in ten members or more, they are targets of fire from every corner of the neighborhood. We have a report from Houston, where one gang lost twelve of sixteen members."

Another reporter interviews a resident of a neighborhood in a small Missouri town. The resident says, "We have a 24/7 watch group. If we see any strangers coming into the neighborhood, especially strangers with more than one in the car, we start out by blasting our air horns. Most residents also have bull horns to warn people to stay off their property. Once the strangers are warned, if they don't get off the property, they get one warning shot and only one warning shot."

The reporter asks, "Has anyone been injured or killed?"

The resident says, "None of our neighbors have been injured or killed. Ninety percent of the intruders leave once they hear the air horns. There have been a few groups of five or more who tried to approach properties, but none of those got into any houses. One group of six kept walking toward a house, even after the warning shot. When two of them were shot in the leg, they also left."

The news anchor thanks the reporters and breaks for commercials.

Anderson says, "This is so surreal that it's like watching a Twilight Zone episode."

Lydia replies, "It's so scary that it makes you wonder when it will come to our neighborhood."

"The one reporter compared the robberies and vandalism to a plague of locusts. It's totally catastrophic," replied Anderson. "It could be months or much longer before things begin to stabilize, if at all."

Lydia asks, "You don't think this will be the new normal, do you?"

Anderson says, "It's hard to get my head wrapped around it, but I think one outcome is America becoming an isolationist nation. Our country may not have much choice. Once the dust clears, I hope our nation doesn't fall for any global currency that some national leaders and bankers are trying to promote."

Lydia replies, "I don't know about you, but after thirty minutes of this doom and gloom, I'm not sure I can handle much more."

A Light on the Path

"I agree. Why don't we search for a good movie that starts by 7:00? I think I'll hit the sack by 9:00." Anderson's mood gets serious, "By the way, Lydia, after hearing these reports, we should talk about something."

"I'm all ears."

Anderson says, "You're probably familiar with the outside lights I keep on. There are also some detector lights that sense movement. Whether its day or night, it might be best that you don't answer the door for now. I can look out to see if it's a friend or stranger. Some people check doors to see if they're unlocked."

Lydia says, "I'm glad you shared that. I also need to be more careful at home."

"While we are looking for a movie, I have two things to run by you for tomorrow. For dinner, I would like to take you to the Smokey Mount Restaurant in Mount Holly. They have good American food like barbecue, chicken, steak and pork chops. They even have black eyed peas and sweet potato casserole! Also, earlier in the day, if we're in the mood, I'll build a fire in the fire pit. We can roast hot dogs or just enjoy the fire."

Lydia replies, "They sound like good times to me!"

Anderson says, "In the guide so far, the movies that start at 7:00 are Rocky, Pale Rider, Fried Green Tomatoes, and Ground Hog Day. The movies that already started by 6:30 are Back to the Future, Forrest Gump, Day after Tomorrow and As Good as It Gets."

Lydia replies, "If they're on a movie channel with no commercials, why don't we pick one that starts at 7:00?"

"They're all good movies," replied Anderson. "Do you want to choose between Ground Hog Day and Rocky?"

Lydia says, "I like them both; how about Ground Hog Day?"

"That's a good choice."

Lydia looks at the wall clock and says, "We have about fifteen minutes. I'm going to the bathroom, then get a bottle of water from the fridge. Do you want anything?"

Anderson says, "While you're in the bathroom, I'm going to fix a cup of black tea, and I might pop some skinny popcorn."

Lydia replies, "I'll stick with the cold water. The popcorn sounds tasty!"

When Lydia comes back, the movie is almost ready to begin. They begin enjoying the popcorn.

Anderson says, "Saturday morning is going to get here too quickly."

Lydia replies, "I know. It would be nice to stay longer."

Chapter 9 - Back in Indiana

As Anderson finishes preparing breakfast, he thinks, "It's hard to believe that Friday has come and gone. I'll miss Lydia, but I also have to get ready for the flight to Indianapolis." He thinks he already heard Lydia get out of the shower. He turns the fire to low and waits on Lydia. In a few minutes, he gets the bread ready to be toasted and makes sure everything is ready to serve breakfast on the dining table.

He goes to her bedroom door. He says, "Breakfast is ready when you are."

Through the door, Lydia says, "I'll be out in a minute." When she comes out, she is carrying her bags.

Anderson says, "Wow, I didn't know you already packed your bags."

She replies, "I got most things ready before I went to bed. I hate to leave after breakfast, but soon I'll be here every day. Are you sure that you can handle that?"

Anderson replies, "It will be my pleasure!"

They sit down at the long country style, dark walnut dining table, and talk about the Indianapolis flight and the sale of Lydia's house over breakfast. After their second cup of coffee, Lydia says, "I think I'll take off in a few minutes."

Anderson carries her bags out, as she holds the door. At her well-kept Impala, Anderson loads her bags in the trunk, and they give each other a hug, Anderson says, "Be careful, Sis. I'll call you from Angela's house."

"Okay, big brother. I'm looking forward to selling the house and being here." She gives him another hug. Anderson stands in the driveway and waives as she backs her car onto the road. He thinks, "Lord, give her a safe trip. I'm glad I filled her gas tank in Mount Holly yesterday." As he walks back in the house, he thinks, "I'm looking forward to seeing Angela and her family, but I dread the wait at the airports."

He sits down at the computer to check on the Charlotte and Indianapolis forecast for the 23rd and the 26th. The forecast for Indianapolis tomorrow is snow likely; 75% chance of precipitation; a high of 31 degrees and wind up to 15 m.p.h. He plans to leave before 7:30, so he'll be at the Knoxville airport by 8:30.

Anderson busies himself with packing and making calls to his neighbor, Conard; Lydia and Angela. He also calls Kenny, so they can update each other on their Christmas activities. Throughout the day and evening, he also checks the house and Pockets. Before he goes to bed, he packs the Christmas gifts that Lydia helped him pick out in Mount Holly yesterday. As he turns the lights out, he thinks how quickly the Indianapolis trip came around.

A Light on the Path

Even though the cell phone alarm is set for 5:15, Anderson wakes up just before 5:00. He does his early routine of devotions, breakfast and shower. He feeds Pockets and tells her that Conard is going to look after her. He pets her and says, "Pockets, I'll be back by Wednesday." He loads his large luggage bag, carry-on bag and camera bag early. Anderson goes back in the house one more time to check locks and to turn on a few lights.

It's a pleasant and mild morning. Anderson backs his F150 out of the driveway. As he pulls out, he looks at the time: 7:25. He feels good that he left a few minutes early. As he comes out of a curve; up a hill and into a clearing, to his left he can still see the last of the gilded sunrise over the majestic Smoky Mountains. Once he goes through Mount Holly, he takes a short cut to the west to catch I-40. Right after the interstate goes by downtown Knoxville, he takes the Alcoa Highway exit to the airport. He pulls in front of the parking gate and takes a ticket. He parks in the covered garage. As he unloads, he puts the carry-on bag over the check-in bag handle. He throws the camera case over his shoulder and rolls the luggage behind him.

Inside he shows his ticket and checks in the large luggage. He gets on the escalator and goes through security. He thinks he has packed the right size toiletries in the carry-on bag and remembers not to have any drinks or bottled water on him. Everything goes smoothly with the security check. He puts everything back in his pockets and looks at his watch. He has an hour wait before he can board the plane. He buys a cup of coffee and egg biscuit as he waits to board the plane that goes to Charlotte then to Indianapolis.

Anderson thinks, "I was so busy to get checked in that I forgot to look for any extra security at the airport." From his seat, he looks around and notices three national guardsmen in the next few minutes. He grabs his carry-on bag and camera case and goes to gate four. He has about thirty-five minutes before he can board the plane.

After he throws his bag in the overhead and sits down in his assigned seat, he thinks, "the wait wasn't too bad, but in Charlotte I will be waiting another hour." The plane starts taxiing down the runway twenty minutes later. In just a few minutes, he's above the clouds and on his way to Indianapolis by way of Charlotte. Anderson thinks, "I have to go southeast before I can go northwest! It would be nice if I could go to sleep now and wake up when we land in Indianapolis."

As they land in Charlotte, everything looks very familiar to him. He thinks, "I couldn't count all the times I flew from Indianapolis to Charlotte." He guesses that his first flight to Charlotte was around 1965. Most everyone that he has encountered since he arrived in Knoxville, have been pleasant.

A Light on the Path

He mainly hears people talking about the high prices and civil unrest in the country.

Anderson is back in his seat, and soon the plane begins to lift off the ground. Anderson thinks, "Finally, I'm headed directly to Indianapolis." When they get to 30,000 feet, they begin to ride above the clouds. Anderson thinks, "This is about as close to heaven as a person can get." Even though the country is having grave problems, everyone that he notices around him seems to be in a cheerful mood. An older man sitting next to him, tells Anderson about flying to Charlotte out of Indianapolis once or twice a year.

He says, "My son moved to Charlotte from Shelbyville, Indiana, about four to five years ago. He and his wife are raising their son and daughter in Charlotte. I usually come for Christmas, but they're going to his in-laws this year, so I celebrated Christmas with them early this year."

Anderson says, "From Indianapolis, I use to fly to Charlotte a lot on business. Now from my home in Tennessee, I visit places like Maggie Valley, Cherokee, Waynesville and Bryson City."

He replies, "I envy you. I've traveled with my son to Maggie Valley and Cherokee; also, to Asheville and Boone and other places near the Blue Ridge Parkway."

Anderson says, "Its God's country."

He sticks out his hand and Anderson shakes it. The stranger says, "I'm Ricky Cameron."

Anderson replies, "It's good to meet you. I'm Anderson McCollister. Ricky, in my family cemetery, there is a marker with the name "Cameron" on it."

Ricky exclaims, "Is that right? Our family cemetery is in Forest City, Indiana."

Anderson is surprised, "Wow, that is my family cemetery too. My oldest ancestor there is William Albertson from North Carolina."

Ricky excitedly says, "I can't believe we're sitting next to each other. Maybe we're ninth or tenth cousins!"

Anderson laughs as he says, "My family came by way of Richmond to Forest City, to Bluffton, to Portland then to Hartford City. My great grandmother was an Albertson and she married a McCollister."

Ricky says, "That's amazing! I had a great grandfather named Albertson, and his daughter married a Cameron. We also came by way of Richmond, to Forest City, to Bluffton, to Connersville then to Shelbyville."

They talk more about their family tree, and before they realize it, they're descending to the Indianapolis airport in what has the makings of a snow storm. After they land they trade email addresses and shake hands, before they exit through the crowded airplane aisle. Anderson looks at his watch, his flight is five minutes ahead of schedule. Once he exits the plane, he stops and looks out the gate windows. For a few seconds he watches the blowing snow in what looks like a cold wind. It reminds him of his many winters in Indiana.

The Indianapolis airport is now bigger than what it was, but he finds his way pass security and to his delight he sees the smiling faces of Angela and Stephen. He hugs and kisses Angela and give Stephen a hug. Angela asks, "Did you have a good flight?"

Anderson replies, "Yes. I traveled from Charlotte to here with my ninth cousin."

Angela smiles as they head toward the baggage pick-up area, "You'll have to fill me in on that one later. When Anderson spots his luggage and tries to lift it off the carousel, Stephen exclaims, "Man, that's some giant baggage!"

Anderson says, "Santa Claus had me bring this bag of gifts to you."

As they walk toward the exit, Anderson has noticed a lot of National Guardsmen. Just outside one of the main doors, they have two large armored vehicles. Once they're outside, Anderson's sees that his guess is right about the cold wind. The snow is still blowing and to be heard above the wind, he yells, "Now I know why I live in Tennessee!"

They get in their white SUV and Angela says, "On the way home, we're picking up fried chicken, and tomorrow I'll be cooking for Christmas Eve and Christmas."

Anderson says, "Just give me figgy pudding and I'll be happy!" He says to Angela, "When we get to the house, as long as I have your check for the airplane ticket."

Angela says, "There's no hurry with that."

They get on I-70 East and take the Highway 9, Greenfield exit. Stephen pulls in a drive through, and they get a big tub of fried chicken with green beans and mashed potatoes and gravy. Angela says, "Clint is coming in tomorrow afternoon. His girlfriend drove from Knoxville to Terre Haute two days ago, and she is coming with him."

Anderson replies, "That's wonderful! How much snow is forecasted?"

Stephen says, "The forecast for today and tonight is 3 to 5 inches of snow. Tomorrow is only 10% chance of precipitation. They forecasted partly sunny for tomorrow, so we hope the snow will begin disappearing."

Anderson replies, "It sounds like there might be some snow on the ground for Christmas Eve and Christmas."

Angela says, "It will be nice to have a white Christmas this year."

They go just north of Greenfield to their home in a spacious neighborhood. They have a large two-story home with two dormers. Candle lights are on in the two dormer windows and the four windows downstairs.

A Light on the Path

A red door with a green wreath divides the four windows on the front of the house. As they park in their driveway, Anderson remarks, "I can hear the front door say, "Open me and feel the spirit of Christmas here."

They laugh, and Angela says, "That's a good one, Dad."

As the three of them leave their tracks in the snow-covered sidewalk, Angela looks like a dwarf walking with two giants to the front door. As they unlock the red door, they shake the snow off their coats and hats. Ralph, their black lab, greets them at the door. Ralph goes up to Anderson and starts whining. As Anderson pets him, Angela says, "He remembers you, Dad." Anderson talks to Ralph as Stephen takes their supper to the kitchen. Anderson says, "It feels good and comfy in here."

Angela replies, "I want you to be good and comfy the whole time you're here! Ralph is inside, because of the cold weather. You will also have his company this evening, then he'll sleep in the garage tonight."

Anderson looks back at Ralph and says, "You can party with us tonight, Ralph."

As Ralph continues to wag his tail, Angela says, "He likes the attention." Stephen comes in the living room and says, "It's going on 4:30. Do you want to eat now or later?"

Angela replies, "Does everyone want to eat by 5:00?"

Anderson says, "Whenever you want to." Angela goes into the kitchen to get a few things ready." Stephen looks at Anderson and says, "I think I'll take a load off my feet and join you."

Anderson says, "I need to call my sister to let her know that I'm here." Anderson is on the phone for just a couple minutes. Lydia tells him about her family's schedule for Christmas Eve and Christmas. When Anderson gets off the phone, he sees that Stephen has dozed off.

In a few minutes, Angela comes in the room and announces that supper is ready. She says, "The plates and everything are out, so just help yourself." She made a fresh pot of coffee and Anderson says, "The coffee sure smells good! I may be tempted to take one of your Christmas cookies to have with the coffee."

Everyone takes their food into the living room. Anderson says grace and they enjoy taking their time talking and eating. Angela says, "Clint and Sara should be here by 3 or 4:00 tomorrow. After our Christmas Eve dinner, it might be a good time to give Christmas gifts."

Stephen says, "That would be good. Since I've been putting in a lot of overtime, I think I'll catch up on my sleep tonight and start getting ready for bed between 8 and 8:30."

Angela says, "Dad and I can talk awhile. Dad are you staying up until 9 or later?"

Anderson says, "I feel good and relaxed. I feel like I could stay up until the late hour of 10:00."

Stephen says, "There you have it. You can entertain each other."

Angela asks, "Dad, can I get anything else for you."

Anderson replies, "No thanks, it was delicious. I might get some more coffee in about an hour. I think I would like to get some things organized and rest for a while. I'll come back down in about an hour."

Angela says, "That's fine. We'll turn to something good on TV and join us whenever you're ready."

Anderson replies, "Very good. See you soon." Anderson goes to his room and sorts out the gifts and gift bags that he has for tomorrow. He plans to stretch out on the bed for a little while, but when he wakes up, it's almost 7:30.

He goes downstairs to the living room and says, "Sorry about that. I wasn't planning to go to sleep."

Stephen says, "No problem. We've been surfing the channels for the men's college basketball games. We think Indiana State had a game yesterday, but Clint can tell us tomorrow. You did a lot of work in Charlotte. Do you want to watch the Duke and UNC game? It's going into the fourth quarter."

Anderson replies, "That's one of the best rivalries in the country. Let's watch the rest of the game." The game goes back and forth between Duke and North Carolina. They get talking about the team this year at Indiana State. They discuss Clint's work with the team, and what Larry Bird has meant to the team through the years. Before they realize it, the time is well after 8:00.

Stephen says, "I have to excuse myself and get ready for bed." Stephen gives Angela a kiss, and Anderson and Angela wish him a good night.

College basketball highlights are still on. Angela asks Anderson, "Do you want to watch anything else?"

Anderson replies, "No, I'll get some coffee and visit with you."

Angela says, "I'll get it for you, Dad."

When she brings it back, Anderson asks, "How is work and everything with you?"

Angela replies, "Home life is good, but work is kind of frustrating. Peers and superiors act like they want to force their agenda on you, but I'm doing alright."

Anderson says, "Unfortunately, that is too often the way of the world. I would like to get back to that, but I've decided on something to help your Aunt Lydia."

Angela replies, "I would like to hear about it."

"Her financial balance sheet did not look good. She told me that she was having some problems, so I sat down with her. She didn't need money

A Light on the Path

now, but in the next year things didn't look good for her. I felt the good solution for her is to sell her house and to move to my house." Anderson stops and waits for Lydia's reply.

Angela says, "Dad, you always helped your loved ones: Mom, me and now Lydia. I love you and I'm proud to be your daughter."

Anderson says, "In my will, the house and land are yours. Later I want to make a provision saying that Lydia will reside at the house, as long as she can take care of herself. She is also responsible for the upkeep of the house, if something happens to me. Until I add that provision to the will, I am going to notarize the same thing. I will give you a copy and Lydia a copy."

Angela replies, "I totally understand. I've been doing a lot of thinking, since mom passed on. I didn't realize how thorough and thoughtful you were. I was selfish and wanted more of your time, when I was with you and mom. I never considered how much you sacrificed for us."

Anderson says, "You're kind. Don't feel bad. You and I and everyone falls short of the mark. I'm glad you said, "sacrifice", because I think you know who paid the ultimate sacrifice."

Angela says, "Yes, I understand. I know what you believe."

Anderson replies, "I think you know that I am open minded. Quite a few things in life are subjective. Some people think a piece of art is very good while other people don't care for it. A student may think he or she deserves an A, but the instructor thinks a B is generous. An employee may sincerely think that they deserve a raise, but the employer disagrees. On the other hand, there are some things that are absolute. Truth is truth and lies are lies. There is always the right thing to do and the wrong thing to do. God is also an absolute. There is one true God. Christ, who has been proven to be the Son of God, taught that the only way to the Father is through the Son." Anderson waits on Angela's reply.

In a few seconds, Angela says, "Dad, I wish I could be as sure as you."

"You can be sure. Pray about it and study the Bible; especially books like the gospel of John. Jesus is coming soon, and we don't have a lot of time left to be prepared."

Angela asks, "How do you know that He is coming soon?"

Anderson replies, "I know by God's Spirit; by prophecy and by the state of the world."

Angela says, "It's true the world is not looking good."

"In our country, I believe we're seeing a prelude that will pale to what is to come," replied Anderson.

"What is to come, Dad?"

A Light on the Path

"It's in the Bible, including the books of Ezekiel, Daniel, Matthew, Revelation and others. It is also described in modern day books like, "Hope and the Approaching Apocalypse".

Angela says, "I know we disagree with things from evolution to the accuracy of the Bible."

Anderson says, "Let me ask you something, Angela." He pauses for a couple of seconds and sees that Angela is sincere. "If I'm right about the Father, the Son and the Holy Spirit and the Holy Bible, does it matter if we disagree on evolution or any other theory?"

Angela replies, "No."

Anderson says, "Angela, you know that I love you with all my heart."

Angela says, "Yes, Dad, I know you do, and I love you."

Anderson replies, "Jesus Christ made the ultimate sacrifice, because He loves us unconditionally. One day you, as well as I, will stand before God and must answer for our life and what we did. None of us are perfect, that is why the Father redeemed us through Christ. We must follow Christ to be with the Father. When you stand on your own before God, your superiors, colleagues and students of psychology will not be there to support you. Your only support will be the life you lived in Christ. No theories, religions or philosophies of mankind will help you."

Angela says, "You make a strong point."

Anderson says, "Pray about it, and I will be praying for you. You know that I only want the best things for you and the right things."

Angela has tears in her eyes. She stammers a little, while she tries to say, "Dad, I don't know if I'm just missing Mom right now, or something you're saying is trying to register with me."

Anderson replies, "It could be God's still small voice. I know it's getting a little late, but can I say a short prayer for you."

"Yes, Dad."

Anderson bows his head and prays, "Our Father, you know that I love my daughter more than life. I pray that you will show her your light, your Son. May she let the Holy Spirit guide her to Christ. May she follow Jesus Christ. Watch over her and her family and protect them during these perilous times. In Jesus' name I pray. Amen."

Angela wipes tears from her eyes and says, "Thank you, Dad. I love you."

"Angela, we both miss your mom deeply. My prayers and thoughts are always with you."

Angela replies, "Thank you, Dad. You've been a blessing to Mom and to me. I will be thinking about what you shared tonight."

A Light on the Path

Anderson says, "Sweetheart, this old man is beginning to feel his old age tonight. I think I'll retire for the evening unless I can help you with anything."

"I don't need anything this evening. I'm going to sit here a few minutes and think about Mom and possibly what you shared with me."

Anderson walks over and kisses Angela on the cheek.

"Good night, Dad. Have sweet dreams"

Anderson replies, "Goodnight, Hon."

Christmas Eve morning arrives like a phantom jet doing a sky dive. Anderson hears Ralph downstairs. He thinks, "Stephen got up early and took care of Ralph." Anderson can't believe that it's almost 7:00. He wonders if he can help with breakfast. When he walks downstairs, he smells bacon already. He walks into the kitchen and says to Stephen, "A man after my own heart."

Stephen laughs and looks like Christmas in his red plaid robe, "Good morning! I thought everyone would enjoy bacon with their eggs. How do you like your eggs?"

Ralph has glued himself to Anderson's legs and is waiting impatiently to be petted. Anderson says, "Either scrambled or two eggs over medium". Ralph finally gets the attention he wants from Anderson. Anderson says, "He has a lot of energy for a seven-year-old lab."

Stephen replies, "He does for now. I hate to think of the changes coming in about four years."

Anderson says, "I know what you mean. I'm familiar with their physical problems, when they reach that age." Stephen already has the eggs underway.

Stephen asks Anderson, "Could you see if Angela is up? Tell her breakfast is almost ready."

Anderson replies, "Okie-Dokie!"

When Anderson returns to the kitchen with Ralph following, he says, "She'll be here in a minute."

Stephen says, "Good. The table is almost set, and I'll put the bread in the toaster now."

During breakfast, he asks Stephen and Angela, if they would like to go with him to downtown Greenfield. "Of course, I need you; I don't have my car! I would like to see James Whitcomb Riley's estate again and go into a couple of the antique shops."

They both say that they would like to go after they clean up the kitchen. Angela says, "You should find some shops open until early afternoon, but you will probably just get to see Riley's home from the outside."

Anderson says, "That is good. Their grounds are nice, and the snow has stopped, and the sun is shining! I need to shower. If we leave by 9:30, we should have plenty of time to get ready."

Stephen says, "That's a good plan for me. Clint and Sara won't be here until mid-afternoon."

They put Ralph in the garage at 9:30, and they take Angela's silver Chrysler 300. Stephen says, "The last time I got gas in town, a panhandler approached me at the pump. I want to take Angela's car, so I can fill up the tank on the way to Riley's estate."

Anderson asks, "Do the police have stake outs here at the grocery stores and gas stations?"

Stephen replies, "They have some, but I think its hit and miss. The police have a lot of businesses to cover in Greenfield." After they pull out of the gas station, they come to the main light in downtown Greenfield, and turn west.

Angela says, "If the sidewalks are cleared, we can park on the edge of downtown, and walk to the Riley estate. It won't be far to walk back to several antique shops."

They pull over and park. Anderson says, "It looks like we're down to about two inches on the ground." They get out of the car and head to Riley's home. Right before they get to his home, Anderson says, "The bright yellow museum looks good next to Riley's house. They stop and admire Riley's house from the front.

Anderson says, "I always liked looking at the twin chimneys. The white railings on the balcony and front porch look imposing in front of the white house and green shutters. While I'm standing in front of his house, I'm compelled to say from James Whitcomb Riley's famous poem, "…the frost is on the punkin and the fodder's in the shock".

Stephen laughs, and Angela says, "That would put a smile on Riley's face." Anderson says, "I know there's some snow on the estate grounds, but can we walk around the house for a few minutes?"

Angela replies, "Sure we can."

They walk on the Riley grounds, and then hike to two of the antique shops. After they're done with antique and collectible shopping, Angela says, "I better get home, so I can start cooking for Christmas Eve." They get back about noon, and Angela starts on the Christmas Eve preparations. Angela says, "Dad, do you want to watch a ball game with Stephen after he walks Ralph?"

Anderson says, "I need to rest awhile and get some gifts ready for the exchange this evening."

Angela says, "I hope you didn't buy too much."

A Light on the Path

Anderson says whimsically, "I should have bought more! Well, just yell if you need help in the kitchen. If I don't hear from you, I'll come back down before 2:00."

Angela replies, "Okay. Take your time. I hope you're enjoying yourself."

Anderson says, "I'm having a great time. Being here with you is supercalifragilisticexpialidocious!"

Angela laughs and says, "I think it's wonderful too!"

Anderson goes upstairs and puts name stickers on the gifts he bought. He also brought gifts for Clint and Sara. He looks at a special gift again that he brought for Angela. He makes sure he has all the gifts in the small gift bags he brought. He puts green and red wrapping tissue around the gifts and at the top of the bags. Anderson thinks, "I'm about ready for a long winter nap,"

In what seems to be a few minutes later, he hears Ralph rushing up the stairway, but Anderson has been asleep for an hour. It's going on 2:00, and Anderson freshens up and puts on his best red shirt and goes downstairs.

He walks in the kitchen, and Angela is still busy and working hard. She asks, "How was your nap?"

Anderson says, "I was dreaming of sugar plums dancing in my head."

Angela says playfully, "You stole that from Clement Clarke Moore, didn't you?"

Anderson replies, "I kind of rephrased it. Have you heard from Clint?"

"Yes, he called and said he was getting close to Indianapolis. He should be here before 3:00."

Anderson says, "It will be great to see him."

Stephen comes back downstairs with Ralph. He says, "Anderson are you ready to celebrate Christmas Eve and Christmas with some Ariel Red Wine?"

Anderson replies, "Yes, but I refuse to drink more than two liters!"

"Alright, we'll hold you to that," replied Stephen. "Is that a car horn I heard near the drive way?"

Anderson says, "It's either a car or Santa's sleigh."

In just two minutes, Clint and Sara come through the front door. Angela and Stephen hug them. Anderson says, "There's my seasoned college basketball coach."

Clint hugs Anderson and says, "Merry Christmas, Grandpa. I'm glad you could make it. This is Sara." Sara hugs Anderson and says, "Glad to meet you. Merry Christmas."

Anderson barely gets out" Merry Christmas". He's somewhat stunned and Clint says, "What's wrong Grandpa? You look like you've seen a ghost."

Anderson says, "More like an apparition. Maybe I'm getting senile, but frankly, Sara, you look a lot like Ruth, my wife, when she was your age. You have the same warm smile.'

Sara says, "Thank you. That's a great compliment."

Angela says, "Well, get your coats off and visit, while I finish in the kitchen. I'll be done with supper in an hour or so." She looks at Clint, "Do you want an early supper by 4:30?"

Clint smiles and replies, "That would be great; the sooner the better!" After they put their coats up, Clint follows Sara into the living room". As Stephen, Anderson, Sara, Clint and Ralph gather into the living room, they sit down, and Anderson asks Clint, "When do you have to go back to Terre Haute?"

Clint says, "I don't have to be back to work until January 4th. Sara and I are leaving here on Thursday and driving to see her parents in Knoxville. We're going to celebrate New Year's Eve with them. I need to get some things done in Terre Haute, so I'll drive back January 2nd."

Anderson replies, "I'm glad you can celebrate New Year's with them. Wednesday morning, I must leave for the airport by 5:45. I think the trip will be a men's outing, so Sara and Angela don't have to get up so early. I was wondering if you would go with your dad and me."

Clint says, "I would like that. If we take dad's SUV, we'll have enough leg room. The three of us have an average height of 6'5"!"

Everyone laughs, and Sara looks at Clint, "I know you're 6'7". How tall are your dad and grandpa?"

Clint replies, "Dad is 6'5" and grandpa is 6"3"."

Anderson smiles and says, "At least, I use to be. My Grandpa McCollister married an Albertson, and the men in the Albertson family in the 1800s and beyond were 6'4"."

Sara replies, "No wonder Clint sprouted to 6'7"; both sides of his family contributed."

They get so involved in their conversation that they don't realize they've been talking over an hour. Angela comes in and says, "I want to ask my darling husband to set the table, then everyone can wash up for Christmas Eve dinner."

They gather in the dining room, and everyone is wide-eyed as they look at the Christmas Eve spread: ham with pineapple, chicken with melted butter, sweet potatoes with melted marsh mellows, green bean casserole with mushrooms, strawberries and blue berries with whipped cream, and Angela announces dessert will be vanilla frozen yogurt with apple pie. Angela asks Anderson to say grace, and they sit down to enjoy their bountiful dinner.

A Light on the Path

Stephen announces that he'll be serving Ariel Red Wine during the gift exchange this evening.

Anderson asks Sara, "What are your parent's names?"

"They're E.J. and Rachel Black. Dad is from Knoxville, and mom was Rachel Crockett from Jefferson City."

Anderson asks, "Is your mother of Davy Crockett fame?"

Sara replies, "Yes, she's a distant descendant. Davy Crockett hunted in Jefferson County as a boy."

Anderson exclaims, "What a great American hero he was!"

Sara says, "He was. You can visit his parent's cabin in Morristown."

Angela asks everyone, "Are you almost ready for pie a la mode?"

The vote is unanimous. Sara asks Anderson, "Where did you meet your wife?"

"We met in Lafayette, Indiana; at Purdue. We were both undergraduates. I was in business and she was in education. She was Ruth King from Muncie. It was a great blessing in all ways. My hometown, Hartford City, was just eighteen miles from where she lived."

Everyone is stuffed after the pie a la mode. Angela and Stephen clear off the table, and Anderson goes to the living room with Clint and Sara.

Anderson says, "I almost feel like a kid about the gift exchange. It really is more about giving than receiving."

Clint says, "I agree, grandpa. Sara and I both love the spirit of Christmas."

After Angela and Stephen finish in the dining room and kitchen, they join them. Stephen says, "I think we're too full for the wine right now."

Anderson says, "I need to go upstairs and bring my gifts down before the exchange." Clint offers to help, but Anderson can manage the small gift bags. It is already dark outside before he gets the gifts. The short span of time that he is away from the party, he thinks about how much he misses Ruth. He thinks, "Sometimes I can barely get pass the loneliness of her not being here."

When he comes back downstairs, he says to everyone, "Since Christmas is the time we celebrate Christ's birthday, I would like to share something."

Angela replies, "Sure, dad, go ahead."

Anderson says, "About two thousand years ago, a young couple were alone on a cold winter night in a strange town, the town of Bethlehem. They had to sleep in a stable and that is where the great joy and miracle took place, the birth of Jesus, God with us. As I was just now getting the gifts, I also thought of those who came bearing gifts. Sometimes great joy comes out of great loneliness. In spirit my wife is with us. She is Angela's mother and Clint's grandmother. The world is sometimes a lonely place, but Jesus taught that we are in the world and not of the world. When I think of Ruth and her love, I think of Christ and how much He loved us. Even though Christ and my wife are not physically with us this evening, their presence is here in every one of you."

Everyone just stares at Anderson for another second, but then all of them look away and are totally silent for a minute. Angela has tears in her eyes, and everyone is kind of misty. Anderson breaks the silence by saying, "I know that some of us aren't great singers, but can we sing together the first verse of "Silent Night"?"

In soft but tranquil voices, they all sing, "Silent Night, Holy Night! All is calm; all is bright. Round yon Virgin, Mother and Child. Holy Infant so tender and mild. Sleep in heavenly peace; sleep in heavenly peace."

Anderson says, "I thank all of you; that was beautiful. I know we haven't started the gift exchange yet, but speaking of Ruth, Angela's mother," Anderson looks at Angela, "because of her love and my love for you, Angela, I have a special gift for you." He hands Angela a small, plain red gift bag. Angela pulls out a small, long jewelry box. She opens the box and tries to speak, but she is all choked up.

Finally, she can say, "Its mother's favorite jewelry; her diamond necklace. Oh, dad, this is a priceless gift." As she goes over to hug Anderson, she starts crying. She holds her dad a minute then gives him a kiss.

Anderson says, "I love you, Angela. Merry Christmas."

Angela starts crying and hugging her dad again.

Stephen says, "This is already a great Christmas. Let's go ahead and start the gift exchange, and I will serve Ariel Red Wine. As Jesus drank wine in celebration with his disciples, we will drink the same in celebration of His birth."

After they get busy with the gift exchange, Stephen serves the Ariel Red Wine. Anderson receives a beautiful tie from Clint and Sara, and a great hunting knife from Stephen and Angela. Stephen says, "We know that you like to wear a hunting knife in a sheath while you walk in the woods. About a week ago, Angela and I were in one of the shops in town, and we saw this great looking hunting knife with the carved bone handle."

Anderson replies, "It's perfect. It is not quite as big as a bowie knife, but this is also a long hunting knife! Thank you."

Clint and Sara thank him for their gifts. Anderson gives Clint a $300 visa gift card and gives both a mint 1890 and 1900 Morgan silver dollars. Angela and Stephen thank him for their gifts. He gives them a mint 1880, 1899 and 1921 Morgan silver dollars and to each of them a $100 visa gift card.

A Light on the Path

As everyone visits and looks at their gifts, Clint says I have an announcement. As you know, Sara and I have been dating for just over a year, and we have known each other since our second year at UT. We are starting to make plans, and tonight we want to announce our engagement.

Everyone cheers and hugs Clint and Sara. Sara says, "While we announce our engagement this Christmas Eve of 2018, I want to thank every one of you for a beautiful Christmas Eve: one that I will never forget."

Anderson says, "God bless you and bring me great grandchildren! Sooner is better than later, because I'll be eighty in April!"

They all laugh, and Clint says, "Grandpa, we'll start working on that as soon as we get married!"

As they visit, they play some Christmas CDs and check out the holiday, college basketball games. Clint says, "Our guys are doing their best to get back in the NCAA playoffs. They don't want Butler and Purdue to get all the glory."

Anderson says, "I'm all for you and Indiana State, but we want Purdue to get some glory! So what time does Christmas morning get here?"

Clint says, "As early as you want it to, Grandpa."

Anderson replies, "Well, elves and Santa's helpers, I'm ready for a long winter's nap. I'm going to clock out and see some of you bright and early."

Stephen says, "I will start breakfast by 6:30. Everyone can eat when they want to."

Anderson says, "I will see you in the kitchen then."

Everyone says, "Good night."

It was a great Christmas day. Even Ralph got extra Christmas treats. In the evening Anderson makes plans to go back to the airport. Stephen says they'll leave the house by 5:45. Anderson says his early goodbyes to Angela and Sara. Angela says she'll have breakfast for them about 5:00, then she'll go back to bed. Anderson says goodbye to Ralph, and Ralph whines as he says goodbye to Anderson.

The day after Christmas, Stephen, Clint and Anderson finish breakfast by 5:30. Angela and Anderson say goodbye, and the guys load Anderson's bags. It's cold and well below freezing, but a clear day. Stephen says, "The car will be warm in no time." They head out in the pre-dawn hour, right before 5:45. They all have on their warm winter coats and gloves.

As they get on I70 west, Anderson says, "It was a great Christmas and visit."

Stephen replies, "It was great having you. I'm glad Clint and Sara could be with us."

Clint says, "Sara and I had a great time."

A Light on the Path

Anderson says, "You have a lovely fiancée. Clint, when I see you next, I want to give you that picture of your grandma, when she was about twenty-three. It's in a small photo album in my bedroom in the night table."

As Stephen drives down I70 and gets close to Indianapolis, Clint says, "It will be an honor to have grandma's picture. I'll start a family photo album and put it in there."

Anderson replies, "That will be nice. No pun intended, Clint, but I have kind of a dark or serious question for you. With all the trouble in the nation, how are things in Terre Haute?"

Clint says, "Not really bad, but not good either. There have been a lot of break-ins, theft, vandalism and arson in the downtown area and near campus. City officials are estimating that property damage and loss is several million dollars. The police are doing what they can, but the National Guard is spread kind of thin. They have a much bigger presence in larger cities like Indianapolis, Evansville and South Bend."

Anderson says, "Every city, small town and rural area have problems. I hope you're in a protected neighborhood. We have a right to defend ourselves and to protect our families and friends."

Clint replies, "Like you and dad, I believe in gun ownership for protection and for hunting. We have some men in my neighborhood, who have just started a neighborhood watch. I don't think it is around the clock yet, but I think they're taking shifts through the night to watch things. I'm part of their call list, so I will be prepared to help neighbors; "Love your neighbor as yourself".

Stephen says, "I totally agree. Keep on being safe and always take a hard look around you. We need to remind Sara and your mom to do that."

Anderson replies, "That's right. I'm praying for you and your mom and dad every day."

They're already near the airport exit. They pull in front and help Anderson get his bags inside. Anderson says, "Well, you two be safe. I have to go through security, so I'll take it from here."

They shake hands and Clint says, "Have a good flight. I love you, grandpa."

"I love you, Clint."

Stephen says, "Call us when you get home. We're thankful that you could be with us for Christmas."

Anderson says, "It was a great time. Both of you take care and keep lookin' up!"

Things go smoothly at the airport. The flight back is pretty much the reverse of his flight to Indy. They land in Charlotte, and the flight from Charlotte lands in Knoxville right before 1:30. Anderson picks up his large

A Light on the Path

bag and rolls it to the parking garage. He thinks, "It will be nice to be back home."

Chapter 10 – Home Sweet Home

He misses rush hour in Knoxville, and he pulls into his drive way by 3:00. As he sees Pockets walking toward him, Anderson thinks, "This is a nice homecoming." Anderson looks around and gets out of his truck. As he bends over to pet Pockets, he says, "Good to see you, Pockets. Did you guard the old home place while I was gone?" He takes his bags inside and looks around the house. He goes back out to give Pockets food and water. He walks out back to look around. He thinks, "It doesn't look like anything was disturbed outside or inside."

As he warms up a cup of water for some green tea, his cell phone rings. He sees that Conard is calling. "Hello neighbor; I just got back a few minutes ago."

Conard replies, "I saw your truck. Boots was over here every day for food and water."

"Thanks for taking care of her. What do I owe you?"

Conard says, "Just your permission to use your land for my next hunting outing."

"You've got it. Things look like they have been quiet. How have you been doing?"

Conard replies, "I decided to wait until you got back to tell you what happened early Christmas Eve. I think a car woke me up. It was just before 1:00. I got up and used the bathroom, but when I came out of the bathroom, I heard it again. I looked out the window, and it was sitting in the front of your drive. Evidently, it had passed your house and circled back. My handgun was nearby so I grabbed it and continued to watch the car. Within a minute it pulled down by your front sidewalk. When I saw two car doors open, I cracked my front door. They were walking up the sidewalk, when I fired in the air."

Anderson asked, "What happened next?"

Conard replies, "They ran and jumped in the car, and took off like a bat out of hell. When they started backing up, I thought they were going to run off your drive way. When they got it on the road, they screeched their tires like they were running from the law."

"Wow! I owe you one."

Conard says, "I was glad to do it. Since it was dark, they may have thought the shot came from your house."

Anderson says, "That's alright. I'm glad you scared the hide off them. It sounds like we need a neighborhood watch. My grandson's neighborhood in Terre Haute just started one.

"We should start one. How was your trip?"

A Light on the Path

Anderson replies, "It was a wonderful Christmas, especially Christmas Eve, when my grandson and his girlfriend announced their engagement. I thoroughly enjoyed time with my family. All the money in the world couldn't replace that experience."

Conard says, "I'm glad you enjoyed the trip. Let me know when you have time to talk about a neighborhood watch."

Anderson replies, "I will. Thanks again for being a good watchman!"

Conard replies, "I was glad to help. Talk with you soon."

Anderson thinks, "A good neighbor is a great blessing. Let's see; I need to call Angela and tell her I'm home." He uses his quick dial list and leaves her a voice mail. He knows he wants to call Lydia and Kenny today, but his body tells him that he has been up since 4:00 this morning. He lays down on his bed to rest.

When he wakes up, he realizes he has about one hour of daylight left, but he thinks, "My walk will have to wait until tomorrow; I don't have the energy today. I'll eat supper early, but I've been around the cheese, ham and cracker block a little too much lately. Even though I'm not a fan of frozen dinners, I'll pick one and have popcorn and a diet soda with it." After he eats supper, he calls Lydia.

Lydia answers and says "How are you? How was your trip?"

"I'm doing fine, and I had an excellent time. Clint and his girlfriend, Sara, were with us, and they announced their engagement on Christmas Eve!"

Lydia replies, "How nice is that! What better thing could have happened on Christmas Eve?"

"I think Clint agrees. He said something about it going into the record for Christmas Eve of 2018. How was your Christmas?"

Lydia says, "We were making merry, and we had a real good time."

Anderson asks, "Where are you with house plans?"

Lydia replies, "Even though we're between Christmas and New Year's, I'm still calling realtors. I'm telling them that the right realtor for me is not only a good sales record, but I won't sign a sales contract for over thirty days, and I won't take less than $130,000."

"Good for you! It sounds like good salesmanship runs in the family!"

Lydia asks, "How were the national crisis conditions, while you were gone."

Anderson replies, "I didn't have a problem. Clint said that his neighbors just started a neighborhood watch group. Conard and I talked today about getting one started."

Lydia says, "That would be a good idea. It hasn't been bad in Crossville, but the downtown businesses are having more break-ins, and residential areas are having more break-ins. There was a break-in a block from me. The family was gone, but the thieves cleaned out the more valuable items."

Anderson replies, "Be really watchful, and keep ole' Betsy by you. Do you keep plenty of lights on at night?"

"Yes, I have two lights on in front and two lights on in back. I also keep an inside light on near the front door and another one on near the back door. I keep my bedroom door locked, and I have a bright flashlight by me that would temporarily blind anyone."

Anderson says, "That's good to know. Do you remember if we set dates and times for our New Year's here?"

Lydia replies, "I don't remember the times, but I should only stay two nights, since I'm still deciding on the right realtor. New Year's Eve is on Monday, so I could be there by 11:30 that morning. I should probably leave by 10:00 Wednesday morning."

Anderson says, "That will work. Do you want anything special for our New Year's celebration?"

Lydia replies, "I don't think so. I know you'll have snacks and nutritious food."

Anderson says, "I will. I better call Kenny before it gets too late. Call me anytime. I'll look forward to seeing you in five days."

"Me too, big brother. Take care."

Anderson decides to make a cup of coffee right before he calls Kenny. After sitting down with the coffee for a few minutes, he calls Kenny from his dial list.

Kenny says, "Hello brother Anderson; a belated Merry Christmas to you."

"And Merry Christmas, Kenny. Are you and Scooter staying warm and well fed?"

Kenny replies, "No complaints here. How was your trip?"

Anderson says, "I had a wonderful time with my family. My grandson and his girlfriend announced their engagement on Christmas."

Kenny says, "Congratulations. Have they set the date?"

"No, they didn't talk about a wedding date, but I had the feeling that they'll marry before the end of 2019."

Kenny says, "That reminds me that the New Year is just around the corner. Is Lydia coming over?"

"Yes, she'll be here for New Year's Eve and New Year's Day. Were you busy during the Christmas season?"

"Oh, yes. I met some of the retired officers at Salty Sea for dinner, and I saw a lot of my friends in Maggie Valley and Cherokee. The Cherokee Lodge that I'm in had a big get together. It was a real nice party, but I'm not a night owl, so I left before 9:00. It was too busy of a time. I'm ready to just enjoy the farm for a few days."

Anderson says, "I'm glad you enjoyed Christmas. The one thing I haven't done since I left is to get updated on the national news. I was hoping you had been following it for most days."

Kenny replies, "I have. I usually watch it for at least 30 minutes after my chores and then for another 30 minutes or more around 5 or 6:00 in the evening."

Anderson asks, "What are the latest things that stand out in your mind?"

Kenny replies, "There are several things. Insurance companies are now reporting over $300 billion in commercial and residential claims. Deaths from the national crisis have exceeded one thousand. Leading economists are predicting even higher prices by the first of the year. More big cities have martial law, and there is a greater National Guard presence. There has been more reporting on national and banker leaders talking about a global currency."

Anderson says, "Wow, brother; more doom and gloom. My grandson's neighbors have started a neighborhood watch, and Conard and I are looking into one for here."

Kenny asks, "Why did you and Conard decide to look into a neighborhood watch?"

Anderson says, "That's a good investigative question. Of course, I was gone on Christmas Eve, and Conard heard a car about 1 in the morning. He got up and saw that the car had come back around and parked in my drive. He grabbed his handgun and kept watching. When two car doors open, he cracked his door and shot in the air. He said they took off like a bat out of hell."

Kenny says, "I bet they did. You can never be too careful. I know you have a good lighting system."

"I do. Since that happened, I've decided to put more light motion sensors around the house."

Kenny says, "Even though Scooter is not a big dog, he is a good barker, if he hears something. After listening to all this news, I just started strapping my handgun to my belt, when I go out to do my chores."

"You really should. I probably need to wear one outside the house. I already carry one in the woods."

Kenny replies, "With all of the problems, you should wear one outside the house, and keep it in your car, when you go shopping."

A Light on the Path

"Well, brother, it has been a long day. I got up at 4 this morning. Let me know when you can come over, and we'll walk in the woods, and you can teach me nature lessons."

Kenny laughs, "You could probably give me nature lessons about your woods. I'll let you know ahead of time. Hopefully, we can do it by February."

Anderson says, "I may not get back to Maggie Valley as much until Lydia moves in. I'm staying in touch with her more until her house is sold. February would be a good time to get together."

Kenny says, "You've got it, my friend. Until we meet again, and Happy New Year."

"Happy New Year."

When Anderson hangs up, he thinks, "It seems like it has been dark for a good while; I've lost track of time." He gets ready for bed and looks forward to Lydia coming on New Year's Eve.

Monday, December 31st, sneaks up on Anderson. The house is presentable enough, and he has the food and drinks for New Year's, but it seems like New Year's Eve came in like a whirlwind. Lydia arrives by 11:30. They have lunch and take a short, cold walk in the woods. There's no snow, but the predicted high is 33 degrees with a slight wind.

Before their New Year's Eve celebration, Lydia wants to hear Anderson play some of her favorite songs on the piano, including Misty, Just the Way You Are, and Amazing Grace. She loves Anderson's rendition of Amazing Grace. Anderson has his own pet project to share with Lydia. He says, "You know how I like to watch the birds, especially in the bird garden. Take these small binoculars to the kitchen window and watch the birds feeding and perching on the bird bath."

Lydia watches a few minutes and says, "Wow, you can see them really close up and see their markings a lot better."

Anderson replies, "I love watching them through the binoculars. It gives just 5X the normal 20X20 vision, but you can observe so much more. I've looked at markings and colors on the mourning dove that I never saw without the binoculars. I have also identified many birds for the first time like the cute hermit thrush and the beautiful spotted towhee with them."

He also shows Lydia his life list. "Here you mark the date and location of when you first saw the type of bird. You can see that I've identified many from the kitchen window. In parks you can identify a lot of them at the feeding centers. The rangers at parks like Brown County State Park in Indiana help with identification. Some local parks are also real conducive to birds like the Campbell Station Park in Knoxville".

Anderson shows Lydia his computer picture file on birds. She says, "I didn't know that full size screen pictures were available for most species. The full-size pictures of birds like the colorful male and female scarlet tanagers are superb."

Anderson says, "You can usually find those quality of pictures with just the search engine. You save them to your file and voila, you have a slide show! So anywho, sis, I enjoy that hobby and believe it or not I'm doing a new scrapbook with state-of-the-art fixtures!"

Lydia replies, "I know what you mean. The scrapbooks and tools now are greatly new and improved over the ones we had as kids."

Anderson says, "It will be dark soon. Do you want to eat the good food for the evening meal, or do you just want to snack on it throughout the evening?"

Lydia says, "Since it's a special day, let's snack on the good food as well as the snack food throughout the evening. Having popcorn and soda off and on this evening will be like reliving part of our childhood."

Anderson laughs and says, "I remember those celebrations. One New Year's Eve when I was about eleven or twelve, I ate popcorn throughout a late-night Godzilla movie and had three cokes! Do you remember when mom and dad only let us have one coke a week, which was Saturday evening with popcorn?"

Lydia says spiritedly, "I sure do! Through the years I've told people the same thing about the one coke and popcorn once a week. I think mom and dad had that rule until you were about twelve and I was about ten. I guess that was until 1950."

Anderson replies, "I think that's right. Nothing like reminiscing over those good time memories."

They especially enjoy sharing childhood memories throughout the evening. They even find a King Kong movie that they enjoy with diet soda and popcorn! Their midnight comes at the late time of 10:00. They toast the New Year early with diet soda. They get ready for bed, and on their own, they each think of what 2019 will bring.

The first day of 2019 goes by with a flash, and as Anderson fixes breakfast on January 2nd, he thinks, "I can't believe it's almost time for Lydia to go home." He fixes turkey bacon with eggs, but this time he also tries out a new, little smokie sausage.

After breakfast Lydia says, "Your new little smokies were also good."

"I agree. I'll have to get them again."

After breakfast they take their time over coffee talking about the sale of Lydia's house; packing; moving and precautions they both will take during the current national crisis.

Anderson says, "When you're ready, I'll load your bags and follow you to the gas station in Mount Holly."

A Light on the Path

Lydia replies, "That's nice of you. My bags are almost packed. I just have to brush my teeth."

Anderson says, "Take your time. I'll be outside checking on Pockets."

A few minutes later, Lydia comes to the front door and says, "I'm all ready."

Anderson loads her bags, and they go to his regular gas station. Anderson gets out of his truck and fills up Lydia's gas tank. He comes to her window and says, "You're all set. It looks like the police are still watching over the station here. It's Mount Holly's main gas station and convenience store."

Lydia says, "It looks like they do a lot of business here. Thanks for taking care of the gas and for a great time."

"Love you, sis. Be careful and keep lookin' up!"

"Love you, Anderson. You take care too."

Anderson waves as she drives off in her navy Impala. He shivers as he gets back in the truck. He thinks, "It feels even colder than yesterday."

As Anderson drives the foothill curves back home, he thinks, "Time is going by too fast. One day, Ruth, I'll be joining you. Only God knows the day, but I sure will be glad to see you again."

Anderson looks forward to seeing his friends at church again this coming Sunday. Conard and he start organizing a loose knit neighborhood watch group. They call a few neighbors they know and go over home security. They put together a seven-family call list in case anyone needs help, or if anyone observes something different. They feel good that more neighbors will be watching, and some plan to look outside off and on through the night.

Kenny comes over for part of a day in February, so they can have lunch at Anderson's house and walk in the woods. Kenny tells Anderson that the neighborhoods that have had serious problems, put up road barriers and only allow the neighbors to pass. If the neighbor is with someone they don't know, they let them pass. Those neighborhoods have someone at the barriers around the clock and at night, they have at least two men there at a time. Kenny says that some of those neighborhoods have a curfew that starts at 9 in the evening. If anyone comes in after 9, they must be on a list of people who work late or go to evening classes.

Kenny and Anderson stay in touch with each other about twice a month. They also share local and national news. By the end of February, a lot of food and gas prices have almost tripled. Vandalism, break-ins, arson and deaths due to the national crisis continue to rise. World leaders also continue to push their global currency agenda.

Anderson has enjoyed being back in church every Sunday. He loves being with his friends for the worship service. He regularly takes time to talk

A Light on the Path

with Pastor Don, John and Wilma, and his other friends. He especially likes it when they have guest speakers who talk about missions at home and abroad. Anderson is always ready to support missions.

Anderson talks with Lydia a couple of times a week, and he talks with Angela two or three times a month. Lydia is excited to share the good news that her house is sold. She got $132,000 and pays just half of the closing cost. She has thirty days to move and to get ready for the closing. Anderson goes to Crossville to help her pack. After Anderson gets his yard and garden ready for spring, it's time for Lydia to move. She moves on March 13th and must go back for the closing on the 14th.

She calls Anderson on March 12th to work out the details. Anderson says, "Since you have to go back for the closing, I'll drive you. We'll have lunch in Crossville at noon, and you'll be at the closing by 1:00. Wherever you need to go, I'll drive you there and then to your new home!"

Lydia replies, "You're so precious. The movers will start loading by 9:00. They think it will take about three hours. I've cleared out a lot, and what I'm not bringing with me, they'll put in storage on the way. I can only guess that we will be there between 3:30 and 5:00, since we're an hour behind you."

Anderson asks, "Do you need room for anything in the living area?"

Lydia says, "No, since you've organized my bedroom for my dresser and the few smaller things, we can put the rest in the basement."

Anderson replies, "As you know, the basement is large, and there is plenty of room there."

"I only have a few big pieces and about fifteen boxes to put in the basement."

Anderson says, "The statements that you signed about my house and the agreement between you and Angela are in the mail to her for her signatures. She'll sign both copies, then mail them to me. I will go to a notary, so I can sign them and have them notarized. When you get here, I'll give you your copy and mail the other notarized copy to Angela. Later, I'll add that statement to my will."

Lydia replies, "Thank you so much; that's a great blessing."

The move goes well, and Lydia doesn't find any major scratches on her furniture. Anderson takes her to closing the next day. After closing, she is happy as a lark. She goes to her bank and makes a large deposit. She tells Anderson, "Soon I will put some in a short-term annuity, so I can take monthly installments later to add to my retirement income."

As they leave her bank, Anderson replies, "Good idea. You won't have financial problems now. How do you feel?"

Lydia replies, "It feels like a super heavy weight has been lifted off me. I'm so happy about how everything turned out."

A Light on the Path

Anderson says, "I'm happy too, sis. I think we'll be great company for each other."

Lydia says, "Me too, big brother."

On the way home, they have a good time talking. Before they know it, they're turning down their Tennessee road to home.

Chapter 11 – The Arrival

Just a few minutes before they get home, they see the sun set behind the Smoky Mountains, leaving a hazy blue mist hovering over the great mountains. As they pull up the drive way, Lydia says, "It's so good to be home."

Anderson replies, "It sure is." Before he gets out of the truck, Anderson says, "Here's your front door key. Go on inside, and I'll check on Pockets." Lydia makes herself at home, and in a little while, she and Anderson call it an early night.

Anderson continues to walk every day unless there is a lot of wind or rain. Anderson and Lydia have a great time talking, and sometimes Lydia goes with Anderson when he walks less than fifty minutes.

Anderson says, "Can you believe that spring has just arrived?"

Lydia replies, "It is hard to believe. The high was 39 degrees today and the low tonight will be about 30 degrees."

Anderson says, "Even though the forecast says a high of 47 degrees tomorrow, it is also forecasted to be cloudy with a 40% chance of precipitation. Today, we have clear skies with wind at 3 mph, and tomorrow we're to have wind gusts up to 20 mph. Why don't we have lunch a little before noon, then I'll do my long walk of an hour or so after lunch."

Lydia replies, "If you want soup and grilled cheese sandwiches, I can have it ready by 11:30."

Anderson says, "That sounds really good. When it doesn't rain tomorrow, maybe we can walk together for about thirty minutes."

Lydia replies, "It's a date!"

Lydia gets things organized in the kitchen, and they sit down for lunch at 11:30. After lunch Anderson gives her a hug and thanks her for a good lunch. He says, "I need to walk the long, wide ravine again. There will probably be some branches to clear out. It will take just over an hour."

Lydia says, "Okay, be careful. Anderson gets his hiking gear together; grabs his walking stick off the wall in the great room and sets out with Pockets.

There're only a few white clouds in the sky. For the most part, it's a clear day. Anderson thinks, "It's really a nice day with my warm coat on." Anderson guesses that it's already in the high thirties. He passes the fire pit and goes up the trailhead. He looks back for Pockets and sees that she is lying back about twenty yards. He hears a mourning dove cooing. The bushes in the woods are just beginning to sprout, small bright green leaves. Some of the trees have buds, but it's too early for their new leaves.

A Light on the Path

Anderson's View of the Smokies

He's walking the perimeter today, and he can barely see the lake to the left as he heads east. Anderson thinks, "When the foliage is mature it will be hard to see the lake at all from here." From the front of his house, he can see a duck flying from the lake a few times a year. He thinks, "The Canadian geese are so common now. I wonder when they started migrating from Canada?" One of Anderson's favorite sites is watching a long row of wild turkey marching through the woods or in a clearing. His trail now circles to the southeast He thinks, "The long ravine will be coming up in a few minutes. I'll see a trail going downhill right after I pass a very large and very old white oak tree."

Just ahead he sees the trail going down to the wide ravine. Once he starts walking the ravine, it will gradually curve to the south. After he gets through the clearing, pass the horse pasture, the ravine will eventually curve to the southwest. Before he gets to the clearing, he stops two times to clear some medium sized branches. When he gets in the clearing, he takes a bottle of water out of his leather pack. Today he sees a tan palomino, a brown and white pinto and a black horse in the horse pasture.

When he puts his water bottle up, Pockets catches up with him. When he reaches down to pet her, he says, "Where have you been? You're a good girl." After being petted a couple times, Pockets looks around and moves on. Anderson guesses that she is looking for the next large branch or fallen tree to walk on."

A Light on the Path

As Anderson resumes his hike, he is soon on the long ravine trail again. He starts singing the chorus to, "One more river to cross; One more Mountain to climb." He can't remember the rest of the words, but he hums the chorus several more times. He thinks, "In less than five minutes this part of the ravine will begin to curve to the south west." As he looks ahead, where the trail will start to curve, he thinks, "Son of a gun, now I have to make a pit stop at one of my rest areas." About a hundred feet before the ravine trail starts to curve, he stops and leans his walking stick against a hickory. As he is waiting to finish the pit stop, something in his right peripheral vision gets his attention.

Anderson's Trail

When he looks to his right, he notices the big boulders at the bottom of the hill, but where the trail begins to curve, he notices something strange. When he takes off again, it looks like there is a low-lying fog next to the ground. He thinks, "How could that be? It's about 12:30 in the afternoon, and there's only a few clouds in the sky." He looks up again at the sky, but he doesn't see many more clouds. Now he's focused on the trail ahead; trying to figure out what is going on. He passes the familiar boulders on his right, but they seem to continue for longer than normal.

A Light on the Path

He is now walking through the low-lying fog, and his full attention is on the path way. He is still walking through fog, but up ahead he can see a light on the path. When he reaches the light, it seems like he is still headed the right direction, but he never noticed the curve in the trail. He looks back for Pockets but doesn't see her. He assumes she will catch up. He continues down the trail, but now it seems like he is still heading south, instead of southwest. Ahead he now sees a clearing. He thinks, "That's odd, there is no clearing there. After the trail curves southwest, it eventually goes uphill into the woods."

A Light on an Unknown Path

When the path comes into a clearing, there is no trail; just a beautifully landscaped hill to climb. He thinks, "Well, Great Jehosophat! I guess I'll just climb the hill and see what's on top." When he gets to the top, he can't believe what he's seeing. He knows he doesn't have dementia or hallucination problems, but he sees a huge, beautiful meadow that has many small white canopies, like it's a real big art and craft show. There is also a huge building on the other side of all the white canopies. The building reminds him of a grand central station.

Suddenly, he feels warm, and he takes his pack and coat off. He thinks, "Wow, it feels like its seventy degrees. He looks up at the clear blue sky and doesn't see one cloud. The closest white canopy is now about 70 yards from him. He walks over the meadow toward the canopy, and as he gets closer, it looks like a man is at a booth under the canopy.

A Light on the Path

Anderson goes up to the man, who looks about thirty and nicely groomed. Anderson is more than mildly bewildered and says, "Hi, I'm Anderson. What is this? I have never seen any of this before?"

The booth attendant answers, "Good to meet you, Anderson. I'm Joel. Let me look here a minute." He shuffles through a stack of papers and says, "Oh, yes, Anderson McCollister, is that correct?"

Anderson is even more bewildered and stutters, "Well… yes. How did you know my name is McCollister?"

Joel replies, "The paper says that Joseph is expecting you today, March 23rd, by 1:00."

Anderson is shocked and says, "But I don't know Joseph, and I didn't have an appointment with him."

The young man is very cordial. He smiles and says, "Joseph knows you. I'll page him."

When he starts to page him, Anderson excitedly says, "Who's Joseph?"

Joel replies, "He's your host."

Anderson thinks, "I feel like Pockets, when she chases her tail."

Joel pushes a button on what looks like a large pager. He looks up at Anderson and says, "Joseph should be here in just a couple minutes."

As Anderson waits, he looks toward the stately building in the distance. He observes the building for well over a minute, then he notices a person of large stature coming his way. As the distinguished looking man gets closer, he can see that he has a full head of wavy grey and white hair and fine features.

Just before he gets to Anderson, he yells in a booming voice, "Well, hello, Anderson. How are you doing, my friend?"

Anderson is almost speechless. He finally gets out, "Well, to be honest with you I'm confused."

Joseph smiles, "I understand. This is unexpected for you. How was your trip?"

Anderson replies, "My trip? I was hiking around the perimeter of my woods and I ended up here!"

Joseph laughs joyfully, "Oh, Anderson, you always have had a good sense of humor! Most people don't know when they're going on the trip that you just went on."

Anderson just stares at him for a few seconds and asks, "How do you know me?"

Joseph replies, "Well, Anderson, I've known you all of your life. I knew you when you were born at the Hartford City hospital, and when you were an Airedale at Hartford City High."

Anderson asks, "How do you know all of that?"

A Light on the Path

Joseph replies, "This is the first time we've met in person. Do you remember when you were working in Charlotte in 1977, and one night during a heavy rainstorm you hydroplaned on I 85? Your car turned around, and then you were going down I 85 backwards. By that time, you were still going over 50 mph."

Anderson says, "Yes."

Joseph says, "You were right about feeling like the car was ready to roll off the interstate. You always said that you felt like God or your guardian angel grabbed the car and sent it down the next exit ramp; nose first."

Anderson replies with astonishment, "That was you?"

Joseph laughs and says, "Yes, that was me. I'm Joseph, your guardian angel."

Anderson was now beside himself. He didn't know what to say or what to do. He finally asks, "Am I in heaven?"

Joseph laughs loudly and says, "You're certainly on your way! God has a mission for you before you enter heaven. See that big building up there?"

Anderson says, "Yes, you can't miss it."

Joseph continues, "Well. After your mission work, you will be processed in that big building before you enter heaven."

Anderson honestly asks, "Did I die? I don't remember dying."

Joseph lets out another hearty laugh, "That was quite an early spring walk that you went on; wasn't it? As Joseph continues to laugh, he says, "No, you didn't die, but you did pass on. Think about when you walked up the hill into the meadow. Do you remember an extra spring in your step, and where is your walking stick?"

Anderson looks down and says, "I must have left it against the hickory tree. Now that I think about it, I did have an extra spring in my step. What about my family? They will be worried. Lydia is expecting me back by now."

Joseph compassionately puts his hand on Anderson's shoulder and says, "Don't worry. You have already taken care of your sister, and she will be fine. As she calls Angela and Kenny, they will soon be fine also. Anderson, there is a time and season for all things. There is always a time for grieving, but there is also a time when joy returns."

He looks at Joel and says, "Joel, I have some things to do for a while. Give Anderson a chair under your tent and let him relax. Get him whatever he needs."

Joseph looks at Anderson and says, "Give me time to catch up, and I'll be back with you. I know you have more questions, and we'll have plenty of time."

Anderson placidly says, "Okay. Good to meet you in person and thank you."

A Light on the Path

Joseph replies, "God bless you, Anderson. It's good to have you here."

As Joseph walks off toward the imposing building, Anderson makes himself comfortable under the tent.

Chapter 12 – The Search

Lydia looks out the back door and down to the fire pit area, and she still doesn't see Anderson. It's already past 1:30, and he is still not back. She picks up her cell phone in the great room and calls Anderson. She hears a phone ring in the back of the house. She goes to his bedroom and sees his phone on his dresser. She thinks, "Oh, no, he forgot his cell phone. I need to call the police or Kenny right now." She gets Kenny's number on Anderson's quick dial.

Kenny answers, "Hello, my brother."

Lydia nervously says, "Kenny, this is Lydia. Anderson was due to be back from an hour walk over thirty minutes ago. He also forgot his cell phone."

Kenny replies, "Try not to worry. Anderson carries emergency supplies. I don't know how quickly your sheriff's department can organize a search party, but I'm calling friends right now. Two of them have tracking experience like I do. I know Anderson's trails. I'll pick my friends up, then I'll be there in an hour. Try to be calm, and I'll call you as soon as I pick them up. We'll have enough time to search. I'll be there around 3:15."

"Thank you. I'll call the sheriff now from his quick dial," replied Lydia. She thinks, "Thank God Kenny answered."

Lydia calls for a sheriff's deputy, and Kenny gets ahold of his two tracking friends in Maggie Valley. He picks them up at a station on Soco Rd. in Maggie Valley, and Kenny calls Lydia as he drives toward I40. Kenny says, "I have my two tracking friends with me, and we'll be there by 3:15." Kenny looks at his two friends, and says, "Sometimes I wish I still had my blue lights."

When Kenny knocks on the door, Lydia answers right away. She says, "Come in. A deputy is taking my statement, and he has already put out a call for volunteers to search."

Kenny walks over and greets the deputy, "Officer, I'm Kenny Goodpaster, retired North Carolina state trooper from the Maggie Valley area. These are my two friends, Aaron and John, who are excellent trackers."

The deputy says, "Good to meet you. I'm sure that you want to start searching for your friend right away."

Kenny replies, "Yes, sir. We're leaving right away." Kenny looks at Lydia and asks, "Did Anderson tell you where he was going to hike?"

Lydia says, "Yes, he went pass the fire pit and up the trail head and turned left to go east to the perimeter. He was going to follow the perimeter path until it led down into that long, wide ravine."

A Light on the Path

Kenny says, "I know where it is. Was he going to follow the ravine through the big clearing until it went uphill to the perimeter trail that heads west, then back north?"

Lydia says, "That was his exact plan."

Kenny says, "Let's go guys. We'll get our gear out of the Jeep and take off immediately."

They're pass the trailhead by 3:30 and head east to the perimeter trail. They're in the clearing by 4:00. Kenny says, "We have four hours of daylight left. Aaron, you go as fast as you can down the ravine trail and up the hill to the west side. You'll be our front man. John, you stay behind me and be our lookout man. You look for any clues while I follow the perimeter trail. We already have confirmed by his tracks that he went this way."

Aaron forges ahead quickly to get through the ravine and up the hill that curves to the west. As Kenny scouts the trail, John is behind him looking for any tracks or clues he can find. Kenny and John both agree that he continued to follow the ravine once he passed through the clearing. In a few minutes Kenny comes to the boulder area, and he finds Anderson's walking stick against the hickory tree. Kenny says to John, "Anderson never leaves his walking stick. Something unusual must have distracted him." John and Kenny continue to look hard in that area to the end of the ravine.

John says, "His trail disappears. Only a professional tracker or a phenomenon could make tracks disappear."

Kenny says, "It's very puzzling." Kenny's phone rings, "Lydia, we do have one report for you when we get back, but we haven't found Anderson yet."

Lydia says, "The deputy's volunteers just got here. They have powerful search lights. Where do you want them to go?"

Kenny says, "Tell them to prepare their gear until we get back in twenty-five minutes. Tell them to also prepare for a night search that might last until midnight."

As John and Kenny go up the hill, Aaron meets them after the trail curves to the west. Aaron says, "I did double time on the trail and got to the trailhead. I didn't see anything, and then I circled back to meet you."

They hurry back to the house. It's almost 5:00 when they get back. Kenny shows Lydia Anderson's walking stick, and she starts crying.

Kenny says, "Lydia, there is no sign of foul play or any wildlife activity that would affect Anderson. So far, it's a complete mystery."

Kenny turns to the sheriff's deputy and the four volunteers from the local area. Guys we just hiked over an hour and covered the perimeter. We found his tracks, then they disappear on the back side of the woods, where a wide ravine picks ups after a large clearing. Make sure your gear is complete, because we'll be out there for five or six hours. By 9:00, it will be about 32 degrees. If you're dressed for frigid temperatures, then join us. Make sure you have water and protein bars with you. Does everyone have proper gear? We'll meet back here in ten minutes."

The deputy and volunteers all answer in the affirmative. Kenny says, "My guys and I need ten minutes to ready ourselves and to get our search lights."

As Aaron and John go to the truck for a short break and their search lights, Kenny turns to Lydia and says, "I'm taking Anderson's walking stick with me. He will need it when and if we find him."

Lydia says, "I thought I would call Angela in the morning. I don't want to worry her tonight."

Kenny replies, "Good idea. I'm going to recommend to the deputy that he puts out an APB on Anderson right now."

Kenny talks with the deputy and goes to the Jeep to talk with Aaron and John. They meet back in the great room. Kenny says, "Take my cell phone number that I wrote on these papers. I have the deputy's number, so you can stay in touch with both of us. Anderson is the name of the elderly man that we're looking for. He has no mental problems like dementia. He has muscle issues that limit his energy. If you find him, you will need to help him get back. Do all of you know first aid?"

They all answer in the affirmative.

When they head out the door, Lydia says, "Kenny, Pockets showed up here about an hour ago. I'm praying for Anderson, and I'm praying that God will direct you."

Kenny says, "Yes, we're in the hands of God."

They head up the trailhead at 5:30. From the great room, Lydia watches them disappear into the woods.

When the eight men get to the top of the trailhead, Kenny shows them where they need to split up. Since the perimeter has been covered, he organizes a sweep of the woods.

All Lydia can do is pray; look out back every few minutes and drink coffee. She restrains herself from calling Angela until morning. She doesn't want to needlessly worry her.

Kenny calls her after the eight men have searched three hours. "Lydia, we've swept the entire woods on Anderson's property. The closest we've come is when John, Aaron and I searched before 5. It's starting to get dark in the woods, so you may see our search lights off and on until we finish. Most of the time we plan to search neighboring properties on the east, south and west. The east side is mostly woods, the south side is mostly fields and the west side is mostly housing and lots. My friends and I are going to take

A Light on the Path

the south side, since we're trackers, and that is the closest area to the last tracks we've found."

Lydia nervously asks, "What do you think?"

Kenny says, "You never know what to expect. I've done searches off and on for thirty years. I always like it when we find the person in the first few hours. I need to go. I'm guessing that we will finish around 10 or 10:30."

Lydia finds Pastor Don's number in Anderson's quick dial. She calls him in confidence and asks him to pray.

She turns on Anderson's favorite music channel, Spa, on Sirius satellite radio. She continues to look out back every few minutes. She has all the outside lights on. She hopes that Anderson would just walk in and show up on his own.

She looks out back a few minutes after 10, and she sees a lot of search lights, as they come down the trailhead. Everyone congregates out front, and Kenny and the deputy come to the door. The deputy tells Lydia that an APB is out on Anderson. She thanks the deputy.

She says to Kenny, "I want to get my coat and go out and thank everyone."

Kenny holds the door for her. She walks out to the drive way, and thanks the four local men who volunteered. She thanks Aaron and John before she talks to Kenny.

Kenny says, "We've done what we could for now. I'm glad they put out an early APB on Anderson. Are you okay?"

Lydia says, "I'm shook up, but I'm functioning alright. Kenny, thank you so much for your quick response. You're a great friend. Anderson thinks a lot of you."

Kenny replies, "And I think a lot of him. I know that he would do anything for you."

Lydia says, "He has." She gives Kenny a hug and says goodnight.

Right before Kenny gets in his Jeep, he says, "Let me know what I can do. I will stay in touch with the deputy."

As they pull out, Pockets walks up to her, and Lydia reaches down and pets her. She says, "You miss Anderson too, don't you?"

Chapter Thirteen – Spring Takes a New Turn

When Joseph returns, he finds Anderson napping in the chair. Anderson hears Joseph talking to Joel. Anderson looks at Joseph and says, "I've been dozing off, when Joel and I haven't been talking. I thought it would be dark by now."

Joseph laughs loudly and with his booming voice he says, "It never gets dark here! Even though everyone gets restless from time to time, we never get tired!"

Anderson says, "I have a question for you. Do you know if a dream I had about a friend, Russell, was from God?" Anderson can tell that Joseph begins to ponder about his question.

Joseph rubs his chin and says, "I think I have it. I am also Russell's guardian angel. I believe you're talking about Russell, who is about twenty-five to thirty years older than you. Also, you knew him well about twenty-five years ago in central Indiana."

Anderson passionately says, "Yes, that's him!"

"Yes, that dream was from God. It was given to you by the Holy Spirit, as you prayed for Russell."

Anderson says, "Right before Russell passed on, I dreamed that he was much younger looking and at a big and beautiful country estate."

Joseph replies, "Yes, that's where he is! After you do the mission work, I will take you to him."

Anderson asks, "What about Ruth? Where is she?"

With a big smile, Joseph says, "She is in the same area. When we go to see Russell, we'll see Ruth first!"

Anderson jumps out of his chair and leaps for joy, "Praise God! I can't wait to see her!"

Joseph laughs loudly, "See that, my friend. You jumped out of that chair like a thirty-year-old! You probably won't recognize yourself." Joseph laughs and laughs until tears of joy come to his eyes. "Brother, it has been a good while, since I laughed that hard."

Anderson asks, "You mentioned the mission work. How long will it take?"

Joseph replies, "Good question. Here we're not on the same time table as mankind. In your former life, you measured time with a calendar and a clock. To try to answer your question by mankind's time table, it will probably be three to four weeks before we can see Ruth and Russell. By the way, you'll get to see your parents and many others you've known."

"When will I see my parents?" asked Anderson enthusiastically.

A Light on the Path

Joseph laughs, "Hold on my friend. Remember, patience is a virtue. You will see them not long after we visit with Ruth and Russell."

Anderson asks, "Can you tell me about the mission work, and what I will be doing?"

Joseph replies, "Yes. It involves Lydia, Angela and Kenny. First, your former country and military had a process called debriefing. We have a similar process here. We go over what you know about certain subjects, and we share with you what needs to be done. Learning our confidentiality is part of the process. It's also about updates and procedures, so we're both on the same page."

"When do we get started?"

Joseph replies, "Very soon. We will start the process while the people in your former community are still looking for you. You'll continue to prepare yourself while you family and friends gather. They need time to remember you. They also need time to grieve."

Anderson replies, "It will take a while to comprehend all of that. Right now, I still feel like I'm part of their lives. It may take some time to adjust."

"That's right, it will," replied Joseph. "Most everything is new here, so don't pressure yourself. Give yourself plenty of time to adjust. You'll lose track of what you once thought of days and nights. When I come back to start the debriefing, it might be eight to twelve hours based on your old-time system. I guarantee you, that it will only seem to you like a couple of hours, when I return."

"Are we doing the debriefing here or under another tent?"

Joseph laughs, "No, I have a headquarters near what you call the grand central station. I call my work area a campground. When you get there, it will look like a campground to you. There are cabins, tents and a lodge with meeting rooms, rest and relax rooms and rec rooms. I call everyone preparing for mission work like you, "campers". Soon you will meet other campers preparing for mission work."

Anderson says, "This is a dumb question, but this is not like a purgatory, is it?

Joseph's laugh is like a roar. He says, "You're great, Anderson! That is not a dumb question. There is no purgatory, and all the campers are on their final stretch to heaven. I will tell you in the debriefing why more of the saints are doing special mission work before they enter heaven."

Anderson says, "I'm still perplexed. I never believed in purgatory, but this has been too much too process."

Joseph replies, "Exactly! That is why we have the Eternal Processing Center, your grand central station. You remember Enoch, Elijah and Moses

Each of them were processed differently, but none of them had to wait long at all to enter heaven."

Anderson asks, "How long have you been here?"

Joseph replies, "Great question! I was here before Lucifer was thrown out of heaven."

"You knew Lucifer?" Anderson asked.

Joseph replies, "I saw him before he was thrown out of heaven. I didn't know him personally. There are millions of angels. For example, I know Joel here, because we work together. All of us take turns at these hosting bases. Joel, when did you become an angel?"

"I was here for a while before the Father created earth," replied Joel.

Anderson asks, "What about the archangels, Michael and Gabriel?"

Joseph's voice bellows, "You just said a mouthful! Michael and Gabriel are the elite angels in heaven. I've been here a long time, and I don't know them personally. There were a few occasions, when I got to greet them. In your former world, they would be greater than presidents or four-star generals."

Anderson asks, "What about Jesus?"

Joseph replies, "Ahhhh, the Son takes time for everyone. Eventually you will talk with him. The Son, like the Father and the Holy Spirit, has special powers. He is able to communicate with everyone! My friend, Anderson, it has been wonderful talking with you once again. You will be comfortable here until I come to introduce you to the other campers. You will enjoy them and the campground. It will be a great time of sharing, learning and relaxation!"

Anderson replies, "I'm looking forward to it. You've been very gracious and helpful. Evidently, you've helped me all my life!"

Joseph laughs and says. "I have at that, and it has been a great pleasure. Have you been comfortable, since you've been here?"

Anderson replies, "Oh, yes. It's a peace beyond description."

"Okay, Anderson. You and Joel enjoy your fellowship, and soon we'll be going to my base camp."

Chapter 14 – Family and Friends

Lydia called Angela the morning after Anderson's disappearance. Angela took it very hard and was extremely shook up. She didn't know if she could bear it, especially so soon after losing her mother. Angela said that she would have to take some time off work. She needed to be with Lydia and wanted to stay in touch with the police.

An APB was put out the same day in all the local media. Knoxville ran it on their television stations, and it was in the local newspapers and on local radio. Angela was with Lydia for a week, when they decided to have a memorial service at Anderson's church. They decided to delay any funeral service, since there was no body.

With Pastor Don, they planned a memorial service for the next weekend. They planned it for early Sunday afternoon, so family and a few friends could be together with Lydia, later in the day. In the memorial service, they sang two of Anderson's favorite songs, Amazing Grace and The Old Rugged Cross. Pastor Don had a short message, and both Angela and Lydia shared memories of Anderson. Before the closing, Clint also shared how much his grandpa meant to him. Kenny was also there, and he was asked to give the benediction. Conard, John and Wilma and many other friends attended.

Just three and a half months after Ruth passed away, the same people returned to Anderson's house around 4:00 Sunday afternoon. John and Wilma brought the food that the people from Anderson's church provided. When Kenny arrived and had a chance to talk with Lydia again, he said, "It's so sad, but now we have three more hours of daylight compared to December."

Lydia hugged Kenny and said, "Kenny, you've been so faithful and such a good friend."

Kenny replied, "Anderson means a lot to me, and I know he does to you. I will go ahead and greet everyone before they get started with supper." Kenny spoke with Angela and Stephen; and Clint and Sara. He spoke with Lydia's son, Paul, and with Rachel, Faith and Eli. He greeted Pastor Don again, and John and Wilma. Right before the pastor said grace, he spoke briefly with Conard.

Pastor Don prayed, "Lord, we are here together in memory of Anderson. Bless him and be with him. Even though we don't know what happened, you do. Comfort his family and friends. May we look to your Son, Jesus Christ, for all answers. We thank you for the supper tonight, for the church and for all your blessings. We just completed the great celebration of Easter. We thank you for a risen Savior. In Jesus' name we pray. Amen."

A Light on the Path

The church provided baked chicken; a mixed pasta dish, broccoli and cheese; and new potatoes. For dessert, they brought peanut butter and chocolate bars. As they get their food from the dining room table, Lydia brings their water, coffee and diet soda. Everyone is talking mostly about Anderson and remembering many good times with him. No one has a clue as to what happened to him; it's a complete mystery to them.

While Clint and Lydia are talking, Clint says, "When Grandpa was with me at Christmas, he said, "The next time you come over, I want you to have a picture of your grandma, when she was about twenty-three". He said the picture is in a small photo album in his night table in the bedroom."

Lydia says, "When you're almost done with supper, let's go in and try to find it." They finish their supper and go into Anderson's bedroom. Lydia says, "There's the night table. See if you can find it." Clint opens the drawer of the night table, and in the back of the drawer, he finds a small photo album. He turns a lamp on near the bed and sits down to look at the pictures. In a few seconds, he says, "Oh wow, Lydia, there it is. Grandma did look like Sara at her age." Clint shows Lydia the picture.

Lydia says, "That's incredible, Clint. Take the photo album with you and show it to your mom. I know that Anderson would want you to have the picture, and I'm sure your mom will give you many other pictures."

They go back in the great room, and Clint goes directly to Sara, who is talking with Faith and Eli. Clint shows Sara the picture and she says, "Oh, my word, your grandmother did look like me."

Clint says, "I have never known my grandpa to exaggerate. He was always down to earth and honest."

Sara says, "We should frame the picture and always keep it in sight."

Clint shows the picture to Faith and Eli and to other family members. They all agree that she looked like Sara then. Clint says, "I think it was taken in the early 1960s."

Lydia says to Angela, "It looks like everyone is getting filled up. I'll make sure we have plenty of coffee."

Angela says, "I would like to stay one more night before I go back. Is it alright, if Stephen stays with me tonight?"

Lydia says, "You know it is. Basically, it's your house!"

Angela replies, "God bless, dad. He was good to both of us. Clint is going with Sara to her parent's house in Knoxville this evening. He must go back to Terre Haute in the morning. Stephen and I need to leave by 9:00, because we both have to go back to work Tuesday."

Lydia says, "I'm thankful for more daylight this evening. It's getting close to 6:00, and we have plenty of daylight left. Kenny will probably want to leave by 7:00, so he will be back home by dusk."

A Light on the Path

Pastor Don is the first to say goodnight to everyone. Lydia says, "Pastor, we appreciate you being here with us."

Pastor Don replies, "We will greatly miss Anderson. By some miracle, I hope he shows up."

Lydia replies, "I do too."

Pastor Don says, "You know, Lydia. Anderson loves you very much. You're a shining gem in his life."

"Thank you, Pastor. Don't make me start crying."

As he goes out the front door, he says, "Have a peaceful evening, Lydia."

"I'll try, pastor. Have a good night."

John and Wilma say good night to Lydia.

Kenny comes up to Lydia and says, "It's getting close to 7. I need to get back to Scooter and my chickens. Call anytime."

"Thank you, Kenny. Have a safe drive." As Lydia watches Kenny pull out in his Jeep, she thinks, "What a pleasant, early April evening. I wish Anderson were here to enjoy it. I miss talking with him."

After she goes back inside, Clint and Sara say goodnight, and hug Lydia. Clint says, "I wish grandpa was here with you."

She says, "I do too. Your mom and dad will be here tonight. Do you want to take some food with you?"

Clint says, "No thanks. We've had plenty. You enjoy it the next couple days."

"Goodnight you two. You look good together. Clint, let me know about your team for next season."

Clint replies, "I will. Take care."

Conard gets ready to go home and says, "Lydia, let me know if you need anything. Our neighborhood watch group is active, and I want you to feel safe."

"Thank you, Conard. I'll talk with you soon. Have a good night."

Paul comes up to Lydia. "Mom, Rachel and I were talking about us coming to visit you soon. Would you want us to stay the night, when we plan a time?"

Lydia replies, "I would love for you to visit. I would insist that stay the night."

"Okay, mom. We love you, and we will also be missing Anderson."

Paul, Rachel, Eli and Faith say goodnight to Lydia. Lydia says to Faith, "Don't get in a big hurry with that doctor."

Faith laughs and says, "I won't, grandma. We're taking it slow."

Angela, Stephen and Lydia straighten things up and put the food away. They sit down with coffee and stay up until 10:00 talking about Anderson and family. Angela says, "Aunt Lydia, I guess we need to get ready for bed. We'll probably get up around 6:30."

Lydia says, "Both of you can use the shower, when you get up. I'll start breakfast before 7:30. I want you to have a good breakfast before you get on the road."

They get ready for bed and have a quiet Sunday night.

Chapter 15 – Base Camp

Joseph came back for Anderson, so they could start a debriefing process. Anderson loves the campground and talking with the other campers there. He found out that most of them will also have missionary assignments before they enter heaven. He shares a cabin with three other campers: Larry, Dwight and Richard.

All four of them have enjoyed the lodge, the rec rooms and the meetings with Joseph. Some of the campers are already leading informal discussion groups.

Anderson's favorite experience was right before the church had their Easter celebration. During the time of Maundy Thursday, Christ appeared to all the saints and broke bread with them and had wine. Jesus said that we are also doing this in honor of all the saints that gave their lives for the church and for Him. It was the most breathtaking experience that Anderson has had, when he watched Jesus break the bread, and serve it and the wine.

Anderson is guessing that Joseph will conduct only a few more classes before he can begin his missionary work. When Joseph came back to take him to the campground, he told Anderson that over a period of a few weeks or less, he will be visiting with Lydia, Kenny and Angela at different times.

Anderson asked Joseph, "I thought that since God had given mankind His Word and the prophets, He would not send someone back to warn relatives or others?"

Joseph warmly replied, "I know what you're referring to: The Son's story about the rich man and Lazarus. Also, remember what happened later, after the Son was crucified. In the gospel, Matthew wrote, "... the tombs of many holy people who had died were raised to life. They came out of the tombs after Jesus' resurrection, and went into the holy city and appeared to many people."

Anderson smiled and said. "Good point."

Joseph continued, "Also, Lazarus was speaking to Abraham, and not to God. Keep in mind that God has absolute power and authority. The Father, Son and the Holy Spirit have power over all things."

Joseph gave Anderson a rough timeline on when he would see Lydia, Kenny and Angela. Joseph said, "By mankind's calendar, you should be finished with this missionary assignment in less than three weeks. The Spirt of God has directed me to tell you that you have been a good and effective witness to your sister, friend and daughter. God wants you to complete your witness by sharing with them what you have learned here."

Anderson said, "I understand that the Apostle Paul was not allowed to share what he saw in the third heaven."

A Light on the Path

Joseph laughed and said, "You haven't seen the third heaven yet."

Anderson replied, "Another good point!"

As Anderson recalls the conversation that he had with Joseph about his assignment, he gets ready for a missionary class in the rustic lodge, that he and his roommates find so captivating. They all agree that whenever they must leave the lodge, they feel reluctant to go.

They enter the huge vestibule, heavily decorated with God's wonders of nature: beautiful stones, large leafy plants and stunning pictures of wildlife. They go into a meeting room with other campers. Joseph conducts the meeting.

He says, "Greetings, missionary campers. I trust all of you are comfortable by now and have gotten use to your new surroundings. I want to congratulate all of you, because this will be your last group class before you go on your missionary assignments. I know that some of you were guessing there would be a few more classes. I will be meeting with you individually before you leave. All of you will come back, once you complete each assignment. Some of you will be leaving and coming back several times, while others will be leaving just once or twice. Are there any questions?"

Larry asks, "How will we leave and how will we get back."

Joseph gives a hearty laugh and says, "I'm sure all of you are wondering about that. I will cover that before we dismiss. I will go ahead and tell you that the door to leaving and coming back is a portal."

Dwight says, "So it's something like we've seen in science fiction movies?"

Joseph laughs and says, "Something like that. Before I share those details with you, I want to talk briefly about free will. You are created in the image of God. If you did not have free will, as well as those who remain on the earth, you would not be the image of God. Because of free will, we have need of things like witnessing, teaching, visitation and all types of missionary work. When you go on your missionary ventures, I ask that you do your best to appeal to the free will of those you will be visiting with. By now you have a good understanding of God's Word. You also have good witnessing skills. When you go on your assignments, it is necessary that you pray and let the Holy Spirit lead you. Are there any questions?"

One of the other campers asks, "Do we have any special powers of persuasion, since we are now here?"

Joseph replies, "Good question. You know about prayer, and you know about the work of the Holy Spirit. I cannot stress enough how important they are. Your enhanced power of persuasion is the fact that you have passed on; you have been here, and you are returning to share the good news."

A Light on the Path

Richard says, "I don't have a question, but honestly, I'm eager to hear about the portal."

Joseph belts out a loud laugh, "I bet you are! Nothing like honesty; it is the best policy. When I meet with each of you individually, we will rehearse the steps of using the portal. When it's time for you to enter the portal, I will have surveyed the proper location at a favorable time of day or evening on earth, as well as an appropriate weather condition. In our one on one meetings, you can help me determine what those factors will be; any questions?"

Anderson says, "I assume in the individual meetings, we will learn how we return through the portal. I'm curious about when we will be leaving."

Joseph replies, "Yes, we will go over necessary portal information. All of you will be leaving soon. Some will be leaving sooner than others. Very soon, I will be in touch with all of you to let you know when we will meet. At the end of our individual meetings, you will be leaving for your assignments. You don't need to take anything, because you won't be gone long, especially on your first outing. If there are no other questions, I will close the meeting."

Joseph hesitates and looks at every one before he continues, "It looks like everyone is ready at this point. I encourage all of you to use the lodge rec and relaxation areas before you go back to your cabins. You don't have long before you leave, but you have plenty of time to enjoy the lodge and each other while you're here. After you've had time to fellowship and rest, I will be in touch with all of you. Let us now thank our Holy Father for all things. Father, we are here before you, and we thank you for being with us. Give us the wisdom and faith we need to accomplish each missionary journey. Amen and Amen!"

Everyone greets Joseph as they leave the classroom. They all love his friendliness and jovial laughter. Everyone stays a good while at the lodge; enjoying the rec rooms and each other. When everyone is ready to leave, Anderson walks out of the lodge with Larry, Dwight and Richard. As they head back to the cabin, a courier approaches them and hands Anderson a letter. All of them stop as Anderson reads the letter. Anderson looks at his friends and says it's from Joseph. He says I will be one of the first ones to leave. He also says to rest at the cabin, and he will meet me there.

Richard, Dwight, Larry and Anderson talk about their assignments and the portal. Once they get to the cabin, Anderson gets quiet and lays down on his bunk bed. He starts to think about Lydia and what he is going to say. His mood becomes introspective and prayerful. After he has drifted off for a while, he can hear Joseph's booming voice, as Joseph walks in the cabin.

A Light on the Path

Joseph says, "I've come for my one on one with Anderson." They go outside, and Joseph says, "We'll walk to my office inside the lodge." Anderson is still in a quiet frame of mind, and Joseph understands.

They walk through the lodge's large vestibule and down the main hall to the rear section of the lodge, which is Joseph's office complex and quarters. They walk into a large room that is designed like an informal conference room. They sit down, and Joseph says, "I have a feeling Anderson that you might want to visit with Lydia after things get quiet there for the evening; maybe a couple hours after she gets ready for bed. Of course, it's a hunch. As your guardian angel, I was familiar with your routine."

Anderson replies, "Yes, you're right; that is one of the things I've been thinking about."

Joseph says, "In that case, we have plenty of time to prepare. Right now, she is home, and it's early evening there. We can cover all your questions and plans before you depart. Have you thought about a timeline in which you want to visit Kenny and Angela?"

Anderson says, "Yes, I would prefer that I do the visits in less than two weeks in their time. I would like to visit with Kenny less than a week after I visit Lydia. I would then like to visit Angela a few days after I visit with Kenny. Kenny doesn't need any announcement of my coming, but could Lydia call Angela in about a week, and tell her that I will be calling on her in a few days. I don't want to scare Angela, since she lost me soon after she lost her mother."

Joseph replies, "I follow you. I'm sure that you can trust Lydia not to say anything to Kenny for a week, and to call Angela a week after your visit with her."

"Yes, I know we both want the visits to be as effective as possible. I understand that this is about their life in Christ and their eternal life."

Joseph replies, "The Lord knows that there are many people who are borderline. Many of those people have had someone in their lives like you. Now they must be nudged. The Father is allowing this, because he wants those people, who have some understanding, to know the rapture of the church is coming real soon. Of course, only the Father knows the day and the hour, but the time of the rapture is so close, he wants as many people as possible to follow Christ. It is not our place to tell people that the rapture will occur in seven months or fourteen months and so on. You can tell them that the world will approve a global currency that will give way to the mark of the beast. Once the mark of the beast is instituted, everyone will need the implant in the forehead or arm to buy or sell. Those who don't make the rapture before the mark of the beast is instituted will have a second chance. Let them

A Light on the Path

know that it will be much better for them in their current life, if they are ready in Christ before the mark is used worldwide."

Anderson says, "Yes, I understand. I believed that from my studies in my former life."

Joseph says, "Since we have plenty of time. I will go ahead and tell you, Anderson, that you are being considered for a missionary captain. The responsibility will carry over after you are processed for heaven. As a missionary captain, you would be doing what you have seen me do, except for the actual portal work. Each time you have an assignment, you will come back through the Eternal Processing Center and work with various needs at our hosting stations and at the base camp. During those assignments, you will be working out of my base camp."

Anderson replies, "I would enjoy that."

Joseph laughs and says, "The Father and Son expect that you will! They know that all your former life, you encouraged and helped people. As an adult, you continued to help people spiritually as well as financially. Saints who will continue to work as missionaries are called missionaries, missionary captains and missionary overseers. One of the overseers is one of your favorite people in your former life."

Anderson asks, "Who is that?"

Joseph replies, "Billy Graham. He joined us last year, on February 21, 2018. Like Enoch, Elijah and Moses, he was processed real soon into heaven. The Father and Son had a special place for him as a missionary overseer."

Anderson replies, "Praise the Lord! That's wonderful! Will I have a chance to see him and to talk with him?"

Joseph says, "Not only will you do that, but he will be your direct overseer. He will be working with many missionary captains, and he and you will be an excellent team."

Anderson says, "This is already like I hoped heaven would be."

Joseph says, "Besides seeing your friends and family, there was something else you hoped for. The Lord knows you have a great love of nature. You remember that God's Word says the lion will lie with the lamb, and the Word describes trees along a river. Well, there will be all kinds of God's creation for you to enjoy."

Anderson exclaims, "It is everything that I hoped heaven would be! I need to find out what else I'm allowed to share with Lydia, Kenny and Angela."

Joseph says, "Yes, we've covered part of it. In God's grace, lead them to Christ. The same way you did in your former life. Encourage them to follow Christ in all ways, including going to church; spreading the gospel and helping others. I believe you can accomplish leading all three to Christ. In turn, they will help others. Remind them to be prepared; the Lord is coming real soon. From your missionary journeys, the three of them will form a much closer relationship; based on God's Word. Do not get into details about your life here currently. You can say something general like how well you like it."

Anderson says, "I know you still have to tell me how to return through the portal. Do we have time for any other questions?"

Joseph checks and says, "Yes, we have time."

"Can you tell me about your duties, and how you get back and forth as a guardian angel."

Joseph belts out a laugh, "Good questions, Anderson. First of all, guardian angels don't need a portal. Somehow God created us with a built-in portal. The Father, Son and Holy Spirit have many phenomenal powers. They can communicate directly with all the guardian angels, and as you know, there are millions of angels. Secondly, all the guardian angels have subs who are also guardian angels. It never gets boring. We get a break when we come to conduct a base camp. We always have another angel filling in for us. Right now, it may seem complicated to you, but with God's power and how He created us, it is not as complicated as it may seem."

Anderson says, "Thank you for the insight."

Joseph asks, "Are you ready to find out how you return through the portal?"

Anderson replies, "Yes, I am."

Joseph explains, "There is very little to entering the portal and returning through it. I will be watching, so I know when you'll be ready to return. Tell me where you plan to be during the time you're gone."

Anderson replies, "I will go to my great room at my home. After I visit with her, how do I make my exit?"

Joseph says, "When you get ready to return, tell Lydia that it's time for you to go, and walk through the door of the great room to the back deck. As soon as you take a few steps out of her sight, I will bring you back."

Anderson says, "That sounds easy. Where do I go through the portal from here?"

Joseph says, "Very simply, we are in another dimension. You will be going from this dimension back to where you lived. Our portal is a dimensional door. Physically it would be difficult to explain, but I set the dimensional door for your place on earth at the current time, and you just walk through the portal."

Anderson asks, "Is the portal door here?"

Joseph laughs and says, "It sure is. In your former world it's something like turning on your TV. You might say that I turn on the remote, and instead of a screen lighting up, the door appears!"

A Light on the Path

Anderson smiles and says, "General Electric would like to have that technology!"

Joseph says, "So Anderson, very soon I will set the portal and reveal it, and you will simply walk through the door that appears, which kind of looks like a hologram. After you walk through the door, you will be in your great room! Because of the fibromyalgia, I'm checking now to see if Lydia has had time to relax her muscles and has turned out the lights and gone to bed."

After Joseph checks, he says, "Anderson, are you ready?"

Anderson replies, "I am."

Joseph says, "Okay, stand up and face the wall I'm pointing to. Keep your eyes on that wall, and you will soon see the portal door appear. Joseph makes his settings, and says, "When the door appears just step through it."

Right away the portal appears, and Anderson walks through it.

Chapter 16 – The First Visit

The next thing Anderson experiences is standing in the middle of his great room. He looks around and sees his recliner and notices that Lydia is keeping on the same lights out back and in front. He walks to his recliner and sees that the TV remote is where he always kept it; on the end table by the recliner. He sits down on the recliner and picks up the remote. Since Lydia is used to him listening to the Spa channel on Sirius satellite radio, he turns the TV on; sets it on a low volume and changes it to the Spa channel.

Anderson leans back in the recliner, but he doesn't hear Lydia moving, so he turns up the volume. Lydia has taken Anderson's advice and keeps her bedroom door locked for security reasons. A few seconds after Anderson turns up the volume, he hears Lydia say loudly, "Who's there?"

Anderson says, "Lydia, it's me, Anderson."

Lydia leans over in her bed and grabs her handgun on the night table. She says, "I have a gun. Do you want to be shot?"

Anderson laughs and says, "No, Lydia, I don't want to be shot. You don't need the gun."

Lydia just sits quietly in her bed for a few seconds; pointing her gun toward the bedroom door. She slowly swings her legs around and stands up. She is still quiet for a few more seconds and says, "Are you still there?"

Anderson says, "Yes, Lydia, I haven't gone anywhere."

She walks closer to the door and stops and puts her ear next to the door. She says, "Anderson, if that's you, what happened to you?" Anderson says, "I will tell you when you come out, but I did pass on."

Lydia replies, "What do you mean, you passed on?"

Anderson just laughs, "Okay, Lydia, ask me something that only you and I would know."

Lydia thinks a second and says, "Recently we were talking about the poor family that had a refrigerator in their yard."

Anderson says, "That's right. It was when I was about 8 or 9 and you were about 6 or 7. One of the young children got in it and the door closed, and the child suffocated."

Lydia unlocks her door but hangs on to the gun. She comes out of her bedroom, but before she goes in the great room, she says, "Turn on a light so I can see you."

Anderson replies, "Okay, I turned the lamp on by the recliner."

She walks into the great room and says, "Oh, my gosh, it is you, Anderson, but you look thirty-five years old!"

A Light on the Path

She rushes over to Anderson, and he stands up and says, "I think we can hug. She proceeds to hug him and says, "Oh, how I have missed you. What happened to you?"

Anderson says, "Have a seat and I'll tell you." Lydia sits down, and Anderson says, "First of all, I did pass on, but I didn't die: that is why only my walking stick was found and not my body."

Lydia is shook up and says, "Are you saying that you've been in heaven?"

Anderson laughs and says, "Pretty much. I can't say a lot about it, but I can tell you how I got there, and why I'm here."

Lydia says, "I'm confused, but that doesn't matter, because I'm just glad to see you. How did you get so young looking?"

Anderson laughs, "At first I wasn't aware of it. When I leaped out of a chair, someone pointed out the extra energy that I now have with that and other things like walking. Evidently, the youth returned about that time. I can tell you what happened, when I passed on and why I didn't show up here. You know where the large clearing is by the horse pasture, on the back side of the woods."

Lydia replies, "Yes, I do."

"I had been clearing a few branches out of the long ravine, and I continued down the ravine after the clearing. Soon I had to make a pit stop at one of my rest areas. I leaned my walking stick against a hickory tree by the rest area. Do you remember where those large boulders are on the right, not far pass the clearing?

Lydia says, "Yes."

Anderson continues, "Where I stopped, they were immediately ahead of me on the right. I also noticed a strange low-lying fog on the path ahead of me. It was even stranger, since only a few clouds were in the sky. As I continued down the path, I'm walking through the low fog, and it felt like the path never curved to the southwest. It felt like I continued walking south, when I saw a light on the path ahead. The path opened to a large, beautiful meadow, and the rest I can't share at this time."

Lydia asks, "So the path went to heaven, like a fourth dimensional path?"

Anderson says, "Something like that, but what I can share now is the message that the Lord has for you."

Lydia is surprised and asks, "God has a message for me?"

"Yes, Lydia. I can tell you that I met my guardian angel, and you have one too. The Lord wants you to serve him by going to church; spreading the gospel and helping others."

A Light on the Path

Lydia replies, "Oh, yes! Anderson. Whatever the Lord wants. You already shared things that convicted me of shortcomings in my life. I just need to take the next step."

"Lydia, that's the main reason I'm here tonight. The Lord is coming soon, and the rapture of the church will occur very soon. The Lord also wants you to know that soon a global currency will be approved and soon after that, the mark of the beast will be institutionalized. Everyone to buy and sell, will have to take the mark, which is an implant in the forehead or arm. Those who don't take the mark will have a second chance for heaven, but the Father wants you to follow Christ, so you can avoid those events by being taken in the rapture."

Lydia replies, "Oh, yes! I want to be taken in the rapture. Since you have been gone, Anderson, the country and the world have gotten even worse. The third world countries are suffering greatly, and leading countries like ours are experiencing the same kind of violence. Most of them also have great inflation. The inflation, vandalism, robberies, arson and murder rates are even worse than when you were here."

Anderson says, "I've confirmed that war, famine, pestilence and natural disasters will increase as well."

Lydia replies, "Yes, there have been more reports of those as well. The third world countries are experiencing more famine and pestilence. There have been more severe earthquakes in China, Turkey, the United States and other countries. Russia conflicts with a lot of countries, and there has been an increase in conflicts worldwide."

Anderson says, "God's Word prophesies that all of these things will happen before the rapture. After the rapture, it will be worse. As we're taught in the gospels, Jesus wants us to confess our sins, so he can forgive our sinful ways. He wants us to follow him by obeying His commands. We are in a new covenant of God's grace, love, forgiveness and salvation."

Lydia asks, "What do I need to do?"

Anderson says, "Say a prayer, and I will be praying with you. Tell God that you have fallen short of His glory, but you want to ask for forgiveness. Tell him that your desire is to live in Christ and to obey his commands. Lydia, God will forgive you, and the Holy Spirit will be your guide and counselor. He promises you eternal life, if you follow Christ."

Lydia begins to pray, "Our Father in heaven, thank you for guiding Anderson to me. Thank you for your love and his love. I know that I am a sinner like all men and women. I desire to be forgiven, because I want to live in Christ. Guide me daily in Christ. May I become a lighthouse like Anderson, and lead people to you. Thank you for your Son and eternal life. In Jesus's name we pray. Amen."

A Light on the Path

Anderson is quiet for a few seconds, and Lydia is sobbing. Anderson says, "Oh, thank you, Father. Thank you for giving us your Son. Thank you for bringing Lydia into the fellowship of believers. I know that she will be faithful daily. I know that she will go to church and encourage others. May the Holy Spirit lead her to help others. The Lord is coming real soon. May Lydia, Angela and Kenny form a close bond to encourage each other and to lead others to Christ. In Jesus's name. Amen."

Lydia says, "Anderson, I really can't express how much you mean to me."

Anderson replies, "Sis, you've always meant a lot to me. Just imagine how much more Christ means to us. In Christ, we are not only stronger together, but we're also stronger individuals."

Lydia says, "Yes, we are. I will try to do all that I can. You have been a good example, and I'll start with going to your church every Sunday."

Anderson replies, "That's a good start. It helped me to study the Bible; read a devotional and pray first thing in the morning. It would help me to start the day off right. Daily devotions will help you mature as a Christian. Remember to give regularly. It's more blessed to give than to receive. Pastor Don can give you good advice. Also, you might start studying the gospel of John. It was my favorite. All four of the gospels will help you."

Lydia says, "I will do those things. Anderson, how long can you stay?"

Andersons replies, "I have to go back tonight. I can't stay a long time. You will eventually get sleepy, because it's already midnight."

"Right now, I feel like I could stay up all night."

Anderson says, "You might feel that way for a little while, but soon you will get tired. I know how fibromyalgia works."

Lydia says, "You're probably right. What can you tell me about your recent experiences?"

"It has been wonderful. I have very little impatience there. Peace is much greater. I haven't seen Ruth yet, but I'll get to see her after I visit with Kenny and Lydia, which I'll explain before I leave."

Lydia replies, "Oh yes, I want to hear about those visits. I'm glad you get to see Ruth soon. Have you seen anyone else?"

Anderson says, "I found out that our parents are there!"

"Oh, Anderson, that's great news! Have you seen them?"

Anderson replies, "I will get to see them after I see Ruth. I also know that Russell, on old friend, is there."

Lydia asks, "I think I remember you talking about him. He served in World War II, and right before he passed away, you had a dream about him."

Anderson says, "Yes, that's Russell. Lydia, believers have little time left to share the gospel. It's necessary to be prepared. In the gospel of Matthew,

Jesus said, "So you also must be ready, because the Son of man will come at an hour when you do not expect him." Also, in Matthew, Jesus said that his coming would be like the days of Noah before the flood. People were eating and drinking and marrying. Even though there are many tragedies in the world, people continue in their routines. Most people and many believers are not watching for the coming of the Lord."

Lydia replies, "I believe you, Anderson. With what you have shared before and now, I do believe the Lord is coming soon, and I will be watching."

"That is good to know. I'm very thankful, that you are now following Christ and looking for him," replied Anderson.

Lydia says, "Even before church Sunday, I will be sharing with Paul, Rachel, Eli and Faith about the Lord coming soon."

Anderson replies, "Yes, that is superb! I will assume that they will be following Christ like you. Before you tell them about my visit with you, wait until you here from Angela about my visit with her."

"Whatever you say, Anderson," replied Lydia.

Anderson says, "I need to share some things with you about my upcoming visits with Kenny and Angela. Also, when you share with Paul, Rachel, Eli and Faith, hopefully they will follow Christ. It's important that you don't talk with Kenny about my visit with you, until I visit with him. Wait one week, then you and Kenny can share about my visits with both of you. Also, in one week, call Angela, and tell her that I will be visiting with her within a few days. Tell her in one week, because I don't want to scare her after her loss of her mom and me. I think Stephen usually goes to bed by 10, and Angela usually goes to bed between 10 and 11. Tell Angela in one week that I will wait until she is ready to go to bed. Right before she turns out the last light upstairs, she will see a light downstairs, then she will know it's me."

"Wow, I think I can remember all of that!" replied Lydia.

Anderson laughs and says, "You'll be fine."

Anderson continues, "Lydia, it's important for Angela, Kenny and you to stay in touch with each other after my visits. It's good to encourage each other; pray for each other and motivate each other, since you don't have much time left to do God's will. Hopefully, you can see each other at times. Stay in touch by email, text and phone calls as much as you can."

Lydia replies, "I definitely will. The closer relationship we'll have, because of Christ and your visits will compel us to stay in touch often. You're such a great blessing. I'll be glad when I get there too. I will enjoy being with you again. I don't know when you have to leave tonight, but again I want to thank you so very much for all that you've done for me."

A Light on the Path

Anderson smiles and says, "Lydia, you know that it's my pleasure. I wouldn't have it any other way. There is one more thing that I want to share with you before I go. Because the Lord is coming soon, it seems like more and more believers who have passed on will be coming to visit those that they have witnessed to. I'm not implying that all believers will be coming back on what they call missionary journeys, but some will. I was with several that I know for sure are coming back to share with at least one or two people. One is from Indiana. Another one is from New York, and one is also from east Tennessee. I met two from North Carolina and one from Georgia, who will also be on missionary journeys. Eventually there will be more stories reported about believers who have come back. Do your best to get the gospel message out. Do it with love, kindness and gentleness."

Lydia replies, "Anderson, I totally agree with what you say. You can count on me, and report that I will do my best."

"I know you will, Lydia, you were always a trooper. I love you, and I will continue to pray for you. I would like to pray now, since I have to leave real soon."

Lydia replies, "Yes, Anderson, let's pray."

Anderson prays, "Father, thank you for your Son's love and sacrifice. Be with Lydia as she shares your Word. Watch over her and guide her. Your kingdom come and will be done. Thank you for Lydia's commitment and life in Christ. In Jesus' name we pray. Amen." Anderson stands up and goes over to hug Lydia. He says, "God bless you, Lydia; I love you."

"I love you, Anderson."

Anderson says, "In a second I'm going out the great room door to the back deck. For just a few seconds I will be out of your sight, and I will be going back. In a few seconds, you will know that I've gone back. Take care and keep lookin' up!"

Lydia says, "Thank you, Anderson. I will be looking forward to seeing you again."

Joseph is already watching as he sees Anderson walk through the door to the back deck. When Anderson takes a few steps to the left, Joseph opens the portal door for Anderson to walk through."

Chapter 17 – Return to Base Camp

As soon as Anderson steps into the portal, he is back into Joseph's conference room. It seems like it takes him about two seconds to get oriented. Joseph says, "Welcome back, Anderson. You're one step closer to being a missionary captain. How was your visit?"

Anderson replies, "It went well. The transportation beats frequent flyer miles and security checks."

Joseph laughs and laughs. "Oh, Anderson. I always loved your humor."

Anderson says, "Lydia made the commitment to follow Christ and to be prepared for the Lord's coming. It was a joy seeing her again."

Joseph says, "After you left, I had other activities to attend to. When I tuned back in, you were getting close to the end of your visit. Did Lydia make any comments about church and her family?"

"Yes, she will be going to church and witnessing to her family and others, but she won't say anything to them about my visit until after I visit with Angela."

Joseph replies, "Good. It sounds like you accomplished your mission goals."

"Lydia also said she would be giving and helping others."

Joseph exclaims, "Excellent! It sounds like a successful journey to me. Basically, Anderson, you'll be able to rest and enjoy the base camp until you're ready to visit Kenny. We'll have two one on ones before you visit Kenny. The first meeting will be for any questions or concerns you have about the journey you completed and about the one coming up. The second meeting will be like the one on one we had right before you left to visit with Lydia."

Anderson says, "I enjoyed being with Lydia, but I also like the base camp. Before our first meeting, will I be free to use the rec rooms at the lodge and to visit with other campers like Richard, Dwight and Larry?"

"Yes, Richard, Dwight and Larry will be available most of the time. Like you, their first missionary journeys only take about two hours of earth time. When do you plan to visit Kenny?"

Anderson replies, "In one week, from my visit with Lydia. During the morning hours, he does his chores on the farm. About 8 to 9 in the morning, I will find him at his chicken coup."

Joseph says, "Very good. There are some things about the lodge and rec rooms that I want to show you. I know that you and your friends have used the chairs and some videos and games, but there are some things I haven't shown you, that you'll like."

Anderson replies, "What are we waiting for?"

A Light on the Path

Joseph laughs and says, "That's the spirit! We'll go into the hall now, and I'll show you one of the rec rooms that you probably haven't seen." They pass the big rec rooms that Anderson has seen and used. Next is a closed door that is off the vestibule. Joseph opens the unlocked door. They enter, and Joseph closes the door behind them. Joseph says, "The entire room is dedicated to God's eternal kingdom of wildlife, domestic animals, water life, plants and trees. It also contains a lot about the immense phenomena of the galaxies. In the other rec rooms, you and your friends saw God's state of the art videos and games about other things in His kingdom. Here you will find the most fantastic videos of nature and wildlife that you have ever seen. You could spend hours of earth time in here, and not scratch the surface of this room's library. Anderson says, "I have never been to a museum or other venue that showed the beauty of nature like this room. Is this what I will find in heaven?"

Joseph replies, "Yes, you will find all of this in heaven. Think of this area: the base camps, the hosting stations and the Eternal Processing Center as Ellis Island. It is an induction area for the believers, the true followers of Jesus Christ. We are all part of God's kingdom; angels, the saints in heaven, the new saints in the base camps and missionary captains, who see that new saints and older saints accomplish their missions on earth as well as in heaven. Anderson, the longer you're in God's kingdom; the more you will learn about your eternal life."

Anderson exclaims, "It's overwhelming!"

Joseph says, "It takes a long time to understand the extent of God's splendor. Only God knows about all his kingdom. One thing that you may be somewhat familiar with is the New Jerusalem, the holy city described by the Apostle John in Revelation. Christ will reign from there during the millennium. You will recall that the War of Armageddon ends with the return of Christ and His victory on earth. At that time, the New Jerusalem is established. The City is as high as it is long and wide. Take one third of the United States: from Maine to Northern Florida and from the Atlantic seaboard to a line from Chicago to St. Louis, and that is the width and length of the New Jerusalem. Remember though, it is many, many times bigger than that dimension, because it is also as high as it is wide and long."

Anderson replies, "God's kingdom is unfathomable!"

"Yes, it is. Most believers on earth don't think about all the unbelievers that will still be alive after the great tribulation ends. When Christ's establishes his kingdom on the new earth, there will be over one billion unbelievers still alive on earth. Remember the scripture about the saints: they will fall on the sword, and it will not harm them. The scripture is talking about saints like you, Anderson, during the millennium of Christ's reign on earth. The unbelievers are mortal without Christ, but the saints have eternal life in Christ"

"I always thought that the millennium after Armageddon was a time when saints would be evangelizing God's Word to the unbelievers on earth," said Anderson.

Joseph replies, "That's right. Heaven has many realms. The Apostle Paul went to the third heaven. What you have seen so far is a type of entrance to heaven. There is the heaven on the other side of the Eternal Processing Center. There is the heaven in the New Jerusalem, where Christ will reign, and from there His saints go to and fro on earth, sharing God's Word with the unbelievers. Anderson, can you even try to imagine all the realms in all the galaxies?"

Anderson replies, "Absolutely not."

Joseph says, "Only God knows what is in all of His realms."

Anderson says, "And that is just fine. I'm just glad and thankful to be in heaven through Christ and His church."

Joseph says, "It's not my place to say, but I think the longer we're in God's kingdom, the more we'll find out how extensive God's realms are. Well, Anderson, we could talk about heaven for a long time. Unfortunately, I have some things I must get done, and you have the stimulating experience of the nature room awaiting you."

Anderson asks, "It looks like the nature videos are catalogued by subject. Do the devices to watch them work the same way as in the other rec rooms?"

Joseph says, "Yes, and when you sit down in the main chair you'll see the control for the different types of formats they are shown on. Also, there is a control marked planetarium and another one marked galaxy, and a remote beside it, so you can make your own changes."

Anderson remarks, "And a planetarium and galaxies too!"

Joseph replies, "Yes, and there's much more I'll show you soon."

Anderson says, "I guess in heaven, I should expect infinite resources!"

Joseph laughs and says, "You've got that right!"

"Thank you, Joseph. I'll hang out here for a good while, then I'll look for Richard, Dwight and Larry in the bigger rec rooms or in the cabin."

While Joseph goes back to work, Anderson looks over the large library of nature videos. The video titles fuel his curiosity to look even longer at the great variety. The botany section has individual videos on specialized subjects like pine trees, cypress trees and cedars. Wildlife has individual videos on subjects like the life of the grizzly bear and habits of wild turkeys. Other nature videos explore different types of land like the mountains of India;

A Light on the Path

woods in northern Michigan and the wetlands of Central Indiana in the 19th century.

Anderson watches videos on wildlife and different kinds of woods for a long time. He begins to look at the controls for the planetarium and the galaxy exhibits. He thinks, "Here I would call the technology divine art instead of state of the art." He tries out the planetarium exhibit for a while, but when he investigates the galaxy exhibit, he is completely mesmerized. He sees many galaxies, their stars and their other phenomena for the first time. The ceiling in the nature room takes him on an unknown voyage.

Even though the new experience in the nature room is breathtaking, he needs to stretch and walk around. He decides he'll walk to his cabin first to see if any of his friends are there. His walk is refreshing, and it seems like he is back at the cabin in no time. When he walks in, he sees Richard stretched out on his bed. Anderson says, "How is the missionary business?"

Richard tilts his head to look at him and says, "Hi, Anderson. Things went well. I went on my first journey, not long after you left the cabin."

Anderson asks, "Who did you visit with?"

Richard replies, "My wife; she survived me. She is a retired psychology professor, who got caught up in humanism. Two of her best friends were a psychiatrist and a psychologist. I had witnessed to her for years. I know that my passing influenced her. When I showed up and shared things that Joseph suggested, she finally gave into God's ways and accepted Christ as her savior."

"Praise God!" replied Anderson. "How are you feeling?"

Richard replies, "I couldn't feel better!"

Anderson says, "Humanism has been one of Satan's most effective tools. It basically replaces God at the center of our beliefs with the value of humans. Some of the ancient Greeks taught the philosophy. Today it's in fields like psychology and medicine; in government agencies; in public schools and colleges and many other areas of society. Richard, you probably know that some people during the renaissance coined it humanism. Unfortunately, there are many people who call themselves Christians, but they have replaced the divine teachings of the gospel with humanism. The third person I'll be visiting is my daughter, and she is also an active psychology professor."

Richard asks, "Is she caught up in humanism like many people in the field of psychology?"

Anderson replies, "Yes, she is. The good news is the passing of her mother had a positive, spiritual impact on her. She also grew closer to me spiritually after her mom passed."

Richard says, "That sounds promising. Do you think she will give her life to Christ?"

Anderson replies, "Yes. I visit her in little over a week in earth time. I think she is ready to yield to God's will. I recently got back from my journey to visit my sister. She also gave her life to Christ.

Richard says, "That's good to hear. Humanistic beliefs can be so enigmatic. Most people don't refer to it as humanism, and most don't realize that humanists place humans at the center of their beliefs instead of God."

Anderson replies, "It's deceptive. People get caught up in it because it seems right, but they don't realize that they give God a subordinate position in their lives. As we know, we are not to put any other gods before out Father."

Richard replies, "Well put."

Anderson asks, "Do you have any more missionary journeys?"

Richard says, "At this time, I don't think I have more. It sounds like I will be going through the Eternal Processing Center soon. What about you?"

Anderson says, "I have two more. I should be done after that. I look forward to catching up with you in the next heavenly realm!"

Richard replies, "Me too. I enjoy being here at base camp, but I'm also looking forward to what's next."

Anderson says, "If I don't see you soon, I will look you up. I'm going to walk back to the lodge to see if Dwight and Larry are in one of the bigger rec rooms. Take care, Richard."

"You too, Anderson."

As Anderson walks back to the lodge, he wonders if Dwight and Larry have completed their first missionary visits. He thinks, "The most logical place to find them would be at the lodge, unless one or both of them are on a missionary journey." When he walks into the biggest rec room, he finds them playing one of his favorite video games. It allows the player to fly like a bird to any city or countryside on earth.

Anderson says light heartedly, "Where are you world travelers off to?"

Larry says, "We just landed in the highlands of Scotland, and we're enjoying the scenery, but we're already debating about where we'll fly to next."

Dwight says, "I've noticed three more scenic highlights in the highlands than Larry, so unless Larry finds four more real soon, I'll be deciding where we go next."

Larry says, "Let's put it on pause, and catch up on our missionary journeys."

Anderson asks, "Have both of you been on your first journey?"

A Light on the Path

Both Dwight and Larry answer in the affirmative. Dwight says, "Richard left not long after you met with Joseph, then I left, and Larry just got back."

Anderson says, "Tell me about them."

Dwight says, "I went back to Indiana to see my best friend. He is a vet with a disability. He has been fighting bitterness for years, since he left the army. I've witnessed to him off and on for years, and I'm sure my wife did after I passed on. The last couple years he has mellowed with age. I have always tried to help him, and when I returned, it blew his mind! You should have seen his face! He knows about Christ, the church, the rapture and many other things of God. After I shared with him, he made the commitment to Christ. We praised God together and had a great time of celebration!"

Anderson exclaims, "That is what I call a great victory!"

Larry says, "I have a cousin in Tennessee, who is three years younger than I was. Most of his life it seems like he blamed God for everything. Through the years, I would tell him about God's grace and mercy, but he was spiritually blind. I think I was able to reach him during my visit, because despite his former attitude, we remained friends. It also blew his mind when I showed up. He was really shook up for several minutes. I was so thankful, when he opened the door to Christ. What about your journey, Anderson?"

Anderson replies, "All of our lives my sister and I have been close. We grew up in the same home church. I think two things affected her negatively in life. Our parents we're busy, and she felt that they should have spent more time with her. On top of that, she married a controlling man, who ended up leaving her for a much younger woman. I don't think she blamed God, but inside I believe she was hurt so much that she just hadn't surrendered to Christ. She is a very sweet person, and even before I passed on, I think she was getting closer to God. She also gave her heart to Christ."

Dwight exclaims, "Praise God! We have a lot to celebrate. How do you want to celebrate, since we don't have cravings here for things like chocolate milk shakes?"

Anderson says, "We could have ice cream, if we want it, but I just wanted us to share our stories and have a good time of fellowship."

Larry says, "That we will!"

Anderson says, "I have a lot of time before my next journey. What about both of you?"

Dwight replies, "I have one more. I'll be done in a few days based on earth time."

Larry says, "I have one more too, and I will be done in less than a week based on earth time. How about you, Anderson?"

A Light on the Path

Anderson replies, "I have two more. One in about a week, and another one a few days later."

Larry says, "That's splendid! We will all be processed in less than two weeks. Richard will be processed real soon, and, Anderson, you will be the last one. We'll have to get together then and have another celebration."

Both Dwight and Anderson say, "We will".

They decide to walk back to their cabin to check on Richard. On the way, they pass a few other white cabins and the vast meadow of vivid green grass with the country charm of white and yellow wild flowers. As they walk through their cabin door, they don't see any sign of Richard. They walk over to his empty bed and see a note. Anderson picks it up, and reads it out loud:

"To my buddies; Anderson, Larry and Dwight,

Joseph came by, and he's walking me to the process center. I will see all of you in about two weeks, EARTH TIME!

Best Wishes,

Richard Cameron."

Anderson says, "Good for him."

Dwight says, "He's taking the big step. We'll have to address him as Richie Rich now."

Larry says, "That's fine, if we can call you Dwight the Light."

They all laugh. Dwight asks, "Is this what they call heavenly humor?"

Anderson replies, "I think it's just humor."

Larry says, "In church we use to say that believers have more fun and laughs than anyone."

Anderson says, "I can attest to that! What do you think about unwinding here while we rest, and when we go back to the lodge, I have something special to show you."

Larry asks, "What's that?"

Anderson says, "The nature room."

Dwight replies, "Where's the nature room?"

Anderson says, "It's right off the vestibule, as you start down the hall. It is the most spectacular venue on nature that you have ever seen. There is the most phenomenal exhibit. I have never seen anything like it. It takes place above you, like a planetarium, but it makes the planetarium look like the invention of the wheel. It's about the galaxies, and no pun intended, but it's out of this world! You'll feel like you're flying through the galaxies. You will see all of these incredible wonders of space."

Dwight says, "It sounds better than riding on the Enterprise."

Anderson replies, "It is, and there is also this huge library of remarkable videos on nature. You'll love it."

Larry says, "Time is on our side, so let's go when we're done here."

A Light on the Path

Anderson says, "I think I want to stretch out in my bunk and meditate about my upcoming missionary visits."

Larry says, "Good idea. I think I'll do the same."

All three of them quietly meditate on their beds for quite some time.

After a long rest, they're ready to go back to the lodge to enjoy the nature room. As they wait for their next missionary assignments, they enjoy talking with each other; walking in the meadow; relaxing at the lodge; playing the advanced video games and using the nature room. Anderson shows them how to use the controls for the planetarium and the galaxy exhibit. They love flying through the galaxies and watching the outstanding nature videos. Dwight has a passion for watching a video on the Colorado Rockies, and Larry's favorite is the Redwood Forests in Oregon and Northern California.

As Joseph directs Dwight and Larry on their next missionary journeys, Anderson waits his turn. Finally, it's time for Anderson to visit Kenny.

Chapter 18 – The Second Visit

Anderson meets with Joseph in the conference room. Joseph asks, "Are you ready for your second journey?"

Anderson replies, "I'm looking forward to it."

Joseph says, "Just to confirm things: you know your mission goals, and you know God's message for Kenny."

Anderson replies, "Yes, I do."

"Very good. You told me earlier that Kenny does his chores in the morning. I think you said that he usually works in the chicken coup area between 8 and 9."

Anderson says, "Yes. I think my approach to first seeing Kenny would be easier on him, if he saw me walking across the field. As you face the house, the field and the chicken coup are just to the left."

Joseph replies, "Excellent. I'll tune in to his location, and see if he's at the chicken coup. It's just a few minutes after 8:00 a.m. his time." Joseph looks down at Kenny's farm and tunes in to the field and the chicken coup. He says, "Yes, I see him inside the fenced yard by the chicken coup. If you're ready, Anderson, I'll fix the portal at the same place here in the room. I'll align the portal, so you'll be in the field. Are you ready to walk into the portal, Anderson?"

Anderson says with expectation, "Yes, I'm ready to go." He walks into the portal and right away he's standing in Kenny's field. He can see Kenny in the yard by the coup. It looks like he's cleaning the area. Anderson is about seventy yards from Kenny. Once Anderson is about forty yards away, Kenny sees him walking toward him. At first he doesn't recognize Anderson, but when Anderson gets about twenty yards away, he yells, "How is my friend doing?"

At first, Kenny just stares and doesn't know what to think. Scooter barks just a few times, then he starts wagging his tail. As Anderson gets close to Kenny, he says, "Kenny, don't you have anything to say?"

When Anderson is just a few yards away, Kenny asks, "Are you a ghost?"

Anderson laughs and says, "No, I'm not a ghost; it's really me."

Kenny says nervously, "What happened to you? I have never seen you so young looking!"

Anderson replies, "That's right. I was about sixty, when we first met."

Kenny asks, "How did you get here? I didn't see your truck pull in."

Anderson laughs again and says, "I know it's perplexing, Kenny, but don't worry; everything is alright. You've heard of state of the art. Well, I got here by divine art. I'll tell you what happened, but how have you been doing?"

A Light on the Path

Kenny says, "I'm doing fine. Lydia and I have been worried about you. The day you disappeared, we searched for you about six hours. You met Aaron and John a couple years ago. They came with me and helped with the search."

Anderson replies, "Thank them for me, and you can tell them what happened to me."

"What did happen to you?"

Anderson smiles and says, "I went on quite an early spring walk. It turned out to be an incredible journey, instead of the regular hike."

Kenny says, "I found your walking stick. What happened from there?"

Anderson replies, "So far, Lydia is the only person who knows what happened to me. I went to see her a week ago. After I leave you today, call Lydia right away. I'll explain before I leave."

Kenny says, "Sure I will."

Anderson says, "It's getting warm already. Could we talk in your house?"

Kenny replies, "I'll be ready in a minute. I'll put some feed out for the chickens, then we'll go to the house."

Anderson pets Scooter, while Kenny finishes.

They walk across the field together. Kenny says, "I can't get over how young you look. Evidently, something incredible did happen to you."

Anderson replies, "It sure was incredible. I have a lot to tell you. Maybe we could get a cold drink in the house, and I'll tell you what happened." As they walk in Kenny's house, Anderson still enjoys the aroma from Kenny's pipe.

Kenny says, "Have a seat. Do you want some ice water or a diet soda?"

Anderson says, "I think I'll have a diet soda; it has been a while." He sits down near the kitchen by the old upright piano. Kenny brings back the diet sodas and sits in his recliner. Anderson enjoys his first sip of the cold drink.

Kenny says, "You must have quite a story. We had a memorial service for you. It was at your church about two weeks ago. I can imagine the look on their faces, if they were with us now!"

Anderson laughs and says, "Yes, brother; it has been some mind-boggling journey, since that day in the woods. I had just cleared a few branches from the wide ravine before I got to the big clearing. After I walked through the clearing, I had to make a pit stop, so I leaned the walking stick against the hickory tree at my rest area."

Kenny remarks, "Yes, that's where I found it!"

Anderson continues, "While I was there, I noticed a strange low lying fog on the pathway ahead. As I continued down the trail, the boulders to my right seemed to continue longer than normal. At that time, I started walking through this low lying fog, while there were only a few clouds in the sky. As you know, the trail eventually curves to the southwest, but it felt like the trail continued south. I stayed on the trail, and soon I saw a light on the path ahead. When I got to the light, the path opened to a large beautiful meadow. I didn't understand where I was, so I climbed the hill to see where the meadow would lead me. At that point you wouldn't believe what I saw!"

Kenny asks, "Was it an ethereal experience?"

Anderson replies, "It sure was! It looked like a big art and craft show, with the white canopies over the booths. In the background was this huge building like a grand central station. It was the entrance to heaven."

Kenny says, "Oh, come on; you're pulling my leg."

Anderson replies, "Oh, no; you know me, Kenny. I'm going to tell you the straight, unpolished, unedited, honest, truth. I've been in the heavenly realm that is located by the entrance to heaven. There is something else. I met my guardian angel, and you have one too!"

Kenny remarks, "This is almost too much for me to smoke my pipe over."

Anderson says, "While you're pondering what I shared, I will go ahead and tell you the message God has for you."

"God has a message for me?"

Anderson replies, "He sure does, Kenny. God says, "Kenny I've known you since you were in your mother's womb. I created you in my image. I am God, the creator of all things. I created the cougar, the bear and the owl. I created the cedar, the pine and the oak. I am the one true God. I want you to follow my Son, the Christ, who died for you and rose again that you might have forgiveness for your sins and eternal life. I want you to obey his commands and follow my Son. Put aside your trust in man's cultural traditions. From this day, I want you to follow me."

Kenny sits in his recliner spellbound. His eyes have welled up in tears, and they're flowing down his cheeks. He sobs with emotion as he says, "Anderson, you were right. Inside, I felt you were right. Now I know it with all my being. Yes, I will follow Christ. I have already been baptized, but I will repent of my sins, and follow Jesus as my savior. I would be one of the last to impede God's work. I will do what needs to be done. This gives me a new mission in life."

Anderson says, "Praise God, brother. I have prayed for a long time that you would see that the Father, Son and Holy Spirit are all you need. In your new mission, you can take the message to many people like Aaron and John. You can share it with the Cherokee and with all people."

A Light on the Path

Kenny replies, "Yes, yes; there are so many people I want to share this with. Now I know why there a few reports on the national news about believers in Christ, who have passed on, returning to visit a friend or relative. It is happening to me right now!"

Anderson says, "It sure is, Kenny, and I'm sure glad for you!"

"Anderson, you have been a precious friend; unlike any friend I've had."

"Kenny, you have been a great blessing to me as well. Let's thank the Lord now in a praise offering. Our Father, guide Kenny every day. May Lydia, Angela and Kenny form a unique bond that is a great witness to your love and grace. May many people find Jesus through them in this late hour. In Jesus' name we pray. Amen."

Kenny says, "Thank you, Anderson, from the bottom of my heart."

Anderson replies, "Thank you, Kenny, for being a faithful friend. We have more to cover, but I have plenty of time. I will get back to you about Lydia and Angela before I leave. I wanted to get an update from you on the state of the nation and the world. Lydia said there is more famine and pestilence than usual in third world countries. She said there have been more earthquakes in several countries, including the United States, Turkey and China. She said that Russia conflicts with a lot of countries."

Kenny says, "Yes, that's right. Every day it seems like the breaking news is the bad news. Our country is reeling out of control. The officials can't keep up with all the spiraling robberies, vandalism, arson and murders. Neighborhood watches have become a mainstay, instead of the exception. Murders number over 2,000 since the civil unrest started. Now officials are predicting that the murder rate before the end of the year will be much higher than the number killed on 9/11. I believe all the greed and lies of companies are calling their hand. There's no doubt that God is judging the world. Gas prices are now triple of what they were three to four months ago. Food prices are almost as bad. The world bankers and government leaders are talking like a world currency will be a given instead of a suggestion. Russia has precipitated a lot of the world conflicts, but so has Iran and North Korea. Already there is an aggressive alliance against those countries, which includes our country, Japan, South Korea, Great Britain, Israel, France and Poland."

Anderson replies, "I would expect as much. There will certainly be a reckoning in the world. I have another message for you that I have shared with Lydia and will also share with Angela. I cannot say what day or hour the rapture of the church will occur. Only the Father knows, but he is sending missionaries like me, because there is little time left before the rapture of the church. I cannot say it will be in a few days, seven months or fourteen months, but it will be soon. God wants the church to be ready. He says that too many are straddling the fence. He wants the church to wake up and be prepared."

Kenny says, "I totally believe that. Not to change the subject, but how did you get here?"

Anderson laughs and says, "If I were you, I would also be curious about that. Some things I can share, and some things I can't. I can tell you that heaven is everything you've dreamed about and everything the Bible promises. Of course, I shared how I got there, but other things I can't share at this time. The main thing that God wants me to relay is the message that His Son is coming very soon for His church. God wants you and other believers to actively tell people that He is coming soon."

Kenny asks, "How long can you stay, and will you come back?

Anderson replies, "I can stay today as long as needed. Whether I come back before the rapture remains to be seen. I will go ahead and tell you that I will be visiting Angela within a few days. It's important that you call Lydia after I leave. The reason for your call is Lydia is going to call Angela after she hears from you. She will tell Angela that I will be at a specific place in her home at a certain time within a few days."

"I do know that God wants Lydia, Angela and you to form a bond of fellowship. You can text, call and email each other as often as you like. Since you don't live far from Lydia, maybe you could see her every month or two. You won't see Angela as often, but if the rapture is over a year away, maybe the three of you can get together a couple times.

Kenny says, "I can promise that I will drive to see Lydia at least every two months. Hopefully we can get together eight or nine times a year. We have a powerful message, and I want us to get the word out."

Anderson replies, "Wonderful! Getting the message out is of prime importance. Share with Angela also about our visit. Get her number today from Lydia and wait almost a week before you call her. Encourage each other and pray for each other. Once Angela hears from the three of us, I think she will become a new person in Christ. Kenny, Lydia's commitment to Christ and yours mean everything to me."

Kenny says, "My friend, I owe everything to you, and of course, to Christ."

Anderson asks, "Is anything new in your life? Has everything been okay?"

Kenny replies, "Nothing new, except you showing up today after your memorial service! Everything has been as usual, but now I get the best news I've had all my life. Imagine being in touch with God!"

"I've been working with my guardian angel, but the Holy Spirit continues to guide me. By the way, do you have a paper and pen?"

A Light on the Path

Kenny replies, "Yes, I have a pad and pen on my table."

Anderson says, "Good. Write down these scriptures about the end time: Matthew 24, 1 Thessalonians 4: 16-18 and the book of Revelation. Also, for a great spiritual guide, write down John, chapters 14-16. The whole book of John will help you daily. Where did we leave off about all the changes in the world?"

Kenny replies, "I think we were talking about a world currency looking like it will come to pass."

"Oh, yes. I'm to tell you, Lydia and Angela that it is coming soon. Once they institute it, they will start working on an implant that you must have to buy or sell. It will go in the arm or the forehead. The Bible calls it the mark of the beast. Before they start requiring the implant, the rapture of the church will take place. The rapture could happen at any time, but if they have the world currency in place first, you will know that the rapture will happen soon afterwards."

Kenny says, "I'm glad to know. I already knew that wars, famine, pestilence and earthquakes would increase in the end time."

Anderson says, "That's right. The end time is the end of the old era, but the new era is coming soon, and you will be part of it!"

Kenny exclaims, "Thanks be to God. I have a mission now that will take me to my eternal home!"

Anderson replies, "You've got that right. You know, Kenny, I haven't been gone long, and heaven is a wonderful place, but I have missed some of the changes from winter to spring. We were going to take a hike on your property this month or go turkey hunting. I won't be able to take a hike, but I miss seeing the redbud trees and the dogwood trees this time of year."

Kenny says, "My friend, you've come to the right place. All we must do is walk about one quarter of a mile; around the garden in back to the tree line that is part of the woods. Before you get to the woods, you'll see several red bud and dogwood there, as well as to your left, on a hill with a slight grade."

"That's perfect. I should get back after that. While we walk to the tree line, my guardian angel told me to share some scriptures from Matthew 24. They will help prepare you for the rapture. Besides, 1 Thessalonians 16-18, Matthew 24: 39-41 is another main rapture scripture. It talks about two being in the field and one will be taken, and one will be left." As they walk by the garden, Anderson finishes sharing what Joseph wanted Kenny, Lydia and Angela to know. He says, "Jesus tells us in verse 44 that we must be ready. He says the Son of man will come at an hour, when you don't expect him. Also, before verse 39, Jesus tells us that it will be like the days of Noah. People won't be expecting it. They will be living their lives like always; eating and drinking and marrying. Kenny, God is telling us that we must be prepared and be looking for Jesus. He is telling us to not get caught up in the routines of life."

As Kenny talks to Anderson about the Matthew 24 scriptures, they come to the tree line where there are close to nine or ten redbuds and dogwoods. Anderson listens to Kenny as he looks to his left and sees more redbuds and dogwoods on the hill that Kenny mentioned.

Anderson replies, "Yes, Kenny, you've got the idea. Share it with all that you can. Share the scriptures too, when you have the opportunity. Thank you for bringing me out here. The dogwoods and red buds are beautiful. I'm in the habit of seeing these trees as spring sets in. It's kind of like seeing the autumn leaves as winter is on the horizon."

Kenny says, "You're welcome, my friend. You're welcome to come anytime, but it sounds like I might be coming where you are the next time we meet!"

"Yes, Kenny, I know we will be together in heaven. I will be praying for you. I know in my heart, that Lydia, Angela and you will be preparing and encouraging others to get ready."

Kenny replies, "You can count on it! I will stay in touch with Lydia and Angela. I will be sure to call Lydia, as soon as I walk back in the house."

"Kenny, may God bless you and keep you. I will be lifting you up in prayer. Let the Holy Spirit guide you at all times. God wants us to go to church; to help others and to spread the gospel."

Kenny says, "I will do those things, my friend."

"Well, brother, my heavenly transport will pick me up about the place where you first saw me. I know that we've walked just far enough north to be somewhere behind the chicken coup."

"That's right. We'll just turn around here and walk due west, and we'll be back at the chicken coup in no time."

"When we get there, Kenny, if you would walk to your house, I need to keep walking west in the field, so I can catch my ride." Anderson looks at Scooter; pets him and says, "Scooter, you take care of Kenny."

When they get back to the chicken coup, Anderson hugs Kenny and says, "I'm looking forward to seeing you forever, brother."

Kenny says, "Until we meet again, my friend."

Kenny walks toward his house with Scooter, as Anderson continues to walk west in the field. Kenny looks back now and then and still sees Anderson about twenty-five to thirty seconds later. When he looks back the next time, he thinks he sees Anderson disappear into thin air.

As soon as Kenny walks into his house, he calls Lydia.

Lydia answers the cell phone, "How are you doing, Kenny?"

Kenny replies, "I'm doing really well now, since I had a special visitor."

A Light on the Path

Lydia asks, "Was Anderson there?"

"Yes. He told me that he visited you a week ago. When he left, I was walking back toward the house; I turned around and it looked like he vanished into thin air."

Lydia replies, "Yes, when he left here, he walked out the back great room door and just disappeared. It sounds like his visit was a good experience for you."

Kenny says, "It meant everything. It opened my eyes, and I made things right with the Lord."

"I did too. I told Anderson that I would wait on your call before I called Angela. Did he tell you that he is going to visit Angela within a few days?"

Kenny replies, "Yes, he said he didn't want to scare her. When I first saw him, I thought he was a ghost! He plans to meet her at a certain place in the house around a certain time."

"Yes, he explained that to me. I think letting her know about his upcoming visit will help her, since she lost her mom and dad within three months of each other."

Kenny asks, "Lydia, did Anderson tell you that he wants us to form a fellowship, and stay in touch regularly, because the Lord is coming soon?"

Lydia replies, "Yes, he did. He wants us to tell people to be prepared; help others; go to church and spread the good news."

"Exactly! It sounds like he shared a lot of the same information with both of us."

Lydia remarks, "Have you stopped to realize how extraordinary these visits are?"

Kenny replies, "Even though he just left, I realize it's phenomenal! He didn't even die. He just walked a pathway to heaven!"

Lydia replies, "I believe it's happening, because the rapture of the church is very close."

Kenny says, "I agree. We should tell everyone we can. Did you hear any of the national news reports about these visits happening to other people?"

Lydia replies, "Yes, it sounds like it's happening in different places around the country. I've been waiting to call Angela, so I could start sharing my experience with others."

Kenny says, "I know you need to call Angela now. Since she will know in a few minutes, what do you think about calling Pastor Don? I could pick you up about 10:30 Sunday. Maybe he would let us have five to ten minutes to share the news about Anderson's visits."

Lydia says, "Yes, we should do that as soon as possible. I'll call Angela, and then I'll call Pastor Don. I'll let you know what he says. Thanks for calling, and I'll let you know about the church service."

A Light on the Path

Kenny replies, "Until then, Lydia."

Lydia has butterflies in her stomach; just thinking about sharing such a mystifying experience with Angela. She looks at the time and wonders if Angela is home. She dials Angela's cell phone number.

"Hi, Lydia, how are you?"

Lydia replies, "I'm fine, but I don't know how you will react to what I need to tell you. Are you sitting down?"

"Why, yes. I had an early class today. I gave a test, and now I'm grading the papers. What do you mean about how I will react?"

Lydia says, "Well, I have an unusual experience to share with you, and Kenny had the same experience. Of course, you know that your dad's body was never found."

"Of course, I know. Did someone find some evidence?"

"Yes, Kenny and I sure did find evidence. Did you ever think of what may have happened to him?"

Angela replies, "It has crossed my mind that he was abducted or drug off by a bear. You're not going to tell me that he was abducted by aliens, are you?"

Lydia says, "Oh, no. He wasn't abducted by aliens; It was a lot more pleasant than that."

Angela says, "Tell me, Lydia, what you and Kenny know."

Lydia replies, "He walked into heaven."

"Walked into heaven! Why do you say that?"

Lydia says, "We saw him, and he talked with us."

There's a long pause, then Angela says, "Are you saying that he is an angel?"

Lydia replies, "Not an angel, but he's something like that. He's coming to see you, Angela."

"Coming to see me! Are you kidding me, Lydia?"

"No, Angela. I wouldn't kid about something like this. Your dad will be there within a few evenings after Stephen goes to bed. He thought 11:00 would be a good time for you. He wanted me to tell you, so you wouldn't be scared."

Angela says, "I don't know what to say. I guess my response is a mixture of unbelief, bewilderment and shock."

Lydia replies, "Think of it as good news. Your dad is in heaven, and he has something special to tell you."

Angela asks, "When did you see him?"

"A week ago. It was around midnight. I had just gone to sleep in bed, and I heard sound from the television. Your dad had turned on the Sirius

A Light on the Path

Radio Spa Channel, which was familiar to me. When I saw him, he was sitting in his recliner in the great room."

Angela replies, "This is just too much! When did Kenny see him?"

"This morning. He left Kenny's house less than two hours ago."

Angela asks, "Does he have transportation?"

Lydia says, "None that we're familiar with. He just disappears into thin air."

Angela says, "Do you think it's an apparition?"

Lydia replies, "No, it's your dad. We've talked with him, and he makes perfect sense. You won't believe how young he looks."

Angela says, "So, he is coming to see me within the next few evenings around 11:00? Did he say where?"

Lydia replies, "Yes, in your living room. He will turn on a light, so you know he's there."

"I still don't know what to say, Lydia. Thank you for telling me."

Lydia says, "I know it's a puzzling surprise, but you'll be fine. Once you talk with your dad, you'll even be joyful! I'll be praying for you. Have a good night."

"You too. Lydia. Take care."

Lydia collects her thoughts while she gets ready to call Pastor Don. She looks up his number and calls his cell phone. She listens to it ring several times.

"Hello, this is Pastor Don."

"Hi, Pastor. This is Lydia, Anderson's sister."

"Hi, Lydia. It was wonderful seeing you in our worship service Sunday."

"Thank you, Pastor. It was nice being there. In fact, I plan to attend every Sunday. I called you, because Kenny would like to come to worship with me this Sunday."

"We'll be glad to have both of you."

Lydia continues, "I have a favor to ask you. Something very spiritual has happened to Kenny and me. It happened to me a week ago, and to Kenny this morning. It is Christ centered, and something we would like to share this Sunday. If it is alright with you, could we have five to ten minutes of your service time to share this with your people? I know they will be glad to hear what we have to say."

Pastor Don replies, "Of course, you can. Even if you need ten to fifteen minutes, we'll look forward to it. Sometimes I get long winded, so it will be a nice break for the congregation to hear a ten to fifteen-minute sermon from me."

Lydia says, "You will be glad to hear what we have to say, Pastor. I think it would be good for you to hear about it, when your people do."

"Lydia, I pray for you every day. It's a joy to have you with us. Do you need anything?"

"I'm doing fine, Pastor. Have a good night."

"God bless you, Lydia. See you Sunday."

Lydia thinks, "Thank God; that is set. I'll call Kenny now."

Kenny answers, "Hi, Lydia."

"Good news, Kenny. Pastor Don said we could have ten to fifteen minutes this Sunday."

Kenny replies, "Very good! I'll pick you up right after 10:30 Sunday. After service, I'll take you out to dinner, and then I'll take you home. I'll return home about 4:00, so I can finish my morning chores."

Lydia says, "That will work. Why don't we each give a testimony for seven minutes. If we time it while we practice, we won't run over the fifteen minutes."

Kenny says, "Sounds good. Our testimonies should encourage them to tell others. It will also be interesting to hear how our testimonies are alike and not alike."

Lydia replies, "We should be all set. We have less than two days. I've been on the phone a lot, so I'll wish you a good night."

Kenny says, "I'll see you Sunday; Lord willing. Good night."

Lydia is ready for a rest. She leans back in Anderson's recliner. She starts thinking about what she wants to say Sunday morning, when she falls asleep.

Lydia wakes up almost an hour later and gets a pad and pen to make notes for Sunday. She looks at the great room clock. It's already 5:00, so she decides to make some soup and coffee. When she sits down at the dining table with the soup and coffee, she thinks, "Now I'll be alert while I get ready for Sunday."

After she works on her notes, she watches the evening news, then the history channel. She goes to bed early. She thinks, "I'm going to finish the notes and outline early tomorrow, so I can go over them tomorrow evening.

When Lydia wakes up, she is refreshed from a good night's sleep. She immediately starts thinking about her notes for Sunday. After she makes a trip to the bathroom, she thinks, "Once I make coffee, I'll be ready to tackle the notes again."

Her day goes as planned. The notes and outline are done early. She can enjoy the day as she reviews her testimony. The day ends quickly. She decides to shower early in the morning, so she can relax and review her notes before Kenny arrives.

A Light on the Path

Kenny pulls his Jeep into her driveway at 10:32 Sunday morning. He gets out and walks to her door. As he walks on the porch, Lydia opens the door. "Good morning, Kenny. How was your drive this morning?"

Kenny replies, "Good morning. It was nice. I enjoyed the country sunshine."

Lydia says, "Come in. I'll be ready in a minute. I think I'm kind of tense and a little nervous about giving my testimony."

Kenny replies, "I'm a little nervous too."

Lydia says, "Do you mind going first? It might help me with my jitters."

Kenny laughs and says, "I'll be glad to."

It's a scenic trip, as they drive through the Smoky Mountain foothills to the church in Mount Holly. Both Lydia and Kenny comment about how enchanting the dogwood trees are. Kenny says, "Anderson was just admiring the dogwoods and the redbuds at my house. He wanted to go outside just to see them."

Lydia says, "I wish I could have been there to enjoy that with him. I can't complain. I got to visit with him just a few nights ago."

Kenny says, "We live in unprecedented times, Lydia."

"That is certainly the gospel truth. After our testimonies this morning, others will be thinking that," remarked Lydia.

They pull in early at the Mount Holly church. So far, there's just a few cars in the lot. Kenny says, "Who owns the candy apple red, 1957 Chevy Impala?"

Lydia replies, "It belongs to the piano player and her husband. He's a contractor, and she is also the children's director. It's so sad that most churches have very few children today."

Kenny says, "It's a sign of the times."

When they walk in, Pastor Don greets them. Lydia says, "It looks like we're ten minutes early."

Pastor Don says, "That's good! You can greet everyone that's early. We just love to have new people!"

John and Wilma are already there; the piano player, Pastor Don's wife and another couple. John and Wilma's two grandchildren are with them. They're a bundle of energy. Lydia says to Wilma, "It might be a while before I have great grandchildren. They must be a great joy to you."

Wilma says, "They are. We're fortunate they live in Knoxville."

John says, "They're as cute as can be, but they're hard to keep up with."

It's getting close to service time, and people are starting to file in. It looks like they're going to have about thirty people this morning.

A Light on the Path

Pastor Don opens the service, and they sing, "What a Friend We Have in Jesus". Lydia says to Kenny, "I bet Pastor Don knows this is one of Anderson's favorite songs."

Before the sermon, Pastor Don goes to the pulpit and says, "Today, we welcome back Lydia, Anderson's sister, and Kenny, Anderson's close friend for twenty-five years. Most of you have met Lydia and Kenny. They have something special to share with you today. We're going to ask Kenny to come first.

Kenny walks up to the pulpit, and humbly says, "Today, I remember Anderson, as I have something very important to share with you. By show of hands, I would like to see how many of you have heard reports on the national news about some believers returning from beyond the grave, to visit friends or relatives." Over half of the people raise their hands. "Friends, I won't mince words. It's true, because Anderson visited both Lydia and me." There are some gasps and a lot of surprised faces, looking at their friends and family members.

"It is crucial that you know; these events are happening, because Jesus is coming soon." Several people shout out, "Praise the Lord!" We found out where Anderson went; to heaven. A body was not found, because he passed directly from this life to the next life." One zealous lady stands and rings out, "Thank you, Jesus!" "Anderson appeared at my house, outside of Maggie Valley, a few days ago. He appeared at his house, where Lydia is, just over a week ago."

"Anderson said that God wants you to know Matthew 24. Pay close attention to Jesus' coming in the chapter. It will be unexpected, and it will be like the days of Noah; people marrying, drinking and eating. The famines, pestilences, earthquakes, wars and conflicts have increased, because His coming is soon. God wants you to be ready for the rapture of the church. As you prepare yourselves, God wants you to help others, go to church and spread the gospel."

Some of you know that "What a Friend We Have in Jesus" is one of Anderson's favorite songs. It tells us to take everything to God in prayer. The end of the song says, "Rapture, praise and endless worship; Will be our sweet portion there." Friends take inventory of your lives and make things right with God. Jesus is coming real soon! May God be with you and guide you."

Loud applause fills the small sanctuary. Many of the people shout praises to God. As Kenny takes his seat, the applause continues. Lydia comes to the pulpit.

Lydia says, "Good morning fellow believers, friends of Anderson's. Everything Kenny says is true. We've compared our conversations with Anderson, and they have the same information. We're sharing this today,

A Light on the Path

because God, the Father, the Son and the Holy Spirit, loves you, Anderson loves you, and I love you. God wants you to be ready. Anderson reminded Kenny and me that only the Father knows the day and the hour. God is concerned especially about all the believers who are straddling the fence. Many are not committed, and many are not obeying the commands of Christ.

We must follow Christ, if we are going to make heaven. It's urgent that you make things right with God. You must follow Christ every day. God is a God of love, grace and forgiveness. God wants you to make things right with him today. If He came for the church right now, would you be ready? Anderson said that it is not for him to say that the rapture will happen by tomorrow, in seven months or fourteen months, but it will happen soon. God sent Anderson to Kenny and me, so you would be ready. Please make things right with God before we leave today. After we leave, share the gospel message with others. God bless you and thank you for having us today.

When Lydia finishes, there is a temporary hush in the sanctuary, then it explodes with loud praises and applause. People are happy and shouting. As Lydia takes her seat, people are still praising God. As Pastor Don stands at the pulpit, he waits on all the people praising God. He also joins in with the applause and thanksgiving to God. The praises begin to subside after several minutes and people take their seats.

Pastor Don says, "Can somebody say, "Amen". The congregation responds with many boisterous amens. Pastor Don says, "I can't stop smiling; I feel like there's a river of joy flowing inside me!" The people stand again and start praising God.

Now the pastor starts laughing and says, "That's okay. Sing praises to God; worship Him!" In another minute, the people sit down. Pastor Don says, "I had planned to shorten my message today, but now I'm going to make it even shorter! We have one piece of unfinished business left. Before we leave, we need to make things right with God. Just over a year ago, we lost the world's greatest evangelist, Billy Graham. His favorite altar song was "Just as I Am". Evelyn, will you come and play, while we sing and come to the altar to make things right with God."

As they sing, everyone comes forward to the altar. They tarry at the altar for a long time of prayer, crying and shouting praises. When they finish, Pastor Don gives the benediction. Everyone comes up to greet and thank Lydia and Kenny. As they leave, Pastor Don says to Lydia and Kenny, "God bless you and thank you for the best service we've ever had." Kenny says, "It's an honor, Pastor." Lydia says, "Thank you for letting us speak, and keep lookin' up!"

A Light on the Path

When they get into Kenny's Jeep, Lydia says, "I almost hate to leave, but we have to move on." Over dinner they have a great time talking about the service today and the events of the past week.

Chapter 19 – One More Valley to Cross

While Lydia has been busy being in touch with Angela, Kenny and Pastor Don, Larry waited for Anderson to return from his last missionary journey. Larry was in the big rec room, when Anderson walked out of the conference room. Larry asks, "How did it go, Anderson."

Everything went well, Larry. My good friend gave his life to Christ. He has been a believer, but he had also mixed his belief in Christ with his traditional beliefs. He is a person of impeccable character, and a great example of the Cherokee people. The problem was mixing his faith in the one true God with spiritual teachings he learned as a child. Fortunately, he saw the light of Christ, and now has a Christ centered life.

Larry says, "He must be proud of his Cherokee heritage. I would be."

"He is a Cherokee that his people can also be proud of. He has a rich heritage," replied Anderson.

Larry says, "Dwight went through the processing center after he finished his last journey."

Anderson replies, "I'm glad you waited on me. The fellowship will be nice. How did your visit go?"

Larry replies, "My sister grew up in the same home church. After high school she went to an Ivy League College. Before she finished her first year of college, she called herself an existentialist. Years later her existentialism philosophy morphed into humanism. As you know, today humanism is influencing most every part of society. I call it the spiritual pandemic. Of course, she is retired now and is in her late seventies. I have shared the gospel message with her through the years. She started to mellow some about ten years ago. She quit being real defensive and would politely listen. They say a golden key can open any door. My surprise visit was the golden key."

Larry continues, "Of course, the Holy Spirit turned the golden key. When I first arrived, she was doing dishes in the kitchen. I didn't want it to be a gotcha experience. I stayed in the living room, and yelled out, "Hey, sis, have you got any coffee?" I didn't hear any movement or any sounds. I walked into the kitchen, and for a few minutes, I think she froze in time. Several times I said, "Hey, Sis, its Larry. After five or six times, she said, "Larry who?" She still made no movement.

In my life, I haven't seen anyone so startled. After three or four minutes, she said, "You sound like my brother, who isn't with us anymore." I couldn't help but laugh. She finally calmed down. I explained what was going on. I let her know that God wanted her to be prepared. She opened her life to Christ. It was a tremendous experience to see her accept Christ as her savior. I think I cried more than she did."

"Wow, Larry, that's a wonderful report. So, where do you want to go from here?"

Larry replies, "I told Joseph I wanted to wait on you. He said that I could be processed whenever I was ready."

Anderson asks, "When do you want to be processed?"

Larry replies, "I think after we talk awhile. I know that Dwight, Richard, you and I will have a reunion before long. I don't want to do anything special now. After we talk, I will be ready to go through the processing center. I just have to give Joseph a heads up and wait on him."

Anderson exclaims, "Terrific! I really appreciate you waiting for me. Our friendship means a lot. When you leave for the processing center, I only need to wait about three earth days for my last missionary assignment. I'll be visiting my daughter."

Larry says, "I know that will be a great joy for you."

Anderson replies, "I'm excited about seeing her. Like your sister and millions of others, humanism infiltrated her thinking many years ago." As they talk about their missionary journeys, they sit down in the majestic vestibule of the lodge. They also speculate about what awaits them on the other side of the processing center.

Anderson says, "I realize that we will see family members and old friends. I already know that I will see my wife, my parents and an old friend. I'm sure there will be many others that we will be reunited with."

Larry says, "I sure am looking forward to it. Do you realize we have the rest of eternity! I knew that I had plenty of time before I needed to go through the center."

Anderson replies, "You're totally right. I'm sure for eternity, we won't have to rush too many times."

Larry remarks, "Don't you think there will be lodges and vestibules as nice as this on the other side?"

Anderson replies, "It's hard to imagine how they could be more splendid, but I know we'll see many things like this. Imagine, Larry, a stone fireplace or wildlife portraits more magnificent than these!"

Larry said, "The galaxy exhibit in the nature room may just scratch the surface of what we'll see soon."

Anderson replies, "I'm sure you'll right. Why don't we take a walk; check on the cabin; then take a hike through the meadow?"

Larry replies, "Good idea. A nice walk will be a good change of pace."

They check on their cabin and take a quick look inside. Larry says, "We probably won't see this cabin too many more times."

Anderson replies, "You never know if we'll be back for future missionary journeys."

A Light on the Path

"That's a good point, Anderson."

They take a long walk through the meadow and pass the white canopies. Anderson sees Joel, and they stop and chat a few minutes with him. Larry says, "To me, this is already heaven, but we know it's only the outskirts of it!"

Anderson says, "Yes, and you'll be on main street soon!"

Larry replies, "And before you know it, you'll be right behind me. Well, Anderson, I think I'm ready to go through the center. Why don't we walk back to the lodge, and see if Joseph is there?"

They walk through the vestibule and down the hall to the door to Joseph's office complex and quarters. A note on the door says, "Be back soon, please wait in the big rec room or the vestibule." They decide to go back to the vestibule and continue their conversation.

They sit down again, and Anderson says, "You know, Larry, recently I was thinking about the angels who visited Abraham and Lot, as recorded in the book of Genesis. They ate and drank both with Lot and Abraham. Our make-up now isn't exactly like the angels, even though we look about the same. I realize they have some powers that we don't have, but the Bible says that we have become greater than the angels. I believe it's because of our relationship with Christ. I was also thinking about how we don't need food or drink for sustenance, but a cold drink or a hot drink is still so refreshing!"

Larry replies, "Yes, that is one of the things that boggles the mind at this point. I'm sure we'll never stop learning."

Anderson says, "Remember the saying in our old earth days, "when we stop learning, we're history."

"That's a good one. I also remember an old saying that was a play on words, "time wounds all heels!"

They're laughing when Joseph walks up. He says, "Can I get in on the fun?"

Anderson is still laughing when he says, "We're reminiscing about some old earth humor; a humorous saying, "time wounds all heels."

Joseph laughs loudly, "That is a good one!" In Joseph's jolly way, he says, "What are you boys up to?"

Larry says boldly, "I'm ready to go through the processing center."

Joseph belts out, "Excellent! Congratulations, Larry. As you know, Anderson will be joining you soon."

Joseph looks at Anderson while Larry stands up, "Anderson, make yourself at home. You have free reign of the lodge. Even when you lay down, you have the seclusion of the cabin, or you can stay here. There's a comfortable couch in one of the bigger rec rooms.

Anderson replies, "Thank you." He looks at Larry and says, "It has been good. See you soon, brother."

Joseph and Larry walk out of the lodge to the Eternal Processing Center.

Anderson thinks, "I can use the quiet and the rest right now". He goes to one of the bigger rec rooms and lays down on the most comfortable couch he has ever been on. He wakes up, when he hears some activities in the biggest rec room. It's Joel playing some games with one of the new campers. Anderson says, "How ya doin', Joel?"

"Hi, Anderson. This is one of our newest campers, Judy. She is preparing for her first missionary journey." Joel looks at Judy and says, "Anderson has been on two journeys, and will be going on his third one soon."

Judy says to Anderson, "Congratulations! That is a great accomplishment."

"Thank you, Judy. God's speed on your upcoming journey. I'm sure I'll see both of you soon. I'm going to get a little R&R now."

Anderson decides to walk to his cabin, where he knows he'll have some solitude for a while.

A good bit later, Joseph returns to the lodge from the processing center. He looks in the rooms that Anderson likes, then he sees Joel. "Hi, Joel. Have you seen Anderson recently?"

Joel says, "I think he went to his cabin a good bit ago."

Joseph walks to the cabin. Anderson is lying prostrate on his bunk. Joseph says, "I see you found solace in your old cabin."

Anderson replies, "Yes, just for right now. I'm not lonely. I just wanted some quiet and peace for a short time."

Joseph replies, "That's good." Joseph walks over to him and hands him something long and thin wrapped in white paper.

Anderson asks, "What's this?"

"Open it, my friend."

Anderson unwraps it. It's a name plate with gold letters that says:

Anderson McCollister

Missionary Captain

Anderson just looks at it and says, "I don't know what to say."

Joseph smiles and shakes Anderson's hand. "Congratulations, Anderson. You deserve it, and those letters are real gold!"

Anderson says, "Thank you so much. I'm virtually speechless."

Joseph laughs and says, "We'll go over the details later. Basically, I need help with the base camp from time to time. You won't be spending most of your time here, but I will appreciate your help."

A Light on the Path

Anderson says, "I'm glad to help."

Joseph says, "After you finish your last journey, and I take you for processing, I need to get back to my guardian angel work. I have two angels taking care of my clients now. They're ready for a break, and I need to finish my vacation here. Later, you might also look at base camp as a vacation."

Anderson replies, "I'm sure I will."

Joseph says, "When you do your first base camp, you'll oversee three or four campers. You'll do about everything that I did, except for the portal work. There will be angels working the hosting stations, who will do the portal work for your campers. We'll have plenty of time to go over everything before you do your first base camp. When you're in charge of campers, you'll be using my office. Your new name plate will go on that desk!"

Anderson says, "It will be an honor."

"By the way, Anderson, right before you go through processing, I will take you through the center. It not only has shops; it has more facilities than you could imagine."

Anderson replies, "I would love to see it. Before I leave to visit Angela, will you be available most of the time?"

"I sure will be. Let me know, if you need anything. I know your time is getting close to your third missionary journey."

"Yes, it is. I'll be in touch with you, so we can meet before I leave."

"Excellent. I need to leave soon as well, so let me know when you're ready."

"I want to go over the things I need to share with Angela, then I will pretty much be ready", replied Anderson.

"I'll be in my office complex and quarters most of the time. Have a good rest and study."

"Thank you, Joseph." Joseph walks out of the cabin to return to the lodge.

Anderson thinks, "I'll finish relaxing here, then I'll start reviewing my visit to Angela before I go to the lodge." Anderson starts reflecting about Angela's life, especially when she was a child. He wonders if he truly learned unconditional love. Many thoughts come to him about their relationship. As he thinks about Angela, he prays for her, and he asks God to guide the conversation during his visit with her. Anderson meditates for a good while. Suddenly, he thinks, "I'm ready to go!" He jumps out of his bunk bed and heads toward the lodge.

As he walks down the hall at the lodge, he can see Joseph's door is open. He steps just inside the doorway, and yells, "Joseph!"

He hears Joseph's voice, "I would recognize that strong voice anywhere." Joseph steps into his foyer, "Are you ready to go?"

Anderson replies, "Yes. I was wondering what time of day or night it is in Greenfield, Indiana?"

Joseph says, "Let's go into my conference room, and I'll look. Joseph sits down and investigates some device like a computer. He looks up and says, "It's about 7 in the evening there."

Anderson replies, "I have plenty of time. I want to arrive close to 11 this evening. I just need to meet with you a few minutes before I leave. I think I'll wait in the nature room. I love the atmosphere there."

Joseph says, "Good planning. I'll come and get you before it's time for you to leave."

Anderson walks in the nature room and sits down on the chair with the controls. He starts up the galaxy exhibit. He thinks, "I'll just float through space until it's time to go." He wonders if the main part of heaven has places like the nature room with the galaxy exhibit.

Chapter 20 – The Third Visit

After Anderson has traveled through several galaxies, Joseph walks in and says, "Are you ready Joseph? It's about 10:30 p.m. Greenfield time."

Anderson replies, "Yes, I'm thrilled about going. I've been somewhat anxious lately, but the galaxy travels calmed me down."

Joseph and Anderson walk into the conference room. They both sit down. Joseph says, "We have plenty of time to cover anything you want to."

Anderson says, "I can only think of two things. We might talk longer than some of the visits, since she's my daughter and she needs the Lord. Also, the pick-up location is the same as the arrival location; my daughter's living room."

Joseph says, "No problem. I have extra time to get the portal set, so just relax. You have about 10 to 12 minutes more in earth time." Joseph gets the portal set while he hums a song. Ten minutes later he says, "Its ready, Anderson. You'll enter the portal at the same position in the room. You know how to step into it. Are you ready?"

Anderson replies, "I'm ready." The portal shows, and as soon as he steps into it, he is in Angela's living room. He looks around and sees that Angela has left a dim light on in the adjoining kitchen. He sees the recliner and turns on the floor lamp before he sits down. Evidently, Angela was watching for the light; Anderson can hear footsteps in the upstairs hallway. At the top of the stairs, Angela says, "Is that you, Dad?"

Anderson replies, "It's me, Angela. Everything is okay."

Angela comes downstairs in a light blue robe. At the bottom of the stairs, she peers into the living room and looks at her dad. She says, "Oh, my gosh, Dad, you look thirty –five years old!" She runs over to him and gives him a long hug. She looks up at him and says, "You look like you did, when I was ten to twelve years old!"

Anderson replies, "It's great being with you, Angela."

She asks unassumingly, "Dad, is this a miracle?"

Anderson smiles and says, "I would call it a miracle; at least, in the way I use to look at miracles."

Angela says, "I'm so happy that you could come and see me. Did you pass on?"

Anderson laughs and says, "Lydia may have told you some things, but I will say that I had the most unusual early spring walk!"

Angela says, "Yes, I know about that. They searched a long time, and I went down right away to be with Lydia. I'm so glad something bad didn't happen. For you, this must be a real good thing."

A Light on the Path

Anderson says, "It's different, but it's everything I hoped heaven would be and more. Your mom is there, and your grandparents."

Angela asks, "Have you seen them?"

"No, I'll see them when I go back. I had to see Kenny, Lydia and you before I have the reunion with them."

Angela says, "This is what the world calls a game changer. I've heard reports about some people like you visiting friends or family. I've heard of other visits in Indiana, Tennessee, New York and Texas. Has this become common?"

Anderson replies, "I don't know if it has become common, but I do know that it is happening across the world. I got to know three people, and they each went to see people in New York, Indiana and Tennessee."

Angela asks, "Do you know why this is happening?"

Anderson replies, "It's happening, because the Lord is coming soon."

Angela says, "I wondered about that. I have been more introspective, since your visit at Christmas. I was sad after mom passed on. You got me to reflect on my life, when we talked at Christmas time. After you passed on, I was hurt, but I started to look at things more spiritually."

Anderson says, "I'm glad to hear that you are looking at things spiritually."

Lydia replies, "I started thinking about experiences as a child, teenager and adult. Dad, you inspired me in many ways, and I honestly did not realize it until recently. I thought about the great times as a young child. Things like all the times you and mom took me to Kings Island. I remembered how much I enjoyed all the attention and fun during those young years. I remember Hanna-Barbera's Happy Land at Kings Island. I thoroughly enjoyed all the cartoon characters there: Yogi Bear, Scobey Doo, Huckleberry Hound and Fred Flintstone. Believe it or not, Dad, I enjoyed it so much and missed it years later, that I didn't want heaven to be another fantasy land."

"Sweetheart, you know that I have always told you the truth. You can rest assured that heaven is no fantasy land. I've been there, and it's everything I've dreamed of."

"You were right about my peers. They don't have my best interest at heart, like you do. Now I know that God does too. I've let too many educators influence me in secular ways, especially those in the field of psychology. It is true that humanism is a like a god to them. I never told you that I saw qualities of you in Stephen, and that was the main reason I married him."

Anderson replies, "A father could have no better compliment from his daughter. Thank you. You mean more than the world to me."

A Light on the Path

Angela says, "Dad, I also thought about Mrs. Wright, my second grade Sunday School teacher. Do you remember those full colored poster pictures we use to have in the class room; like of Jesus and the disciples?"

Anderson says, "Yes, I do. We had them also in the 1940s. I also remember Mrs. Wright and her husband. He commuted to Muncie and worked as a toolmaker at the Chevrolet plant."

Angela continues, "There was something about those pictures that became etched in my mind. Maybe I needed a visual aid to realize that God is real. How could I get away from church and the Bible with experiences like that?"

"Angela, Satan also knows that the Lord is coming soon. He is throwing everything in his book at people. The list is long, but it includes false religions, cults, philosophies like humanism, sexual immorality, greed and envy. The people of the world are better at judging others than judging themselves. God judges us. People can't judge God, but they try to judge God in their hearts and their conversations."

Angela says, "I agree. Dad, you would have been a good preacher."

Anderson says, "All of us have a calling. The goal is to fulfill it before we pass on."

Angela replies, "I admired you for a lot of reasons. You were a devoted and faithful husband and father. You were successful in business. You were active in church. I realize now that you do love God, and you have been obedient to him."

"Angela, we have so much to be thankful for. Having you as a daughter is an indescribable blessing. I have also been blessed with your mother; with good parents; with wonderful friends and with a Creator who knows every need I have."

Angela says, "I wish I could see things through your eyes."

"Angela, God has given us individual minds and hearts. He wants each of us to make things right with him, and to be ready for him. Jesus is coming soon. In Matthew 24, Jesus says that it will be a time when we don't expect him. His coming is so close that He wants to bring in a remnant, who haven't made a full commitment to follow him."

Angela asks, "How do I start following Jesus?"

Anderson replies, "Recognize that God is the Father and Creator. Repent of the ways of the world and the ways of the flesh. Acknowledge that Christ saved you and make a commitment to follow him. Angela, it's an eternal commitment, and there's nothing like it."

Angela replies, "Oh, Dad, I believe, and I want to do those things. I want to be with God and with you and mom for eternity. I do repent of my worldly ways, I accept Jesus as my savior. I will do what God wants me to."

A Light on the Path

Anderson says, "Let's pray together. Father, we come humbly before you. We lay aside our sins and dedicate our lives to the ways of your Son. I know you forgive Angela, and you love her. Show her your ways. Be with her always. May she always find shelter in your arms. She commits her life to Jesus Christ. In his name, we pray. Amen."

"Dad, I will be eternally grateful for all you have done, especially coming to me tonight. Once again, you have made sure that your daughter has what she needs. I love you."

"I love you, Angela. Get the word out in any way you can, that Jesus is coming soon. It's a simple message that means so much. Stay in touch with Lydia and Kenny. Pray for them and encourage them. Meet with them, when you can."

Angela replies, "I will. Dad is all of the civil unrest and problems in the world a sign that Jesus is coming soon?"

"Yes, it is. Jesus taught us that only the Father knows the day and the hour. God is concerned that everyone possible be ready for the rapture of the church. Matthew 24 and 1 Thessalonians 4 tells us about the rapture. The book of Revelation and Matthew 24 also tell us about the signs of the end of this era. Men, women and children who know Christ are just beginning to enjoy freedom and everlasting life with Jesus."

Angela asks, "Do you know if these problems in our country and in the world are going to get worse?"

Anderson says, "I only know that they will probably get worse. I know they are signs of the end of this world. I know that a global currency is coming that will lead to the mark of the beast."

Angela says, "There is more talk about a global currency. I think it's frightening."

Anderson replies, "It's frightening for those who aren't following Jesus. Once the global currency is in place, the global organization will tap into every living person, and require that they take the mark of the beast. People who take the mark are doomed. Encourage people to follow Christ before the global currency is established. The rapture of the church will happen before the mark of the beast is required. We want people to be prepared in Christ before that happens. Tell people, Angela, that Jesus can come at any moment. Tell them not to procrastinate. God's Word says, "Now is the day of salvation."

"Yes, Dad, I will. The things you're telling me are coming back to me. I know I learned about them, when I was growing up in church."

Anderson asks, "Did Clint learn those things when he was young?"

A Light on the Path

Angela replies, "I think he learned a lot of it in church. When we didn't take him, his friend, Luke, and Luke's parents took him. They lived just a block from us."

"I remember Luke. I want you to tell Clint something for me. I want him to know it came from me. It's something that only Clint, Luke and I know about."

Angela replies, "I'll be sure to tell him. This should be very interesting."

"Angela, I want you to tell Clint that his grandpa wants him to get things right with God and to be ready for the Lord's coming. He will know that it came direct from me, when you relay this story to him. You might remember when Stephen and you had to go to a three-day business convention in Louisville. You asked me to stay with Clint and Luke during those three days."

Angela says, "Yes, I remember that."

Anderson continues, "Clint and Luke were fifteen then. In the summer they had gone to the Indiana State Fair, and they met two seventeen-year-old girls from Dayton, Ohio. About 3:30 that Friday in October, Clint told me that he was going to Luke's house, and they would be back later. I didn't realize they were coming back about twenty minutes later and took your other car. At the time, I was probably talking with your mom on the phone. Of course, they had learning permits, but not regular driver's licenses. When they returned about midnight, I was up, and Clint said they had gone to Dayton to take the two girls to a movie. You can tell Clint that I remember the IU sweatshirt he was wearing that night."

Clint begged me not to tell you, and he promised he would never do anything like that again. I promised him I wouldn't tell, but that night I made Clint sleep on the couch. In the morning, I had him make breakfast, and I had Luke do the dishes."

Angela laughs and says, "It might have been a good thing that you didn't tell; at least for him. I probably would have grounded him for a month."

"Tell Clint that I told you that story, so he will know that I came back from heaven to tell you, Stephen and him that the Lord is coming real soon. I know you will also tell Stephen about my visit."

"Oh yes, I'll tell him over breakfast in the morning. I am confident that he will believe me, because he knows about the people who have returned to warn loved ones. Also, he already knows that Lydia and Kenny said you had come to visit."

"Angela, the Lord wants his people to follow his commandments; to help others; to support the church and to spread the gospel. Ask Clint and Stephen to do the same. I know that Kenny, Lydia and you will have a

A Light on the Path

productive and joyful time, when you meet. With the time you have left, the three of you decide how you can best share the good news. I wish I could be there."

Angela smiles and replies, "If you could be there, we would ask you to chair the meeting."

"Angela, I will have to leave soon. Would you make me a cup of coffee? I know you keep the little cups of mild and medium roast."

Angela says, "I sure do. A little cream and Splenda like always?"

Anderson says, "Yes, that would be perfect."

Angela comes back in the room after she starts the coffee maker. She asks, "How do you get back, Dad?"

Anderson laughs and says, "The way I came! It's like a door to another dimension. I can tell you firsthand, there is a fourth dimension! I think my transport will be ready after we finish our time together with coffee. I can also tell you firsthand that you have a guardian angel."

Angela says, "I'm glad to know that. I know you can't tell me a lot about heaven right now, but do you know who your guardian angel is?"

"Yes, I do, and it's just amazing how superb everything is in heaven."

Angela says, "I'll go get the coffee. I made you mild roast."

She brings in the coffee, and Anderson says, "When we finish the coffee, it's alright for you to be nearby, but not in the same room. Don't stand in the kitchen and watch me leave. Just rinse out the cups, and I'll depart before you know it."

"Dad, I know this is silly for me to ask, but do you know for sure that I will get to see you and mom in heaven and others I know?"

"Yes, Angela, I know for sure. You don't have to worry. A scripture that has helped me for over twenty years is Romans 14: 23, "Whatever is not of faith is sin." With faith in Christ, it will take you all the way!"

Angela replies, "That's so good to know. We have assurance then that anyone who follows Christ will be in heaven for eternity."

"Yes, we have that assurance, Angela. Believe me; I want you to be in heaven as much as anyone. I'm here this evening to make sure that you will be in heaven. Following Christ is the whole key. Make Him the center of your life. He is God, and He is the one who saved you. You can make sure that Clint and Stephen will be in heaven. Like everyone else who believes, they just need to follow Christ daily. Encourage everyone to study the gospel of John. It's a great guide for daily living in Christ."

"Dad, thank you so much for all that you have given. Since we've about finished our coffee, I think it's time that I give you a real big hug."

They both stand and give each other a hug that expresses how much they mean to each other. Anderson says, "Angela, there's nothing like having

A Light on the Path

a passion for the things of God. Jesus told us that it is more blessed to give than to receive. God blesses us in every way. I've always wanted the best for you, and I will be thinking about you daily. I'm looking forward to our reunion in heaven."

"Me too, Dad. I love you, and I appreciate everything you have done. Thank you so much for being here this evening. I know you have to go, so let me give you one more hug."

As they hug, Anderson says, "I love you, Angela."

As Angela gathers up the coffee cups, she says, "I'll see you soon, Dad."

As Angela walks into the kitchen, the portal appears in front of Anderson. He steps into it, and he is gone in a second."

Angela doesn't hear anything, but she senses her dad left. She looks back into the living room and sees that he has departed.

Chapter 21 – New Beginnings

Angela goes to bed by 12:30 a.m. She is wide awake in bed thinking about her dad's visit, and all the engrossing things they talked about. She goes to sleep about 1:30 a.m.

A little after 7:00 a.m. the smell of bacon wakens her. She thinks, "Bacon is the one thing that will get me out of bed this morning." She takes just a minute to freshen up, since she can already taste the bacon before she goes downstairs. When she gets downstairs, Stephen is putting breakfast on the table. When he looks at her, she is standing near the table looking at him with a big smile on her face.

Stephen says light heartedly, "What is going on with you?"

Angela replies, "Dad visited me last night."

Stephen replies, "So you had a nice dream about your dad last night?"

"No, he visited with me in the living room."

Stephen hesitates then says, "Let's sit down to breakfast before it gets cold, and we'll talk about his visit."

After they sit down, Angela says, "I want to say a prayer."

After she prays, Stephen says, "There is something different about you."

Angela says, "Yes, there is. I committed my life to Christ after Dad and I talked a while."

Stephen says, "You're sure it wasn't a dream?"

Angela replies, "We both heard on the news about people across the country being visited by loved ones who had passed on. We also know that dad visited Lydia then Kenny. Last night he visited me."

"Wow, that's a lot to take in. I certainly need to ponder what you're saying."

"I'm a little surprised, Stephen, that you have some doubt, since you know dad visited Lydia and Kenny. He told me something last night that only he, Clint and Clint's old friend, Luke, knew for years. After I share it with Clint, he will tell you that only his grandpa could have told me that."

Stephen asks, "What was that?"

"I'll let Clint tell you the story after I tell him what his grandpa told me last night. It happened during the time you and I were at the business convention in Louisville, when Clint was 15."

Stephen says, "I remember that convention. I do remember your dad staying with Clint and Luke while we were gone."

They finish breakfast, and Angela calls Clint. He has just gotten up, since its Saturday. After Angela tells Clint what his grandpa told her last night, Clint says, "Holy Cow! Grandpa must have been there last night."

A Light on the Path

Angela says, "He even remembered the IU sweatshirt that you had on that night."

Clint replies, "I forgot about that, but he's right. What else did he say?"

"He wants you to be right with God, and to be prepared for the Lord's return. He said it will be soon."

Clint says, "Yes, I believe I'm right with God, and I will do my best to be prepared. I do believe you, mom. Does dad believe you?"

Angela replies, "I want you to talk with your dad, so he will know for sure. Will you also tell Sara about your grandpa's visit and the message he gave us?"

"Yes, I'm calling her today, and I will tell her. I love you. I'll talk with dad now."

Angela gives the phone to Stephen. He says, "Hi, son."

"Dad, grandpa would have been there last night for mom to know that story. Grandpa never told the two of you what happened that night during his lifetime. He made a promise, and I promised never to do anything that crazy again. You know that he is a man of his word. I'm amazed that he even remembered what I was wearing that night."

Stephen says, "Clint, it's hard to believe, but I believe you, and I believe your mom. To be honest, I'm stunned."

Clint replies, "I'm stunned too, but it's the truth."

"Do you want to talk to your mom again?"

Clint says, "I have to get dressed to meet a couple friends for breakfast in about fifteen minutes."

"Okay, Clint. I'll tell mom. I'm sure she'll call you soon. I love you."

"Love you, Dad. Bye for now."

Stephen hands the phone back to Lydia and sits down at the kitchen table.

Angela says, "Stephen, I know it's hard to comprehend, but it really happened. I'm glad you believe Clint and me."

"Yes, I do. Later today I want to find out everything your dad said. Right now, I need to walk Ralph. I put him in the garage yesterday evening."

"Have a good walk. I'm going to call Lydia now about Dad being here."

Angela dials Lydia. "Hi, Angela, do you have some good news for me?"

Angela replies, "I have some breaking, good news! Dad was here last night!"

"I'm so glad for you, Angela. Did you recognize him?"

Angela replies, "Yes I did, but he is so young looking! You know, Lydia, Dad's visit was a great panacea for me. Before dad came to see me, I went through spells of sadness after I lost them. Also, after you told me about his visit to you and Kenny, I went through stages of confusion to anxiety."

A Light on the Path

"It is wonderful to hear that his visit was a big help to you. Any other news?"

Angela says, "Of course! I committed my life to Christ!"

Lydia responds, "Praise God, Angela. That is the best news!"

"Dad wants us to meet, so we can get out the message of the approaching rapture and Dad's visits."

Lydia replies, "You could come here. Kenny lives just an hour away, and you could stay here as long as you want."

Angela says, "Finals start soon. I think I would like to come down next weekend to get things kicked off. After finals, I could come back, so we could get some considerable work done. Would you call Kenny and ask him if he could make it next Saturday?"

"I'll call him right away. What time do you want to meet here next Saturday? When I come back, I'll drive, but this time I'll fly. Since the airline goes to Charlotte before landing in Knoxville, could you pick me up at the Knoxville airport around 1 p.m. Saturday?"

"Sure, I can," replied Lydia.

Angela says, "I'll fly back Monday, since they have to go to Charlotte first."

Lydia says, "I'll ask Kenny to meet us here at 4:00, so we'll have plenty of time. Since it's an important meeting, we should allow about three hours. Kenny should have enough time, since he likes to be back home by 8:30 p.m. this time of year. I'll have food prepared, so we can break for supper between 5 and 5:30."

Angela replies, "Sounds like a good plan. When you confirm the time with Kenny, text me and I'll book the flight."

Lydia says, "I will. When Kenny gets here, you'll have to ask him the details about what happened to my neighbor, Conard, during the neighborhood watch last night."

Angela asks, "What happened?"

"Conard called me this morning and said someone took a shot at him and another neighbor while they were on watch duty last night. I think he didn't give me a lot of details, so I wouldn't get worried. He said he was getting ready to call Kenny and give him the details. Next Saturday Kenny can fill us in."

Angela responds vehemently, "I want to find out what happened!"

Lydia replies, "Well, I'm glad that we have an active neighborhood watch."

Angela says, "Saturday will be here real soon. I'm glad we can meet."

Lydia replies, "Me too. I'll call Kenny, then I'll text you. Love you."

Angela replies, "Love you too. See you soon."

A Light on the Path

Lydia calls Kenny immediately. Kenny sees Lydia's name on his cell phone window, "Hi, Lydia, how are you?"

"I'm doing well, Kenny. Angela just called me. Anderson visited her last night and she accepted Christ."

Kenny exclaims, "Thanks be to God! That's great news, Lydia."

"Angela and I would like to meet with you here. Could you be here by 4:00 next Saturday?"

Kenny says, "Yes, I can. Are we going to meet about the things that Anderson mentioned?"

Lydia replies, "Yes. We all agree it's what we need to do. We're so fortunate that Anderson could come back and be with us; even for a short while. Oh, by the way, Kenny, when we meet, Angela and I would like to know some details about what happened to Conard last night."

Kenny says, "Sure, I will tell you. I think Conard wanted to talk to me, since I'm a retired law officer. Should I bring anything Saturday?"

Lydia says, "If you can, bring a pen and a note pad. I'm preparing supper, so we can take a break after 5. We'll eat during the meeting, if we want to. Can you meet with us until 7:00? I know you like to be home by 8:30."

Kenny replies, "Sure I can. I could stay as long as 7:30."

"That's great, Kenny. I'm glad you can be here. I think we can get a lot accomplished in three hours. Have a safe trip. Call anytime."

Kenny says, "Have a good week. Until then."

Lydia texts Angela right away to confirm next Saturday, so she can reserve her flight."

Kenny writes on his calendar to leave for Mount Holly by 2:45 Saturday.

When Saturday rolls around, Stephen and Angela arrive at the Indianapolis airport at 7:30. Her flight leaves at 9:30. She tells Stephen before she goes through security, "Flying instead of driving this time will give me extra time to get ready for finals."

Stephen says, "Be careful and have a good trip. I love you." He kisses her and watches her go through the security line.

Her flight lands at 1:25 in Knoxville, and Lydia is waiting near the baggage claim area. They drive through light rain back to Mount Holly. They pull in the driveway about 2:45. Lydia says, "All the food is ready."

As Lydia puts her car in park, Angela says, "Here comes Pockets."

Lydia says, "Every time I see Pockets, I think of Anderson."

Kenny loads a few emergency supplies, and he leaves his farm for East Tennessee at 2:45. He thinks, "What a dreary day. I'm glad I'm headed to an important meeting." It's completely overcast and drizzling rain. In no time he's on Soco Rd. and then on 140 West. As he passes by the venerable landscape of the gorge in the North Carolina Mountains, he also thinks of the timeless view of the Smoky Mountains before he gets to Anderson's house. He thinks, "Even though the mountains seem timeless to man, it might be an entirely different story for eternity. The strokes of God's brush give us a whole new perspective." As he passes the Smoky Mountains and gets close to his destination, he also thinks about how mankind has already surpassed the calm before the storm.

He pulls his Jeep into Lydia's drive at 3:45. He thinks, "Good; I like being early." Right before he gets to the front porch, he pets Pockets. Lydia greets him at the door. She says, "Welcome on a beautiful spring day."

Kenny laughs and says, "It's a beautiful day to the earthworms."

When he steps inside, Lydia and Angela give him a hug. Lydia asks, "Do you want coffee, hot tea, diet soda or water?"

Kenny replies, "It's a good day for coffee." Lydia has a pot of coffee ready and pours it in a big mug for Kenny.

Lydia says, "Come on in and make yourself comfortable. We're going to meet at Anderson's long table."

Kenny says, "You know, legend has it that King Arthur met at a round table with his knights many centuries ago. I believe this long table is more important than all of the meetings King Arthur had."

Angela says, "That's an excellent message. I totally agree."

They sit down with their coffee and get out their pads and pens. Angela says, "It looks like we're starting by 3:00. I know we're all thankful that we can be here together after Dad's phenomenal visits with us. I think we all know what Dad wants us to plan before the rapture of the church. Kenny, I might be even more curious than Lydia. Before we get started could you give us the details about last Friday night and the shot that was fired at Conard and his neighbor?"

Kenny says, "I would be glad to. As Lydia knows, the neighborhood watch group out of necessity has gotten more active here. There are now twelve neighbors or more participating in the around the clock watch. We see their post where the circle in the road begins. By now they know Lydia and her car. I stopped to greet them. They also know about me. The neighbor on the corner has provided chairs; a folding table; saw horses for the road and some protection like barrels and sand bags.

Friday night, just after 11:30, a car pulled up to them that they did not recognize. Four young men were in it, and they didn't let them through. Conard didn't know if they were the same men that pulled in Anderson's driveway, while he was visiting Angela during Christmas. It wasn't the same

A Light on the Path

car. If they were the same men, they didn't know Conard, because only Conard knew who fired the shot in the air that night.

The men didn't say much. They said they were out for a drive. When they weren't allowed entrance, one of the guy's said something rude, but Conard didn't hear him clearly. They backed up; swerved the car around and squealed the tires when they took off. Conard's neighbor was watching them closely. He had his hand on his rifle. Suddenly, they stopped quickly when they got about forty yards away. When their brake lights came on, Conard's neighbor raised his rifle to shooting position. Suddenly, one of them must have reached out the window with a handgun and fired a shot. Conard heard the round go by him. As soon as his neighbor heard the shot, he fired his rifle, and they could hear the round hit somewhere on the car. There was this big bang, then the car sped off."

Angela yells, "Wow, it's like an O.K. Corral story!"

Lydia asks, "So Conard and his friend were alright?"

Kenny says, "Yes. Conard told me that there are six shifts around the clock. He and his neighbor friend watch from 8 p.m. to midnight. Two younger men who work the second shift, watch from midnight to 4 a.m. I don't know all the shift details, but Conard said a retired couple he knows, watch from 8 a.m. until noon. He said they have subs too that they can call for fill in. I understand that they have all the neighbors' numbers in their cell phones and can get a message out quickly. Lydia, I know all the people watching have your cell phone number in their phones. You know, people have a right to protect themselves."

Lydia says, "Thank you, Kenny for the report. It's good to know they're watching out for us."

Angela says, "Yes, it is. We also know that we have a job to watch out for people spiritually. We're thankful for the neighborhood watch group and the many blessings that God gives us. Let's go to God in prayer and ask him to guide us and give us wisdom in our meeting today."

Angela prays, "Thank you, Father, for our meeting. We're thankful that the three of us could get together. Bless this house. Thank you so much for Dad, who loves us and is concerned about our welfare and eternal souls. We thank you for letting Dad come back to visit the three of us. We're thankful for the message that you sent with him.

We don't know about large scale marketing, but we ask you to give us wisdom, so we can effectively get out the message that Dad gave us. When we share the message of Dad's visit and the approaching rapture of the church, open the hearts of those receiving the message. Guide us now as we make plans to share your message. In Jesus' name we pray. Amen."

A Light on the Path

Angela, Lydia and Kenny take a couple seconds to look at each other to see who is going to talk first. They all smile at each other and Angela says, "Who has the first idea?"

Lydia says, "The first thing that came to my mind is one of the Knoxville TV stations that has a daily interview show of local people at 4:00. I think there are about five TV stations in Knoxville, including the three traditional network stations."

Angela says, "Good idea. I think there are five or more stations in Indianapolis. There is also a Christian TV station in the Indianapolis area."

Kenny says, "Maggie Valley TV broadcasts come out of Asheville. I think they also have four TV stations in the area. I don't know what to suggest, but I would be glad to contact them."

Angela says, "Why don't we write down what we individually shared, then we'll have record of the television markets in Indianapolis, Asheville and Knoxville. There are several ways to also market on line. I'm no authority on internet marketing, but I know there are blogger groups, social networks and professional networks. A lot of people who have an organization or their own work have a website. Each of us could afford a website, but with the three of us together, we could have an excellent website."

Kenny adds, "That's a superb idea. Pooling our money is a smart way to promote the message. God has blessed all three of us. We could have our own bodacious website and our own emails for our work."

Lydia says, "I'm no computer expert by a long shot, but I think $300 would give us a great start for a successful website."

Angela says, "Wonderful! We're getting there. We will have to organize out efforts. Without a plan, it would just be a slipshod effort."

Kenny says, "There are probably hundreds of Christian radio stations nationwide. We could find out how to reach as many stations as possible. I know some people do it through their computers."

Lydia adds, "There are also some widely televised TV and radio shows that have a Christian theme."

Angela says, "We also need to decide how to promote to local and regional churches. The three of us live in areas that cover a big area. Kenny, could you look into how we could get mailers or other media to reach churches not only in your area, but also the areas of Chattanooga, Asheville and Charlotte?"

Kenny replies, "I would be glad to."

Lydia says, "I have friends and contacts not only in Crossville but west of Crossville. I could look into churches in Crossville, Sevier County and Jefferson County, as well as in the Knoxville and Nashville areas."

A Light on the Path

Angela exclaims, "Excellent! Of course, I live near Indianapolis, and the Indianapolis region has hundreds and hundreds of churches including those in Shelby County, Brownsburg, Zionsville, Carmel, Noblesville, Martinsville and many other areas."

Lydia says, "Let's keep the momentum going. I'll bring the food to you, while you and Kenny discuss things. Do both of you want more coffee or something else?" They all go with more coffee, and Lydia fills their cups. As they talk about places to reach in their own areas, Lydia brings them plates and forks for some good smelling stir fry she made. She also brings them a plate with pieces of celery, carrots and oranges.

They ask Kenny to say the blessing. After Kenny prays, he says, "I would like to make a general comment while we start eating. In sales, they say attitude is everything. In fact, I'm sure I remember Anderson saying that. While we bring people the message of the rapture and Anderson's visits, we should also think about how we share. Basically, it's with a good attitude. God wants us to bring joy to a lost world. The enemy is always lurking in the shadows, but it's up to us to make a difference. I think Anderson said that in the New Testament, we are taught to share the message of Christ with gentleness and respect. We should not be nervous or shy. We're ambassadors of Christ. We are representing the power of the universe."

Angela says, "Kenny, that's an excellent point. We should always remember those things, as we do this work. We are living in perilous times. Many people in our country and in other countries are suffering greatly. We complain that gas is over $6.00 a gallon now and that the death rate from the civil unrest in just our country is over 3,000. God has given us life and financial resources to help others. We don't have a lot of time left, and we should do everything we can."

Lydia says, "Kenny and I are retired, and we have considerable time to work on this mission. Angela are you going to have much time?"

Angela replies, "I'll be done with finals in two weeks, and I'm not teaching any summer classes. Stephen is working full-time, and we have plenty of resources. I just started thinking about teaching only part-time for the fall term. There isn't much time left, and I want to do my part. This evening we can divide up the research and leg work. We could get the website up and running by using the computer and phone. Don't you think we should meet back here in about a month with a solid plan in place?"

Kenny says, "Absolutely. I will do everything I can to be ready in a month. I agree that we could get the website started before then."

Lydia smiles and says, "I make it unanimous! I feel good about the strategy we're developing."

Kenny says, "I feel good about our early progress also. We can maintain our progress by taking one step at a time. I remember Anderson quoting the scripture in Romans that says, "Whatever is not of faith is sin." If we do our job, and go by faith, we don't have to worry. God will lead us every step of the way. Like Anderson, we're working for God now."

Chapter 22 – Spiritual Reunion

While Kenny, Lydia and Angela have been busy with the beginning of their new mission, Joseph has arranged a small celebration party for Anderson's return and the completion of his third missionary journey. Joseph has gotten Joel together with three of the new campers, Judy, Virginia and Marie. As soon as Anderson walks out of the conference room and into the hallway, Joseph says, "Congratulations! Anderson. You are officially now a missionary captain!" Anderson has a big smile on his face as Joseph gives him a hug. Come in the big rec room; we have a celebration ready for you!"

As they gather in the rec room, Joseph announces, "We're celebrating Anderson's official induction as a Missionary Captain. After our small party, I will be going with Anderson to the processing center. To celebrate, we're having angel cake and heavenly punch. Joel, will you give the toast?"

Joel says, "Congratulations, Anderson, on your accomplishment. I had the honor of being the first one you saw in heaven. We toast you at this time for your unwavering commitment to God's kingdom, and to your success at base camp." Joseph, Joel, Anderson, Judy, Virginia and Marie raise their glasses and drink the toast together. Joel says, "Anderson, we would like to hear from you."

Anderson says, "I thank all of you. Joseph has been a great inspiration. My life's journey on earth was not perfect, but all my life, I did love the things of God. Judy, Virginia and Marie, I wish you the best at base camp and in your missionary journeys. I marvel at the idea of eternity in God's Kingdom. I look forward to being with all of you forever."

They all applaud after Anderson's brief speech. Anderson shakes Joel's hand and says, "Joel, I will always remember that you were the first one I met here. Thank you for all of your help."

Joel replies, "I'm looking forward to working with you in the future."

Marie, Virginia and Judy come up to Anderson and shake his hand. Anderson says, "Judy, we met recently. Who are your friends?" Judy says, "This is Marie from Lindsay, Oklahoma. This is Virginia from Rochester, New York. When we met, I don't think I told you that I'm from Rensselaer, Indiana."

Anderson says, "It's good to meet you." He adds blithely, "I'm from Mount Holly, Tennessee, near Knoxville. We could start a travel consulting business from New York to Oklahoma!"

They all laugh. Judy says, "We do represent a big section of the United States."

Anderson says, "Thank you so much for being at this celebration. The fellowship and the love of God means a lot."

Marie replies, "I think the three of us feel the same way. We are happy to celebrate with you."

Joseph comes up to Anderson and his new friends and says, "Has everyone had some cake and punch?"

In unison they say, "Yes."

Anderson asks Joseph, "Do we have plenty of time or do we need to leave for the processing center?"

Joseph replies, "We have time to enjoy all the punch and cake we want, and possibly a little time for a video game." Joseph smiles and walks over to Joel.

Anderson looks at his new friends and says, "Would you say that the party will be breaking up soon?"

They laugh, and Virginia says, "Yes, it sounds like it, but we're not rushed. We know that Joseph has to return to his guardian angel duties."

Anderson says, "Since we have some time left, let's go get some more punch and cake!" They have a good time talking and sharing some experiences. After they finish with the refreshments, Anderson says, "I better get with Joseph. I know he needs to help me at the processing center. It was great talking with you."

Judy says, "We wish you God's speed."

Anderson says, "I wish all of you God's blessings on your missionary journeys."

Anderson walks over to Joseph and Joel. He thanks Joel for being at his celebration party. He looks at Joseph and says, "I'm ready when you are."

Joseph says, "Very good." He looks at Joel and says, "I will see you soon, my friend."

Joseph and Anderson walk through the lodge vestibule, and Anderson says, "Give me a second before we walk out of the vestibule; it's such a beautiful atmosphere."

Joseph says, "It sure is."

After they spend a few seconds in the vestibule, they walk outside into the partially wooded cabin area of the camp. After the camp, they walk into the meadow, passing some of the hosting stations. Joseph asks, "Have you thought about what is west of the vast meadow?"

Anderson says, "No."

Joseph says, "When you first arrived, you were headed south, and you saw the hosting stations in the meadow and farther back you saw the Eternal Processing Center."

Anderson replies, "That's right."

Joseph continues, "As you know, the base camp is to the east. The west side of the meadow gradually slopes downhill like the north side of the

A Light on the Path

meadow. Because of the slope, you can't see the tree line west of the meadow from here. As you walk down hill on the west side, you'll eventually come to seven hundred acres of woods and wildlife."

Anderson exclaims, "No way!"

Joseph laughs and says, "It's so expansive that we didn't have time to go there during your base camp and missionary activities. On the far side of the woods is a small lake and a large creek runs from the lake into the woods. You know about the lion lying down by the lamb in heaven. Well, in the woods, you have cougar, coyote and black bear lying down by the deer and each other!"

Anderson says, "That's astounding!"

Joseph says, "Of course the wild turkey roost in the tree tops. There are also foxes, box turtles, owls, hawks, eagles, quail, pheasant, ducks, geese and much more. Of course, there are plenty of fish, insects, berries, leaves, roots and grass for all the animals."

Anderson asks, "When are we going?"

Joseph laughs loudly and says, "When you have base camp duty, there will be time for you to explore the woods. You just leave word with one of the angels associated with the base camp and give them an idea of when you'll return. They will give you a map of the trails in the woods." They pass the last hosting station before the processing center. For the first time, Anderson can see the grandeur of the building and of the huge front doors and the amazing stone art work on the front of the building. Instead of gargoyles, Anderson sees stone work of Christ, the apostles, cherubims, angels and altars. There is also a large carving of Moses with the Ten Commandments. The last two that catch his eye before they open the huge door is a carving of the Ark of the Covenant and one of John the Baptist baptizing Jesus. Above the door, carved in stone, it says, "All Who Enter Are Blessed by the Light of the Son".

As they walk through the doors and into the concourse, Anderson exclaims, "This is a new definition for massive! I remember seeing pictures of the concourse in Grand Central Station, but there is no comparison."

Joseph says, "I think the concourse is 340 feet by 180 feet. The processing center covers over one hundred acres. There are over 120 shops and about 170 office complexes. I can't show you everything, since we must get you processed. Two of the things that I know you'll like is our Great Barrier Reef Aquarium and our Universe Control Station. I can only take you into the outer office of Universe Control, but you'll even enjoy that. On earth, there are Mission Control Stations. Compared to our technology, Mission Control is something like pre-renaissance technology."

A Light on the Path

The building has four huge hallways that branch from the concourse at 45-degree angles. They cross the concourse to the right and take the back hallway. They first pass some shops, and one of the first shops they pass says, "S. S. & D." in big letters. Anderson asks, "What is S.S. &D.?"

Joseph laughs and says, "Signs, Seals and Delivered. That's where I got your name plate!"

Anderson cracks a smile and says, "Would you believe it. 170 shops, and the first one I notice made my name plate!"

Joseph laughs and says, "You'll have a lot of déjà vu experiences in heaven!"

They pass a lot of shops on both sides of the hallway, then Anderson notices a shop that simply says "Bicycles". Anderson asks, "There are bicycles in heaven?"

Joseph says, "You betcha. Everybody loves them. There is a splendid green way on the west side of the processing center, and they're scattered all around heaven. Just like on earth, people use the green ways for walking, running and cycling. We have people who couldn't run the last twenty to forty years of their life, and they love to run here."

Anderson says, "I can identify with that."

As they pass the last shop, they come to an entrance that has, "GREAT BARRIER REEF" in large, blue neon letters. Joseph says, "You'll love this. We don't have much time today, but you'll know where to bring your family and friends. In heaven there are no admission charges! Inside, the first area is a large room, encircled by very large aquariums. You get a good sample of the variety. As they walk in the beautifully tiled room, Joseph says, "This aquarium is the sea life you see around coral."

Anderson says, "What colorful fish!"

Joseph says, "By standing in the center of the room, you get a good view of the aquariums. To the left of you, are the different sharks that are at the Great Barrier Reef. In other aquariums, you can see sting rays, sea turtles, and many other types of aquatic life."

Anderson says, "No pun intended, but this is an out of the world experience!"

Joseph says, "I never get tired of it. I love coming here. Well, Anderson, we better keep moving. I want to show you the Universe Control Center before you go through processing. The control center is over 80,000 square feet. You'll have time to see the front office and get an idea of how it operates."

Anderson says, "I'm ready."

As they walk out of the Barrier Reef Aquarium, Joseph says, "We're close now to the entrance of the Control Center." Sure enough, just a few

A Light on the Path

office doors down the mega hallway, they come to a pristine office entrance that says, "Universe Control Center". There are no armed guards, but Anderson notices a couple of NFL sized angels, who look like they could throw some supernatural power around. Joseph says, "As you might guess, this is a restricted area, but saints and angels are welcome to come to the large visitor's center. The actual Universe Control Center is on the other side of the visitor's center."

The area is laid out in a one-way winding hall that leads to the end of the universe displays. The halls have plenty of width, so one can easily pass those looking at an exhibit or video. Anderson stops and looks at a video that shows in fast motion the formation of a star. Joseph says, "The next display and video shows the formation of a planet."

Anderson says, "I've always wondered about the veracity of earth scientists who talk about the millions of years on earth, as well as earth being over one billion years old."

Joseph laughs and says, "That's actually a good point. No disrespect to an open-minded scientist, but their assumptions are as wide as an ocean. Many scientists on earth perceive many layers of earth's ground or crust as being millions of years old. Not to be condescending, they don't consider many variables of climate and earth changes. There are changes in the weather like storms, heavy rain, floods, heavy wind, tornadoes, hurricanes and others. There are changes in the earth like earthquakes, volcanoes, decay, landslides, geysers and many other changes. Can you imagine how much the flood during Noah's time changed the structure of earth layers?"

Anderson says, "Those are the kind of things that I've wondered about."

Joseph says, "Frankly their dating methods are inaccurate. Another subject of their inaccurate dating is dinosaur bones. Four to seven thousand years ago, I saw dinosaurs on most of the earth, including in the Middle East, Africa, America and Europe. They are even recorded in the Bible. The Old Testament author calls them behemoths. There have been many warm and cold ages or hot and ice ages on earth. Many times, when an earth scientist thinks an earth layer was deposited one million years ago, it is very likely that is was deposited one to two thousand years ago. The earth goes through significant changes in a few hundred years, and many changes in two thousand years."

Anderson continues to look at more intriguing videos of the universe. He says, "I know we can't stay here long, but even in their visitor's center there is so much to look at. I know it's off the subject at hand, but all of these displays about galaxies and the creation of stars and planets make me think about the creation of mankind and angels."

A Light on the Path

Joseph smiles and nods, "I think I know what you're getting at. Well, since we have limited time right now, I'll try to give some perspective on that. Many angels like myself are new. There are millions of angels that were created roughly 10,000 to 20,000 years ago, based on man's time frame. Of course, God has always been here. Angels like Michael and Gabriel, we call veterans, because only God knows how long they have been with him, as well as millions of others. Now God is building his kingdom with saints. There's over two billion so far!"

A former veteran angel was Lucifer, but he ended up having delusions of grandeur. I think you know the brief story about him. He was kicked out of heaven with his followers before man and woman were created. Heaven has several residents, who are much more powerful than Lucifer. Of course, there is no comparison to God, the Son, the blessed Christ. Others like Michael and the cherubims have much more power than Lucifer had. I'm guessing that God allowed the banished Lucifer to keep some of his powers, because free-will is part of God's make up. Many angels and saints wonder why God allowed Lucifer to keep some of his powers. I believe since God is a God of love, he has a hard time giving up even a disobedient child."

Anderson says, "Your information is just as interesting as the Universe visitor's center. I can always come back here, but now I'm anxious to see my family and friends."

Joseph bellows, "I don't blame you! Let's go, my friend." As they walk out of the Universe Control Visitor's Center, Joseph says, "Before we get to the processing center, there's a couple quick things that I want to share with you. As you know, Anderson, a lot of souls on earth are still in jeopardy. There are many who need to be pointed to the light of Christ before the rapture of the church.

We are spending more time organizing who needs to visit who. As you know, Billy Graham oversees the missionary captains. You might be interested in knowing that several more are helping with the operation, including D.L. Moody, John Wesley and Martin Luther. I know you are willing to go on more missionary journeys after you visit with Ruth, your parents, Russell and other family and friends. You will have plenty of time to enjoy their fellowship. Since we both know that time is short, I know that you'll want to get back to the base camp, when you can."

Anderson says, "Definitely. I'm thrilled to hear that hall of famers are working with Billy Graham."

Joseph continues, "Yes, they are an impressive group of saints. Off the record, I just want to say that I would like to see you help some people that I've been watching over. They include a farmer near Calgary, Alberta; a business lady in Quebec City and a retired merchant in Tucson, Arizona. I'm

A Light on the Path

going to ask that whichever one you do last; you be given an added perk of eight to ten hours of sightseeing. Billy Graham will have the list, so the final decision is his. He'll get input from guardian angels like me, and help with decision making from Moody, Wesley, Luther and others. It's a big undertaking to reach who we can, while there's still time."

Anderson says, "I would love to meet Moody, Wesley, and Luther."

Joseph beams with a big smile, "You will, my friend. You'll meet others as well, like William Tyndale and St. Augustine. Since we'll be at the processing center soon, I want to give you a brief overview. It won't take long. They will give you some orientation on heaven. They confirm your total identity like your name, birth, where you lived and when you passed on. Since there is such a great number of saints, they have counted all of you. Soon you will find out your number; I know it's over two billion!

Hardly no one will see your number, which is on a patch of fabric. They have a method that instantly plies the patch to about the top of a shirt pocket area. The patch is transparent unless a type of black light is used. You get extra patches that can be used on other clothing, if you so desire. I know you're wondering about the purpose of the patch. You won't need it in your heavenly realm, but when you're outside of regular heaven, the Apostle Paul called it the third heaven, just wear clothing that has the patch on it. Eventually the angels at the entrances will know you, like they know me. Because there are so many saints as well as angels, sometimes an angel will need to use the special light to identify you."

Anderson replies, "No problem. I think it's neat that it's transparent, and that it instantly plies to the clothing."

They start to cross the enormous concourse to the opposite hallway on the back side of the center. Joseph says, "The processing center is one of the bigger office complexes. It covers about 70,000 square feet. I'll wait for you in their lobby. I'll help you check in, and once they start, it only takes about an hour in earth time. Once you get done, I'll walk you to the entrance of heaven's gate. From the processing center, it's less than half a mile." They soon arrive at the processing center, which is the first door in the rear east hallway.

As they wall into the large lobby and waiting area, the pictures on the wall remind him of the quality of the big nature pictures in the lodge's vestibule. These pictures are mostly of Old and New Testament events and leaders. They include an outstanding picture of Noah and the animals entering the ark; Joseph's reunion with his brothers in Egypt; David being crowned king of Israel; Jesus at the Sermon on the Mount and Jesus at the Last Supper with the Twelve Apostles. As Joseph leads Anderson to the check-in counter, the last picture Anderson notices shows Christ and the rapture of the church.

Joseph introduces Anderson to the receptionist. Joseph takes a seat and Anderson is directed to an adjoining office, where he fills out some brief paperwork. After a distinguished gentleman interviews him, the same gentleman leads him through the orientation of heaven. After Anderson gets some basic knowledge about heaven. Anderson follows the induction official to another area, where they process the patches for clothing. The gentleman, who calls himself Reginald, says, "Congratulations, Anderson, you are saint number 2,343,782,354. You can see that we have a large church here, and it's growing all the time. We'll have a tremendous influx, when the church on earth is raptured."

Anderson replies, "I guess so! How are you going to handle all of that traffic?" Reginald says, "We have many more hosting stations than what you've seen. Also, we're training millions of saints and angels, so we'll be ready for the large influx of saints. We're expecting close to a billion!" As Reginald completes his paperwork, Anderson counts his blessings that he's a missionary captain. He thinks, "God knows what we're called to do." Anderson shakes Reginald's hand and thanks him. Reginald says, "One more thing, Anderson, we have a white robe especially made for you in this package. Most people wear it on special occasions, like taking communion with the Son. We thank God you're here."

Anderson says, "I thank him too, Reginald."

Anderson walks out of the induction area feeling as light as the wind. When he sees Joseph, he says, "Joseph, I can't explain it, but it seems like all the weight of the world has been lifted off me."

Joseph says, "It has."

They walk out of the processing center, through the concourse to the rear exit. Joseph turns to Anderson and says, "Take a deep breath. When you go through this door, you're going to see the entrance to heaven!"

Anderson feels happier than a five-year-old child on Christmas morning. When he walks through the door, he can hardly believe his eyes. He sees the glory of heaven. He can see the entrance to heaven at the end of a long bridge that must be over a quarter mile long. As they start walking down the bridge, Anderson looks over on each side, and he sees sites almost indescribable. It's like looking at the splendors of earth in one setting. He sees floating, white clouds; majestic mountains, crystal blue lakes; a long, wide river meandering through magnificent woods, lofty red wood forests and other scenes he can't describe in his mind. Joseph says, "I can tell you're mesmerized by the Bridge of Eternal Life."

A Light on the Path

Anderson says, "I don't know what to say except that it is absolutely beautiful! It could only be like this in heaven."

Joseph replies, "You're absolutely right. Anderson, at the end of the bridge and right before the entrance to heaven, is a gazebo and sitting area. We'll sit there just a few minutes before you go into heaven. I have something I need to share with you."

As they get close to the end of the bridge, Anderson can already see the radiance of heaven. The natural light is the most beautiful he has ever seen. There is every color imaginable. Some structures look like they have been built with gems. He can see beautiful estates, landscaping and mansions. There are great oaks and spreading chestnut trees. Everywhere he looks, he sees the beauty of God's glory. They arrive at the end of the bridge, and they take a seat by the gazebo, which is decorated with many more types, colors and shades of roses than he saw at Lake Junaluska.

Joseph says, "Anderson, since I have to get back to my guardian angel work, a friend of mine will take you to where Ruth is and to your other family and friends. I thought you might like a memento from earth." Joseph reveals Anderson's walking stick.

Anderson is dumbfounded. He says, "Where did you get that? How did you produce it? I didn't see it on you!"

Joseph laughs heartily, "Let's just say that miracles aren't uncommon here!"

They get up and Joseph hands Anderson his walking stick. Joseph says, "Don't get the big head. You might feel like Abraham or Moses walking around with this." They both laugh and hug each other. Joseph says, "One more thing; let me know how you like your estate."

Anderson replies, "My estate?"

Joseph says, "Yes, your estate; it's only three hundred acres and a chalet, but you'll probably get a bigger one later."

Anderson exclaims, "I'm overwhelmed! Joseph, you mean a lot to me."

Joseph replies, "And you mean a lot to me."

They walk up to the gate of heaven. Joseph says, "Anderson, this is my friend, Peter. He will take you to your family and friends."

Anderson asks, "Saint Peter?"

Peter and Joseph laugh loudly. Peter says, "No, I'm an angel, not a saint."

Right before they walk through heaven's gate, Anderson hugs Joseph again and says, "Thank you for everything."

Joseph says, "You're welcome. I'll be seeing you soon. Have fun with your friends and family. God is good."

Anderson says, "God bless you."

A Light on the Path

As Anderson and Peter begin to walk away, Anderson looks back and waves at Joseph. With a bigger than life smile, Joseph waves at Anderson, as he walks into heaven.

www.ingramcontent.com/pod-product-compliance
Lightning Source LLC
Chambersburg PA
CBHW071913110526
44591CB00011B/1659